Guide to Louisiana
Confederate Military Units, 1861–1865

Guide to Louisiana Confederate Military Units 1861–1865

Arthur W. Bergeron, Jr.

LOUISIANA STATE UNIVERSITY PRESS
Baton Rouge and London

Copyright © 1989 by Louisiana State University Press
Manufactured in the United States of America

Louisiana Paperback Edition, 1996
05 04 03 02 01 00 99 98 97 96   5 4 3 2 1

Designer: Laura Roubique Gleason
Typeface: Trump Mediaeval
Typesetter: G & S Typesetters, Inc.
Printer: Thomson-Shore, Inc.

Library of Congress Cataloging-in-Publication Data

Bergeron, Arthur W.
    Guide to Louisiana Confederate military units, 1861–1865 /
Arthur W. Bergeron, Jr.
        p.   cm.
    Bibliography: p.
    Includes index.
    ISBN 0-8071-1496-0 (cloth) ISBN 0-8071-2102-9 (pbk.)
    1. Louisiana—History—Civil War, 1861–1865—Regimental histo-
ries.   2. United States—History—Civil War, 1861–1865—Regimental
histories.   I. Title.
E565.4B32   1989
973.7'463—dc19   88-29214
                                                  CIP

The paper in this book meets the guidelines for permanence and
durability of the Committee on Production Guidelines for Book
Longevity of the Council on Library Resources. ∞

Contents

Acknowledgments

A research project of this nature owes whatever success it may enjoy to a large number of people. I wish to acknowledge the following individuals for their encouragement, assistance, and cooperation: Mr. Powell A. Casey, Baton Rouge, La.; Dr. Bert Groene, Southeastern Louisiana University; Mr. M. Stone Miller, Jr., Louisiana State University Library; Mrs. Harriet Callahan, Louisiana State Library; Miss Evangeline Lynch, formerly of Louisiana State University Library; the late Mrs. Mary Oalmann, Louisiana Adjutant General's Library; Dr. John D. Winters, Ruston, La.; Mr. Glenn R. Conrad, Center for Louisiana Studies; Mr. John Price, Northwestern State University Library; Dr. Wilbur E. Meneray, Tulane University Library; and Mr. Bernard Eble, Confederate Memorial Hall.

Two close friends merit special thanks for their part in the preparation and revision of my manuscript. Mrs. Jan Tate strongly encouraged me to put my notes into manuscript form. She then read the first draft and made suggestions for changes, additions, and deletions, which went into my second draft. Jan helped to steer me away from what she called "The Great Confederate Whitewash" school of writing by reminding me that Southern Civil War units, like those of all armies in all wars, had their share of soldiers who did not "fight to the last ditch" but, having once "seen the elephant" or spent desperate weeks besieged in places such as Port Hudson and Vicksburg, decided to go home and remain there.

Larry Hewitt accompanied me on several research trips and made me aware of possible sources of information in places he visited while conducting his own research. He also read my first draft and made helpful suggestions to improve it. Some common interests led Larry and me to collaborate on three books. For all of this cooperation and for his friendship I am most grateful.

It has been a pleasure working with the staff of the Louisiana State University Press. In particular, I want to thank Margaret Dalrymple, Catherine Barton, and Elaine Smyth of the press staff, and Jo-Anne

Naples, who edited the manuscript for the press, for their roles in the process of getting my manuscript into print.

My wife and children have supported me throughout this and other intervening projects. Their love and understanding are appreciated more than they know.

Guide to Louisiana
Confederate Military Units, 1861–1865

Introduction

During the Civil War, the state of Louisiana furnished 111 artillery, cavalry, and infantry units to the armies of the Confederate States of America. These units served in every theater of the war and performed gallantly in numerous battles and engagements. While books and articles present historical sketches of a few individual units, no single publication describes the activities of all of them.

Napier Bartlett attempted to cover all Louisiana units in his book *Military Record of Louisiana*; but when it came out in 1875, he admitted that his work was fragmentary. The historical sketches in Bartlett's book vary in length, accuracy, and usefulness. When the state legislature created the position of Commissioner of Military Records in 1908, it intended that he publish brief histories of all the military commands from Louisiana. Yet when *Records of Louisiana Confederate Soldiers and Louisiana Confederate Commands* appeared in 1920, it contained only an alphabetic listing of military companies. Andrew B. Booth, compiler of the volumes, wrote: "A short but complete history of each of these [companies] is essential, and should be compiled and published in these volumes, for a full understanding of the commands from Louisiana, and for its future historical value. These publications should also include a brief history of all Regiments, Battalions, and Battery commands, their organization, and mentioning the engagements in which they participated."

The office of Commissioner of Military Records passed out of existence before Booth or anyone else could attempt such a publication. My guide fills this void. Considering the continuing interest in the Civil War and the growing interest in genealogy, a guide to Louisiana's Confederate regiments, battalions, and batteries should prove a useful research tool. This book attempts to answer the often-asked question, Where was grandpa when . . . ? I hope also that it will encourage historians to compile for publication more complete unit histories by pointing them toward sources of information for such research.

The list of units upon which this guide is based came from several sources. Records in the National Archives proved the primary source for putting together the list. Record Group 109 (War Department Collection of Confederate Records) includes a series of documents called Compiled Service Records of Confederate Soldiers Who Served in Organizations from the State of Louisiana. War Department personnel compiled these service records of individual soldiers during the early 1900s. Because the personnel had access to the majority of existing muster rolls, hospital records, prisoner-of-war records, and other documents, they identified practically every Louisiana Confederate unit while working on their project.

To supplement the list taken from the Compiled Service Records, I used two other sources. The *General Index* volume of the *War of the Rebellion: Official Records of Union and Confederate Armies* contains a list of all Louisiana units mentioned in that series of books. A state publication—*Annual Report of the Adjutant General of the State of Louisiana for the Year Ending December 31, 1892* (Baton Rouge, 1893)—became the last primary source. This booklet included brief notations on all Louisiana Confederate units that the office of that official could identify. Naturally, I refined my list during the course of researching the unit histories.

This guide omits militia, home guard, reserve corps, and irregular units. Insufficient information on the majority of these units exists to justify their inclusion, besides which few of them saw any active service. Independent infantry and cavalry companies and several Louisiana companies that served in regiments or battalions from other states appear in an appendix.

Under normal circumstances, Louisiana's regiments and battalions received numerical designations that reflected the sequence of their entry into Confederate service. This system worked well with all but a few of Louisiana's infantry units but broke down somewhat in the designation of cavalry units. For example, for most of their service, two units claimed the name 28th Infantry Regiment, and three units used the designation 3rd Cavalry Regiment. The disbanding of one infantry regiment led to the redesignation of two others. These and other problems with unit numbers have led to confusion in tracing the activities of certain units. This guide helps dissipate some of the confusion by discussing alternate and inaccurate designations of units.

The company served as the basic unit in the Confederate infantry and cavalry. On paper, a company consisted of 100 officers and enlisted men; but companies rarely achieved that level of strength, usually numbering from 75 to 90 men when organized. One or more men in a town or rural area would begin forming a company from men in that locale. When a sufficient number of men had volunteered, they would elect their company officers and report to a training camp. At these camps, the state authorities would organize the volunteer companies into regiments and battalions. Normally, ten companies composed a regiment, giving it a strength of nearly 1,000 men. A separate battalion usually consisted of two to six companies and varied in strength accordingly. Each company usually had a nickname adopted at its formation; but upon the organization of regiments and battalions, each company received a letter from *A* through *K*, with *J* always omitted. State authorities attempted, but did not always succeed in, grouping companies by the area from which they originated to give the regiment or battalion a sense of homogeneity.

In organizing its armies, the Confederacy varied from the example of the United States Army. Infantry and cavalry regiments became grouped into brigades of two to six regiments each. A brigade took its name from its commander, and the name generally changed with changes in command. A division consisted of two to five brigades and, like the brigades, took the name of its commander. Two or more divisions made up a corps. In most cases, a corps was known by its commander's name; but in a few instances, the corps had a number. An army contained two or more corps, except for a few small armies composed of from two to four divisions. Confederate armies took their names from the geographical region in which they operated—for example, the Army of Western Louisiana and the Army of Tennessee.

A battery acted as the basic tactical unit for the artillery service and usually consisted of around 125 officers and men. Six cannons (or guns) composed a battery of field or light artillery. When organized into a regiment or battalion, batteries used the designation "company" and had either letters or numbers as identification. Heavy artillery units usually manned large, immobile cannons in a permanent fortification. In such cases, the men of a company or battery might operate as few as one gun or as many as four or five. The companies of a regiment or battalion of artillery frequently found themselves separated and manning guns located a few miles or hundreds of miles apart. Thus, the regimental or battalion organization served a purely administrative function.

Several Louisianians attempted, and to a degree succeeded in, raising units known as legions for Confederate service. A legion consisted of soldiers of all three combat arms—infantry, cavalry, and artillery. Legions had existed as military organizations in previous wars but by the time of the Civil War had declined in popularity because of problems with the command, control, and organization of such a diverse body of soldiery. Nevertheless, the Confederate Congress authorized the formation of at least ten legions within its Provisional Army. No Louisiana legion ever became fully organized and operational as a distinct body, and only one had all three combat arms designated as its component parts. Like other legions in Confederate service, the Louisiana units seldom saw the three arms operate together. Accordingly, this guide will treat the parts separately and make cross-reference notations to connect them with their parent units.

The body of this guide consists of brief historical sketches of each regiment, battalion, and battery furnished by Louisiana to the Confederacy, with the exceptions just noted. The sketches are arranged in the following order: artillery, cavalry, and infantry. Under each arm of service, all regiments precede battalions; and in the case of artillery, batteries follow battalions. Numbered units precede named units, the latter being arranged alphabetically. Units that had both a number and a nickname are listed under the number. Readers should refer to the comprehensive index to find the number by which each nicknamed unit was known.

Each sketch contains a list of field officers, a list of companies (giving nicknames and parish of origin whenever possible) and their commanders, a summary of the unit's movements and engagements, and a bibliography of published sources for that unit. Several of the cavalry and infantry battalions eventually became part of a regiment. Each battalion that maintained a distinctive organization for a time has its own sketch, however brief. Confederate authorities consolidated several infantry regiments and battalions during the course of the war, and each of these new units also has a separate sketch. In all cases, I have made cross-references to all changes in a unit's status by noting the unit's original or successor organization, or both.

The lists of field and company officers are designed in part to help researchers identify a unit when looking through the sources cited. Frequently, a source will speak of "Colonel ——'s" regiment or "Captain ——'s" company without giving the regimental number or company letter. On the subject of officers, the reader should keep one fact in mind. The field and company officers listed did not necessarily exercise constant command of their units in battle, on the march, or in camp. Though carried on a muster roll as unit commander, a man might have spent long periods of time elsewhere—on detached duty, on sick leave, or in prison, for example. Such absences resulted in command devolving on the next officer in the chain of command. Detailing such temporary changes of command is beyond the purpose of this work; and in many cases, they are impossible to document.

Researchers of Louisiana Confederate units will find themselves frustrated many times by confusing or missing information. Try as they may, Confederate officials simply could not keep up with much of the paperwork that is part of running an army. Thus, they did not keep many records up to date, or they made only sporadic attempts to forward to higher authorities documents that would assist us today in following the movements and activities of various units. During the course of the war, many documents fell prey to accidental or purposeful destruction. Records that survived the war are now scattered in a number of archives and libraries, and some of them have disappeared. Because of all of these factors, this work cannot be absolutely authoritative. Perhaps as a result of its publication, however, more information and documents will come to light and make possible a revised edition. With this in mind, the author would appreciate any additional information readers can contribute.

I/Artillery

1st Regiment Heavy

COLONELS. Paul O. Hebert, promoted brigadier general August 14, 1861; Charles A. Fuller.

LIEUTENANT COLONELS. Charles A. Fuller, promoted colonel August 14, 1861; Daniel Beltzhoover.

MAJORS. Johnson K. Duncan, promoted colonel in Provisional Army of the Confederate States; Daniel Beltzhoover, promoted lieutenant colonel August 14, 1861; Raymond Montaigne, died July 24, 1864; Henry A. Clinch, promoted lieutenant colonel April 25, 1865; W. C. Capers; Richard C. Bond.

COMPANIES AND THEIR COMMANDERS

Company A. Henry A. Clinch, promoted major August 14, 1861; John B. Grayson, Jr., transferred to Company F May 1, 1864; William C. Ellis.

Company B. John C. Moore, resigned April 15, 1861; William B. Robertson.

Company C. John T. Shaaff, promoted captain in Provisional Army of the Confederate States March 27, 1861; Frederick B. Brand, transferred to Company D September 6, 1861; John H. Lamon.

Company D. Frederick B. Brand, transferred to Company C April 24, 1861; Randall L. Gibson, resigned September 6, 1861; Frederick B. Brand, resigned December 30, 1861; Rufus J. Bruce.

Company E. James B. Anderson, resigned January 28, 1863; L. B. Haynes.

Company F. Miles F. Squires, killed October 4, 1863; William C. Ellis, transferred to Company A May 1, 1864; John B. Grayson, Jr.

Company G. W. C. Capers, promoted major July 24, 1863; Henry W. Fowler, dropped November 7, 1864; Richard Agar.

Company H. Edward W. Rawle, dropped November 10, 1862; Richard C. Bond, promoted major April 23, 1865.

Company I. Edward Higgins, resigned January 2, 1862; Edward G. Butler.

Company K. Richard C. Bond, transferred to Company H February 9, 1863; Abner N. Ogden, Jr.

Organized February 5, 1861, as part of the Louisiana State Army, the 1st Heavy Artillery transferred to Confederate service March 13, 1861, with 744 men. Regimental headquarters remained at the New Orleans Barracks while the various companies occupied the forts of the New Orleans defenses. Throughout the fall and winter of 1861, Companies B, C, D, E, F, H, and K served in Fort Jackson and Fort St. Philip below New Orleans. Companies A and I helped defend Fort Pike, and Company G composed part of the Fort Macomb garrison. The companies at Jackson and St. Philip fought well against Union admiral David G. Farragut's fleet during the bombardment and passage of the forts and were included in the surrender and parole of the garrisons on April 26, 1862. Company I participated in the brief skirmish with the Union fleet at the McGehee Lines on April 25. Companies A and G evacuated their posts on April 26 and joined Company I at Camp Moore on May 3, 1862. About May 20, 1862, these three companies left for Vicksburg, Mississippi, to help man the river batteries defending that city. They served in a temporary battalion commanded by Major Henry A. Clinch during the first attack on Vicksburg, May 18–July 27, 1862. The officers and men captured at Jackson and St. Philip received their exchanges in the fall, and most of them returned to their command. During the fall and winter of 1862–63, the regiment suffered heavily from sickness; and at one point nearly 500 conscripts augmented its depleted ranks. The men manned the cannons in the lower (southern) river batteries at Vicksburg. On March 11, 1863, Company A moved to Grand Gulf to occupy the upper (northern) battery there. In an engagement with Federal gunboats on March 31, the company distinguished itself by its excellent firing. This company again engaged the enemy on April 29 and participated in the evacuation of the post on May 3. During the siege of Vicksburg, May 19–July 4, 1863, the regiment fired its cannons at enemy gunboats on the river and enemy batteries on the Louisiana shore. The 1st Heavy Artillery marched out of Vicksburg after the surrender there and went into a camp for paroled prisoners at Enterprise, Mississippi. Major General Dabney H. Maury requested the regiment's services at Mobile, Alabama, after it was exchanged; and the regiment arrived there on January 16, 1864. From that time until summer, the companies manned various redoubts along the Mobile land defenses. Twice during July, 1864, the regiment moved to Meridian, Mississippi, to support Major General Stephen D. Lee's cavalry force. At the Battle of Tupelo, July 14, 1864, the men acted as an infantry reserve. The regiment reoccupied redoubts at Mobile in early August, 1864, and late that month the companies moved to two water batteries on islands in upper Mobile Bay. The regiment continued to garrison these batteries until April 11, 1865, when they were dismantled and their men evacuated as part of the evacuation of Mobile. When Lieutenant General Richard Taylor's army surrendered, on May 8, 1865, the 1st Heavy Artillery was camped at Cuba Station, Alabama; and the men received their paroles at Meridian as part of Taylor's army.

BIBLIOGRAPHY

Semper, C. S. "Confederate Who Served from Colorado." *Confederate Veteran*, XX (1912), 469.

"When Vicksburg was Besieged." *Confederate Veteran*, XXXV (1927), 23.

2nd Battalion Heavy

LIEUTENANT COLONEL. George W. Logan.
MAJOR. Eugene Soniat, made battalion adjutant(?).

COMPANIES AND THEIR COMMANDERS

Company A. Daniel Scully.
Company B. C. C. Duke.
Company C. A. D. Parker.
Company D. Christopher C. Davenport.
Company E. Composition and commander unknown.
Company F. Abe A. Cann.

Although authorized in October, 1863, the battalion did not complete its organization until February, 1864, probably at Columbia. The men of the unit came from the northeastern parishes of the state and were both volunteers and conscripts. On March 2, 1864, the battalion was subjected to bombardment from six Federal gunboats at Harrisonburg but probably had no cannons with which to return the enemy fire. Several weeks later, the battalion received two 24-pounder guns and remained near the Ouachita River in case Federal gunboats again moved up the stream. In early April, 1864, the men buried their guns near Columbia and marched to Shreveport. For about one week, the men manned Fort Boggs to help defend the capital city from Major General Nathaniel P. Banks's Red River expedition. The battalion returned to Columbia in late April to retrieve its two cannons, and the men operated near Pineville while the Union army occupied Alexandria. Following the Union evacuation of Alexandria, the battalion remained in the area of the town until early 1865, when it moved to Natchitoches. At the end of the war, the battalion apparently had no cannons and was attached to Brigadier General William R. Boggs's infantry brigade. The men of the battalion disbanded near Mansfield in May, 1865.

8th Battalion Heavy

LIEUTENANT COLONEL. William E. Pinkney.
MAJOR. Fred N. Ogden.

COMPANIES AND THEIR COMMANDERS

1st Company. Ruffin C. Barrow.
2nd Company. Paulin Grandpre.
3rd Company. Thomas N. McCrory.

The battalion originated as the 8th Infantry Battalion, but it reorganized as artillery with only three companies at Vicksburg, Mississippi, shortly after its arrival there, on May 5, 1862. During the first Union attack on Vicksburg, May 18–July 27, 1862, the men manned four heavy cannons in the city's river batteries. From this time until the spring of 1863, the battalion occupied batteries at the center of the city front of river batteries. On April 23, 1863, during a passage of the batteries by Union vessels, one of the battalion's guns discharged prematurely, killing 1 man and severely wounding 2 others. The men fired on enemy gunboats and artillery batteries on the Louisiana shore during the Siege of Vicksburg, May 19–July 4, 1863. Captured and paroled at the fall of that city, the men went into a parole camp at Enterprise, Mississippi. Most of the men eventually made their way to their homes. After being exchanged in early 1864, a handful of men reported for duty at Mobile, Alabama, and served with the 1st Louisiana Heavy Artillery. A larger contingent of men reported for duty in the Trans-Mississippi Department and were organized under Captain Thomas N. McCrory as Company D, Siege Train Battalion. This company may have acted for a time as part of the 2nd Louisiana Heavy Artillery Battalion. The men did duty in Fort Buhlow near Pineville until the end of the war. At the surrender of the Trans-Mississippi Department, most of the men disbanded and went home rather than sign paroles.

BIBLIOGRAPHY
"John W. Daniel, of Louisiana." *Confederate Veteran*, XIV (1906), 82–83.
Moss, A. Hugh. *The Diary of A. Hugh Moss.* [Lake Charles(?), 1948].

12th Battalion Heavy

LIEUTENANT COLONEL. Paul Francis DeGournay.
MAJORS. Paul Francis DeGournay, promoted lieutenant colonel July 3, 1862; Anderson Merchant.

COMPANIES AND THEIR COMMANDERS

Company A, Orleans Independent Artillery (Orleans). John M. Kean, died November 21, 1863.
Company B (Orleans). Felix LeBesque, died June 27, 1863; Henry Castellanos.
Company C, Halifax Artillery (Virginia), detached at Richmond. Samuel T. Wright.
Company D, Bethel Artillery (Virginia). W. Norris Coffin.
Company E, Mohawk Artillery (Alabama). William B. Seawell.

Although composed of men from three states, this battalion is usually accounted a Louisiana unit. It was organized near Yorktown, Virginia, in May, 1862. The battalion served in the Yorktown defenses until they were evacuated. A portion of the unit is said to have fired the last shot from its gun and been the last Confederate unit to leave Yorktown. During the battles around Richmond, May–July, 1862, the battalion manned batteries in the capital's defenses. In August, 1862, the Secretary of War ordered the battalion to Port

Hudson, Louisiana, to man heavy artillery batteries under construction there. Captain Samuel T. Wright's company remained at Richmond and never again served with the battalion. The other companies reached Port Hudson in early September. On September 7, the men fired their cannons at the Union ironclad *Essex* but did not injure it. The men of the battalion helped in the erection and arming of the river batteries at Port Hudson during the winter of 1862–63. They eventually occupied the left (southern) wing of the batteries: Company E at Battery No. 4, Company A at Battery No. 6, Company D at Battery No. 8, and Company B at Batteries No. 9 and No. 10. The battalion engaged Admiral David G. Farragut's squadron when it attempted to run past the Port Hudson batteries on March 14, 1863; 1 officer was killed, and 2 enlisted men were wounded. Just prior to the investment of Port Hudson by Major General Nathaniel P. Banks's Union army, Captain W. Norris Coffin requested that his company receive orders to return to Virginia; but the Secretary of War denied the request. The men served in various capacities during the siege of Port Hudson, May 23–July 9, 1863. A detachment served as infantrymen at the breastworks under Major Anderson Merchant. Coffin's company manned a rifled 32-pounder gun until the cannon was disabled on Brigadier General William N. R. Beall's line near Slaughter's Field. The rest of the battalion remained in the river batteries, where the men engaged the enemy's gunboats and fired occasionally over the land lines into the enemy's works. About 140 men surrendered with the Port Hudson garrison. The officers went to northern prisons; the men who did not return to their homes went into parole camps. Late in 1863, Captain Henry Castellanos collected about 117 men at Mobile, Alabama. There they manned batteries in the city's land defenses. Captain Coffin commanded the remnants of his company, which remained independent until the end of the war, in the Mobile defenses also. A small number of the men were ordered into the 1st Louisiana Heavy Artillery. The remnants of the battalion surrendered at Meridian, Mississippi, on May 8, 1865.

BIBLIOGRAPHY

[DeGournay, P. F.]. "D'Gournay's Battalion of Artillery." *Confederate Veteran*, XIII (1905), 30–33.

Minnich, J. W. "Incidents of the Peninsular Campaign." *Confederate Veteran*, XXX (1922), 53–56.

———. "With the Louisiana Zouaves." *Confederate Veteran*, XXXVI (1928), 425.

Pointe Coupee Battalion

MAJOR. R. A. Stewart.

COMPANIES AND THEIR COMMANDERS

Company A, Pointe Coupee Artillery (Pointe Coupee and East Baton Rouge). Alcide Bouanchaud.
Company B (Livingston[?]). William A. Davidson.
Company C (Pointe Coupee[?]). Alexander Chust.

This battalion of light artillery was organized around August, 1862, near Abbeville, Mississippi. Most of the men had originally served in Captain Richard A. Stewart's Pointe Coupee Battery. The battery was mustered in about August, 1861, and ordered to Columbus, Kentucky. During the Battle of Belmont, November 7, 1861, the men engaged the enemy's gunboats on the Mississippi River. Company B (newly recruited) joined Stewart's battery in early 1862. In February and March, 1862, the men served heavy artillery at Island No. 10 and helped repulse enemy advances on March 7 to 9. The men moved to Fort Pillow on March 18 and served there until June 5, 1862, when the Confederates evacuated the post. From Fort Pillow the men marched to Grenada, Mississippi. The battalion became complete with the creation of Company C from men transferred from existing companies or recently recruited. On December 5, 1862, at least part of the battalion fought in an engagement at Coffeeville, Mississippi. Company B moved to Fort Pemberton near Greenwood in February, 1863, and Companies A and C received orders about the same time to report for duty at Port Hudson, Louisiana. Company B did good service in the defense of Fort Pemberton against several enemy attacks in March and early April, 1863. By mid-April, all three companies were in or around Jackson, Mississippi, and were attached to different brigades of Major General William W. Loring's infantry division. Companies A and C fought in the Battle of Champion's Hill, May 16, 1863. Companies B and C and part of Company A fell back to Vicksburg and became part of the garrison there during the siege, May 19–July 4, 1863. The other part of Company A operated with Loring's division in central and eastern Mississippi through the end of 1863. Most of the men captured and paroled at Vicksburg apparently never returned to duty with the battalion, and Companies B and C ceased to exist. Company A served in the Meridian Campaign, February 3–March 6, 1864, and marched with Loring's division to join the Army of Tennessee in northern Georgia in May, 1864. The company fought at Resaca on May 13 and repulsed an enemy attack at Calhoun on May 18. During the remainder of the Atlanta Campaign, the company participated in all the marches and many of the engagements of the Army of Tennessee. The company accompanied the army into Tennessee in late 1864. Most of the men and all of the cannons of Company A were captured during the Battle of Nashville, December 16, 1864, and the battalion virtually ceased to exist after that date. Of the approximately 346 men enrolled in the battalion during the war, 27 were killed in battle and 28 died of disease.

Washington Battalion

LIEUTENANT COLONELS. James B. Walton, promoted colonel of artillery, detached February, 1864; Benjamin F. Eshleman.

MAJORS. Benjamin F. Eshleman, promoted lieutenant colonel February 27, 1864; William M. Owen, assigned to battalion April 10, 1864.

COMPANIES AND THEIR COMMANDERS

1st Company (Orleans). Harry M. Isaacson, resigned August 16, 1861; Charles W. Squires, promoted major and transferred January 25, 1864; Edward Owen.

2nd Company (Orleans). Thomas L. Rosser, promoted major and transferred June 11, 1862; John B. Richardson.

3rd Company (Orleans). Merritt B. Miller, promoted and transferred February 27, 1864; Andrew Hero, Jr.

4th Company (Orleans). Benjamin F. Eshleman, promoted major March 26, 1862; Joseph Norcom.

5th Company. See separate sketch.

6th Company (Orleans), company did not leave New Orleans. Harman Doane.

Probably the most famous Louisiana unit in the Confederate army next to Wheat's Tiger Battalion, the Washington Artillery traces its lineage back to 1838 in the state militia. Four companies entered

Confederate service on May 26, 1861, and left for Virginia. On arrival at Manassas Junction, the battalion lost 1 officer and 5 enlisted men in its first skirmish, at Blackburn's Ford, July 18, 1861. In the Battle of Manassas, July 21, the battalion performed gallant service and received praise from General Pierre G. T. Beauregard for its "skill, conduct, and soldierly qualities." During the fall and winter of 1861, the battalion occupied camps in the vicinity of Manassas and Centerville; and detachments from the battalion engaged in several skirmishes in that area. The battalion received orders to join General James Longstreet's division on March 5, 1862, and was connected with that general's command throughout most of the remainder of the war. Shortly after this assignment, the battalion accompanied the army on its retreat to Orange Court House and moved to Richmond about April 12. From Richmond the battalion marched down the peninsula and participated in the closing stages of the Yorktown Campaign. The 2nd Company fought in a skirmish at Mechanicsville on May 23, and the 1st Company was engaged at New Bridge on June 5. During the Seven Days' Battles, the battalion was held in reserve and not engaged. The 1st Company engaged several enemy vessels on the James River near Charles City Court House, July 5–7. On August 23, the battalion helped drive the enemy back in a skirmish at Rappahannock Station. The battalion fought at the Battle of Second Manassas, August 29–31; 1 man was killed and 9 were wounded. In the Battle of Sharpsburg, September 17, the battalion helped repulse several enemy attacks. At one point, when the men of the 3rd Company had become exhausted, General Longstreet and his staff assisted in working the guns. The battalion occupied quarters at Winchester, Virginia, after the retreat from Maryland, and on November 22 it reached Fredericksburg. During the Battle of Fredericksburg, December 13, three companies of the battalion occupied positions atop Marye's Heights and helped throw back the numerous enemy assaults on the Confederate lines. The 2nd Company was in reserve during the battle. The battalion occupied winter quarters near Fredericksburg. When the Chancellorsville Campaign began, the battalion once again defended Marye's Heights. On May 3, 1863, the enemy attacked and overran the battalion's position, capturing six guns and 33 men. The battalion arrived on the battlefield of Gettysburg on July 2. The next day, the men participated in the long artillery duel that preceded Pickett's Charge. During the retreat back to Virginia, the battalion fought in an engagement at Williamsport on July 6. After a brief stop at Orange Court House, the battalion proceeded to Petersburg in September to occupy part of that city's defensive works. Not until May, 1864, did the battalion again engage the enemy. The men participated in the successful defense of Drewry's Bluff, May 12–16. After a brief assignment to cover several fords over the Chickahominy River east of Richmond in June, the battalion returned to the Petersburg defenses. The battalion participated in the lengthy siege operations around the city, July, 1864–April, 1865. Small detachments of the 3rd Company played a gallant role in the defense of Fort Gregg and Fort Whitworth on April 2 but were overrun and captured. During the retreat toward Appomattox, the battalion, along with several other artillery units, got separated from the rest of the army. Hearing of General Robert E. Lee's surrender, the men destroyed their gun carriages near Amelia Court House and started making their way toward home. Three officers and 27 enlisted men were paroled with Lee's army at Appomattox. Approximately 719 men served in the battalion during the war. Of that number, 62 died in battle, 2 were killed in accidents, 1 drowned, and 20 died of disease.

BIBLIOGRAPHY

Baker, Henry H. *A Reminiscent Story of the Great Civil War.* New Orleans, 1911.

Bartlett, Napier. *A Soldier's Story of the War; Including the Marches and Battles of the Washington Artillery and of Other Louisiana Troops.* New Orleans, 1874.

"The Battle of Fort Gregg." *Southern Historical Society Papers,* XXVIII (1900), 265–76.

Bayne, T. L. "Our Fellow Comrades." *Southern Historical Society Papers,* XI (1883), 328–30.

Casey, Powell A. *Civil War Campaigns and Engagements of the Washington Artillery.* Baton Rouge, 1986.

"'My Artillery Fire Was Very Destructive': The Charles W. Squires Memoir." *Civil War Times Illustrated,* XIV (June, 1975), 18–28.

Owen, Allison. "Record of an Old Artillery Organization." *Field Artillery Journal,* IV (1914), 5–18.

Owen, Edward. "Reminiscences of Washington Artillery of New Orleans." *Blue and Gray,* II (1893), 43–44.

Owen, William Miller. "The Artillery Defenders of Fort Gregg." *Southern Historical Society Papers,* XIX (1891), 65–71.

———. *In Camp and Battle with the Washington Artillery of New Orleans.* Boston, 1885.

———. "A Hot Day on Marye's Heights." In *Battles and Leaders of the Civil War,* edited by Robert Underwood Johnson and Clarence Clough Buel. Vol. II of 4 vols. New York, 1956, pp. 97–99.

———. "Recollections of the Third Day at Gettysburg." *United Service,* XIII (1885), 148–51.

Severin, John Powers, and Lee A. Wallace. "Battalion of Washington Artillery of New Orleans, 1861." *Military Collector and Historian* (1958), 71–72.

Squires, Charles W. "'Boy Officer' of the Washington Artillery." *Civil War Times Illustrated,* XIV (May, 1975), 10–23.

Walton, J. B., *et al.* "Sketches of the History of the Washington Artillery." *Southern Historical Society Papers,* XI (1883), 210–22, 247–54.

"The Washington Artillery." *Confederate Veteran,* V (1897), 474–75.

"The Washington Artillery of New Orleans." *Land We Love,* VI (1868–69), 150–55.

1st Battery
(St. Mary's Cannoneers)

CAPTAINS. Florian O. Cornay, killed April 26, 1864; Minos T. Gordy.

This battery was mustered into Confederate service at Franklin, Louisiana, on October 7, 1861. The battery remained at Camp Hunter near Franklin until early 1862, when it moved to Fort Jackson below New Orleans. During the defense of that fort and Fort St. Philip, the men performed able service as heavy artillerists. Theirs was the only unit that did not mutiny on the night of April 27, 1862, and the officers and enlisted men became prisoners of war when the forts surrendered. After receiving their exchange, the men gathered at Camp Hunter to be outfitted again as a field battery. One two-gun section fought in the battles at Fort Bisland, April 12–13, 1863. Enemy fire disabled one gun, and the men had to abandon it. The other two sections, with the remaining gun of the third section, participated in the Battle of Irish Bend, April 14. In this battle, the battery lost its flag to men of the 13th Connecticut Infantry. On June 3, the battery engaged the enemy gunboat *Estrella* on the Atchafalaya River and drove it back. The next day, with another battery, Cornay's men engaged three enemy gunboats near the same site. Heavy enemy fire forced the batteries to withdraw. From July, 1863, to March, 1864, the battery joined in the various marches of General Alfred Mouton's Louisiana brigade in south Louisiana but rarely engaged the enemy. The men fired on Federal vessels on the Mississippi River from positions along the levee below Donaldsonville, July 7–10, 1863. At least one gun participated in operations against Federal vessels at Hog Point, near Red River Landing, November 18–21. On December 8, one section of the battery fired on the Federal transport *Von Phul*, causing some damage to that vessel, and then exchanged shots with the gunboat *Neosho*. At the Battle of Mansfield, April 8, 1864, the battery was only lightly engaged in support of the Confederate attack. The battery performed gallant service on April 26 and 27 against three enemy gunboats and two transports on the Red River near the mouth of the Cane River. The heavy, accurate fire of the guns crippled one gunboat and disabled a transport, resulting in its capture. In the skirmish at Mansura, May 16, the battery was the last artillery unit to withdraw from the field, and it covered the army's retreat. The men participated in the Battle of Yellow Bayou, May 18. Following the Red River Campaign of 1864, the battery saw no more fighting. The men accompanied General Camille J. Polignac's division on its march through north Louisiana into southern Arkansas in late 1864. In November, orders officially designated the men as the 1st Louisiana Field Battery. Transferred about that time to General John H. Forney's division, the battery later was stationed near Tyler, Texas. At the surrender of the Trans-Mississippi Department in May, 1865, the battery still occupied its camp near Tyler and had four guns. During the course of the war, approximately 161 men served with the battery.

1st Regular Battery

CAPTAINS. Edward Higgins, resigned January 2, 1862; Oliver J. Semmes, promoted to major November 7, 1863; James M. T. Barnes.

This battery was organized in New Orleans, possibly at Camp Benjamin, on October 29, 1861, with 120 men. Members of the battery had enlisted in the regular army of the Confederacy for five years.

Upon the evacuation of New Orleans in April, 1862, the battery moved to Camp Moore. When General John C. Breckinridge's army passed through the camp on its way to attack the Federals occupying Baton Rouge, the battery joined the column with Colonel Henry W. Allen's Louisiana brigade. In the Battle of Baton Rouge, August 5, the battery fired upon and silenced two enemy batteries and thus established its reputation as an efficient artillery unit. The men moved to Port Hudson after the battle to become part of the garrison there. On September 2, the battery received orders to cross the Mississippi River and report to General Richard Taylor's army. The men fought in a skirmish at Koch's Plantation south of Donaldsonville on September 24 and in the Battle of Labadieville, October 27. Retreating with Taylor's army to the lower Bayou Teche, part of the battery engaged Union gunboats there on November 3. The men went into camp near Centerville for the winter. On April 12 and 13, 1863, the battery helped stop several enemy attacks in the Battle of Fort Bisland. The battery joined Colonel Thomas Green's Texas cavalry brigade as part of the rear guard of Taylor's army during its retreat from Bisland to Opelousas. At Jeanerette, on April 15, one section inflicted heavy losses on pursuing enemy soldiers. The battery continued to operate with Green's cavalry in all its campaigns in south Louisiana during the summer and fall of 1863. On July 3 and 4, the rifled section fired on and crippled enemy transports on the Mississippi River below Donaldsonville. One section attempted to join Green in the Battle of Bayou Bourbeau, November 3; but its horses tired out, causing it to arrive too late. The battery was held in reserve and was not engaged in the battles of Mansfield and Pleasant Hill, April 8–9, 1864. During the retreat of the Federal army down the Red River, the battery operated with General William Steele's Texas cavalry brigade and participated in skirmishing near Cloutierville, April 23–24. The battery fought in the engagements at Mansura, May 16, and at Yellow Bayou, May 18, at the end of the Red River Campaign. In the fall and winter of 1864, the battery served in the 3rd Artillery Battalion attached to General Camille J. Polignac's infantry division. By the end of the year, the battery had transferred to Major Charles Squires's battalion attached to General John H. Forney's infantry division. War's end found the battery stationed at Tyler, Texas.

BIBLIOGRAPHY
Semmes, O. J. "First Confederate Battery an Orphan." *Confederate Veteran*, XXI (1913), 58.
Weinert, Richard P. "The Confederate Regulars in Louisiana." *Louisiana Studies*, V (1967), 53–71.

2nd Battery

CAPTAINS. Richard M. Boone, died of wounds June 15, 1863; Samuel M. Thomas.

Organized about March 1, 1862, at Red River Landing with 130 officers and enlisted men, the battery was to serve as Company B, Miles' Legion Artillery, but often acted independently of the legion. After a short period of training at Camp Benjamin near New Orleans in early April, the battery moved to Camp Moore during the evacuation of the Crescent City. The battery occupied camps near Fayette, Mississippi, from June to mid-August, when it received orders to report to the garrison at Port Hudson, Louisiana. The men participated in bombardments of the gunboat *Anglo-American* on August 29 and of the *Anglo-American* and the ironclad *Essex* on September 7. On December 13, the men moved three of their guns across the Mississippi River and down to a point near Profit Island. The next morning, they opened fire on the wooden gunboat *Winona*, causing considerable damage to it before the *Essex* could escort it to safety. Detachments of the battery and two guns participated in the expedition aboard the cottonclad steamer *Dr. Beatty* against the enemy ironclad *Indianola*, which resulted in the capture of the vessel near Natchez, Mississippi, on February 24, 1863. On May 21, the battery fought in the Battle of Plains Store, east of Port Hudson. During the siege of Port Hudson, May 23–July 9, 1863, the battery helped defend the southern end, or right wing, of the earthwork entrenchments. The men broke up several enemy assaults with their accurate cannon fire. At the surrender of the garrison, the men went home on parole. Lieutenant Maunsel Bennett had escaped prior to the surrender, and in November, 1863, he began reorganizing the battery near Alexandria. Reentering active service on December 12, the men at first had no cannons and acted as a provost guard at

Natchitoches. In March, 1864, probably at Shreveport, the men received two heavy artillery pieces mounted on siege carriages and pulled by oxen. During the closing stages of the Red River Campaign, the battery left behind those two guns and took over two 30-pounder Parrott rifled cannons captured from enemy gunboats. The men fought in the skirmish at Mansura on May 16. On June 8, in a skirmish with three enemy gunboats on the Atchafalaya River north of Simmesport, the enemy fire drove the men away from one of the Parrotts, allowing a landing party to capture it. The other gun burst during the engagement and later had to be scrapped. The battery served in the Alexandria defenses for the remainder of the war, occupying Fort Buhlow near Pineville. Orders issued November 19 designated the men as the 2nd Louisiana Field Battery even though they manned heavy, or siege, cannons. Most of the men disbanded upon the surrender of the Trans-Mississippi Department in late May, 1865, but a few officers and enlisted men received their paroles at Alexandria on June 3.

BIBLIOGRAPHY

Bergeron, Arthur W., Jr., and Lawrence L. Hewitt. *Boone's Louisiana Battery: A History and Roster.* Baton Rouge, 1986.

Tanner, Linn. "Port Hudson Calamities—Mule Meat." *Confederate Veteran*, XVII (1909), 512.

———. "The Meat Diet at Port Hudson." *Confederate Veteran*, XXVI (1918), 484.

3rd Battery
(Bell Battery)

CAPTAIN. Thomas O. Benton.

This battery was organized at Monroe in April or May, 1862. The battery bore the nickname "Bell Battery" because the cannons originally intended for it had been cast from bells donated by planters in Ouachita, Caldwell, and Morehouse parishes. Those guns, cast in Vicksburg, Mississippi, never reached the battery; and Captain Benton finally obtained four cannons from General Braxton Bragg at Corinth, Mississippi. After training at Monroe, the battery received orders to move to the Mississippi River and interfere with enemy shipping in East Carroll and Madison parishes. In early 1863, the battery moved to Harrisonburg and became part of the garrison of Fort Taylor and later of Fort Beauregard. The men fought Federal gunboats at the latter fort on May 10 and 11 and helped drive the enemy back. When Federal land and naval forces caused an evacuation of Fort Beauregard on September 4, the battery fell back to Alexandria. From there, it moved to Bayou DeGlaize near Marksville. The Federal advance up the Red River in March, 1864, forced a retreat toward Shreveport with the rest of the Confederate army. At the battles of Mansfield and Pleasant Hill, April 8–9, the men remained in reserve and did not engage the enemy. On April 26, Captain Benton and his two rifled guns fired on two enemy gunboats on the Red River at Deloach's Bluff and drove them away. The battery participated in a skirmish south of Alexandria at Chambers' Plantation, May 5. The next day, in a skirmish at Polk's Bridge over Bayou Lamourie, three of the battery's four guns became disabled; and the battery saw no further action during the campaign. In the fall and winter of 1864, the battery accompanied General Camille J. Polignac's division on a march into Arkansas. By January, 1865, the battery had returned to Louisiana and established a camp near Collinsburg in Bossier Parish. From there, the men moved to Shreveport. Placing their guns in storage, they reported to Grand Ecore to take over some of the heavy artillery batteries there. The men surrendered at Grand Ecore in June, 1865. Some 108 men served in the battery during the war.

4th Battery

CAPTAIN. Archibald J. Cameron.

Organized about August, 1862, of men from Tensas Parish and Jefferson County, Mississippi, this battery had only four guns. It operated with Colonel Isaac F. Harrison's 3rd Louisiana Cavalry along the Mississippi River opposite Vicksburg and engaged in several skirmishes with General Ulysses S. Grant's Union army in April, 1863. The battery was stationed at Monroe through the summer and fall of 1863, except for a brief period in September, when it retreated to Shreveport because a large Federal force had occupied Monroe. In early 1864, the battery accompanied Harrison's cavalry brigade on its marches through north Louisiana. One section operated with the brigade during the Red River Campaign, March–May 1864, but saw little action, since it was on the north side of the river. After the conclusion of the campaign, the battery moved into southern Arkansas. On July 24, the battery fired on and helped destroy the transport *Clara Bell* at Ashton Landing on the White River. Three days later, the battery damaged the transports *Fairchild* and *B. J. Adams*, part of the Federal Mississippi Marine Brigade, at Sunnyside Landing, Arkansas. As part of the Army of Western Louisiana, the battery returned to southern Arkansas in the fall and winter of 1864. It moved to Marshall, Texas, early in 1865 for repairs. Remaining there until June, it was one of the last organized batteries to surrender to the Federals.

BIBLIOGRAPHY

Rowland, Dunbar. "Military History of Mississippi, 1803–1898." In *The Official and Statistical Register of the State of Mississippi, 1908*. Jackson, 1909, p. 879.

5th Battery
(Pelican Artillery)

CAPTAINS. Thomas A. Faries, promoted major April 17, 1864; B. Felix Winchester.

This battery was organized October 31, 1862, primarily of men from St. James Parish. The battery first engaged the enemy on November 3, 1862, when it fired on four Union gunboats on Bayou Teche below Patterson. Two sections (four guns) of the battery occupied Petite Anse Island during late November. On January 14, 1863, one section participated in an engagement on Bayou Teche in defense of the Confederate gunboat *Cotton*, and three men received wounds. During the Battle of Bisland, April 12–13, the battery performed excellently and received praise from Generals Richard Taylor and Alfred Mouton. One section fought in a skirmish at Vermillion Bridge on April 17. The battery accompanied Taylor's army when it moved back into south Louisiana and the Bayou Lafourche area in June and July, 1863. From July 7 to 10, two guns occupied a position at Gaudet's Plantation on the Mississippi River twelve miles below Donaldsonville and fired on all Federal vessels that passed their location. The entire battery fought in the Battle of Koch's Plantation near Donaldsonville, July 13. The battery went with Taylor's army during its marches in south Louisiana during the fall, usually being attached to Mouton's infantry brigade. From November 18 to 21, the battery engaged in operations against Federal vessels on the Mississippi River at Hog Point, one mile below Red River Landing. Captain Faries led his men from Alexandria to the Ouachita River near Trinity in late February, 1864, and participated with General Camille J. Polignac's Texas brigade in engagements with Federal gunboats near Trinity and Harrisonburg, March 1–4. During the battles of Mansfield and Pleasant Hill, April 8–9, the battery was in reserve and not engaged. On May 12, four guns fired on a Federal tinclad gunboat on the Red River near Mrs. David's Plantation, driving the vessel away. The battery participated in the engagements at Marksville, May 15; Mansura, May 16; Moreauville, May 17; and Yellow Bayou, May 18. The battery followed Polignac's (later General John H. Forney's) division in all its marches during late 1864 and early 1865. On November 19, 1864, the battery was officially designated the 5th Louisiana Field Battery. The men surrendered near Tyler, Texas, in early June, 1865. Of the approximately 183 men who served in the battery during the war, 2 were killed in battle, 5 died of disease, and 1 drowned.

BIBLIOGRAPHY
"Official Reports of Actions with Federal Gunboats, Ironclads and Vessels of the U. S. Navy, During the War Between the States, by Officers of Field Artillery, P. A. C. S." *Southern Historical Society Papers*, XII (1884), 54–59.

5th Company, Washington Artillery

CAPTAINS. W. Irving Hodgson, resigned June 13, 1862; Cuthbert H. Slocumb.

Transferred to Confederate service March 6, 1862, with about 160 officers and men, this battery moved to Jackson, Tennessee, to reinforce the army of General Pierre G. T. Beauregard. Assigned to the brigade of General J. Patton Anderson, the battery played an important role in the Battle of Shiloh, April 6, by driving the Federals from some of their camps and bombarding the enemy soldiers trapped in the Hornet's Nest area. Three guns participated in a skirmish at Monterey, Tennessee, April 29. Two guns fought in the engagement at Farmington, Mississippi, May 9. Transferred to General Daniel W. Adams's (later Randall L. Gibson's) Louisiana brigade, the battery accompanied the Army of Tennessee on its invasion of Kentucky in September. The battery fought in the Battle of Perryville, October 8, losing two caissons. In the Battle of Murfreesboro, Tennessee, the battery was only lightly engaged until January 2, 1863, when it supported an attack against the Federal left flank. The men went with the brigade to Jackson, Mississippi, in May and fought in the campaign there, July 5–25. Returning to the Army of Tennessee, the battery fought in the Battle of Chickamauga, September 19–20; about 33 of its men were killed or wounded. The men participated in the Battle of Missionary Ridge, November 25, and lost their guns to the Federals during the retreat of the army. At Dalton, Georgia, the battery received four new guns in early 1864. In the Atlanta Campaign, the men frequently engaged the enemy. Three of the battery's guns became disabled during the fighting at Resaca, May 14–15, and Dallas, May 26–28. After the battles around Atlanta in July and August, the battery accompanied the army on its invasion of Tennessee. Assigned to General William B. Bate's division, the battery participated in operations near Murfreesboro. The men repulsed a charge by enemy soldiers on December 4 but lost two guns to the enemy on December 7, when the horses were killed. In February, 1865, the battery received orders to report to Mobile, Alabama, to man heavy artillery emplacements there. The men moved to the Spanish Fort defenses in March and fought in the operations there from March 27 to April 8. After the evacuation of Mobile, the battery again received some field pieces and went with the army to Cuba Station. The battery was at Meridian, Mississippi, at the surrender, May 8, 1865. During the war, approximately 382 men served in the battery. Of that number, 43 were killed in battle, 1 died in an accident, and 6 died of disease.

BIBLIOGRAPHY

"Alex P. Allain." *Confederate Veteran*, XVIII (1910), 392.

Bakewell, A. Gordon. "The Luck of the War Game Sometimes Makes Heroes." *Illinois Central Magazine*, IV (October, 1915), 18–20.

———. "Reminiscences of Orderly Sergeant of the Fifth Company of the Washington Artillery, C. S. Army." *Illinois Central Magazine,* III (August, 1914), 22–25.

Chalaron, J. A. "Battle Echoes from Shiloh." *Southern Historical Society Papers,* XXI (1893), 215–24.

———. "Hood's Campaign at Murfreesboro." *Confederate Veteran,* XI (1903), 438–40.

———. "Vivid Experiences at Chickamauga." *Confederate Veteran,* III (1895), 278–79.

Larter, Harry. "5th Company, Washington Artillery of New Orleans, C. S. A., 1862." *Military Collector and Historian* (1953), 101–102.

Lathrop, Barnes. "A Confederate Artilleryman at Shiloh." *Civil War History,* VIII (1962), 373–85.

Richardson, Frank L. "War as I Saw It." *Louisiana Historical Quarterly,* VI (1923), 89–106.

Steely, Frank, and Orville W. Taylor (eds.). "Bragg's Kentucky Campaign: A Confederate Soldier's Account." *Register, Kentucky State Historical Society,* LVII (1959), 49–55.

Stephenson, P. D. "Defence of Spanish Fort." *Southern Historical Society Papers,* XXXIX (1914), 118–29.

———. "Reminiscences of the Last Campaign of the Army of Tennessee, from May, 1864, to January, 1865." *Southern Historical Society Papers,* XII (1884), 32–39.

6th Battery
(Grosse Tete Flying Artillery)

CAPTAINS. John A. A. West, promoted major August 3, 1864; John Yoist.

This battery was organized about December, 1863, from paroled and exchanged prisoners, many from the Pointe Coupee Artillery Battalion, and from men detached from Captain Oliver J. Semmes's 1st Confederate Battery. The battery had two 12-pounder howitzers and two 10-pounder Parrott rifles, all captured from the enemy. At the Battle of Mansfield, April 8, 1864, the battery supported General Alfred Mouton's division, and the rifled section followed behind the attacking soldiers and fired at the retreating enemy. The battery participated in the Battle of Pleasant Hill, April 9, in support of General

Horace Randal's Texas brigade. On April 12, the battery's howitzer section fought at Blair's Landing on Red River. The battery fought at Monett's Ferry on April 23. At Wilson's Landing on the Red River below Alexandria, the battery on May 3 fired on and helped capture the transport steamer *City Belle* with 200 prisoners. Two days later, the cannons disabled the gunboats *Signal* and *Covington* in the same area, leading to the capture of the vessels. The battery fought at Mansura on May 16 and at Yellow Bayou on May 18. From the summer of 1864 until the end of the war, the battery served as part of Major Oliver J. Semmes's Horse Artillery Battalion in central and southern Louisiana. Orders designated the battery as the 6th Louisiana Field Battery on November 19, 1864. The men surrendered at Alexandria on June 1, 1865.

Barlow's Battery

CAPTAIN. William P. Barlow.

This unit was a temporary organization formed at Montgomery, Alabama, in late April or early May, 1864. The guns had been captured from the enemy in various actions. The men of the command were detached and furloughed soldiers unable to rejoin their commands. No proof exists that the battery ever engaged the enemy in combat while it was attached to Colonel John S. Scott's cavalry brigade in east Louisiana. Barlow's men deserted frequently and had to be replaced by details from cavalry commands in the area. In October, 1864, the department commander ordered the consolidation of the battery with Bradford's Mississippi Battery. Barlow resigned and turned over all of his guns, horses, and equipment to the commander of the Mississippi unit. The detailed cavalrymen who served briefly under Barlow returned to their original commands.

Bridges' Battery

CAPTAIN. William M. Bridges.

This battery was organized February 13, 1864, at Charleston, South Carolina, by transferring about 73 Louisianians who had enlisted in the three companies of the 18th South Carolina Artillery Battalion

(Siege Train) to the new command. The battery became Company D of that battalion but frequently went by the name Bridges' Louisiana Battery. From time to time, the men served as infantrymen as well as heavy artillerists. The battery participated in several engagements during the lengthy Union operations against Charleston in 1864. Orders transferred the battery to the command of General John K. Jackson in the Savannah, Georgia, defenses in early February, 1865. Upon the evacuation of that city, the men went to Raleigh, North Carolina, to refit and get new equipment. In April, the battery served as an independent field artillery battery in General William J. Hardee's Corps, Army of Tennessee, and surrendered as a part of that command at Goldsboro, North Carolina, on April 26, 1865.

BIBLIOGRAPHY

Ripley, Warren. *Siege Train: The Journal of a Confederate Artillery-man in the Defense of Charleston.* Columbia, 1986.

Crescent Artillery, Company A

CAPTAIN. T. H. Hutton.

Organized in New Orleans on March 27, 1862, this company manned guns aboard the Confederate ironclad *Louisiana.* The men performed well during the engagements near Fort Jackson and Fort St. Philip in April, 1862. Following the scuttling of the *Louisiana* and the surrender of the forts, the men of the company became prisoners of war. The company reorganized at Jackson, Mississippi, in late December, 1862, and, armed with muskets, acted as a provost guard in that city for several weeks. In early 1863, the men reported for duty in western Louisiana and received orders to go to Fort DeRussy on the Red River. The company manned some of the fort's heavy guns during the engagement with and capture of the Federal ram *Queen of the West* on February 14, 1863. Placed aboard the cottonclad *Webb,* the men participated in the capture of the Federal ironclad *Indianola* on the Mississippi River on February 24. Major Joseph L. Brent, commander of the expedition that captured the *Indianola,* praised the men for their gallantry and skill and named Lieutenant Thomas H. Handy of the company as prize master. On May 4, the men worked the guns of the gunboat *Grand Duke* during an engagement with the Federal gunboat *Albatross* on the Red River near Fort DeRussy. Following the evacuation of that fort, the men moved to Shreveport and garrisoned Fort Boggs. They moved from there to Grand Ecore in August, 1863, and manned guns mounted overlooking the Red River. In early February, 1864, the men again found themselves at Fort DeRussy, manning the water battery there. They fought in the defense of the fort on March 14; 4 officers and 25 enlisted men became prisoners when the fort surrendered. The remnants of the company served heavy artillery in the Alexandria defenses in the fall of 1864 and winter of 1865. On November 19, the men were designated Company C, Siege Train Battalion. From then until the end of the war, they garrisoned Fort Buhlow near Pineville. Approximately 118 men served in the battery during the war.

Donaldsonville Artillery

CAPTAINS. Victor Maurin, promoted major July 11, 1864; R. Prosper Landry.

An old state militia company founded in 1837, the battery organized for Confederate service in August, 1861, and arrived in Richmond, Virginia, on September 5 with three 6-pounder guns. The government furnished three rifled cannons and ordered the battery to Yorktown. During the Federal operations against Yorktown, April 5– May 4, 1862, the battery occupied a position at Wynn's Mill. At the Battle of Williamsburg, May 5, the three 6-pounders were engaged in defending Fort Magruder late in the action. The battery suffered no significant casualties. On June 1, the battery played a small part in the Battle of Fair Oaks. During the Seven Days' Campaign near Richmond, the battery served with General James Longstreet's division. The men saw action only at Gaines' Mill, June 27–28, and Glendale, June 30; 1 man was killed and 3 were wounded in those battles. The battery was attached to General Richard Anderson's division of Longstreet's Corps, Army of Northern Virginia, for the Second Manassas Campaign. On August 23, the battery had one section (two guns) engaged in skirmishes at Beverly Ford and Rappahannock Station but suffered no casualties. The battery fought at Sharpsburg, September 17, and again had no men injured. During the retreat from Maryland, the battery lost one gun, overrun by a Federal attack, and had 1 man killed and 2 wounded in a skirmish at Shepherd's Ford, September 18. At the Battle of Fredericksburg, December 13, the battery occupied cannon pits to the left of the Plank Road on Marye's Heights. One gun became disabled because of a broken wheel, and casualties amounted to 1 man killed and 6 wounded. The battery was not engaged in the Battle of Chancellorsville. In the reorganization of the army, the battery was assigned to the III Corps. At the Battle of Gettysburg, the battery saw action only on July 1, 1863, near Cemetery Hill. The men fought in the skirmish at Williamsport, Maryland, on July 6 during the retreat from Pennsylvania. The battery was involved in both the Bristoe Station Campaign, October 9–22, and the Mine Run Campaign, November 26–December 2. During the spring and summer of 1864, the battery participated in all of the operations of Robert E. Lee's army, including the Wilderness, Spotsylvania, and Cold Harbor operations. The men occupied various fortifications in the Petersburg defenses during the operations there from the summer of 1864 to the spring of 1865. The battery was included in the surrender of Lee's army at Appomattox, on April 9, 1865. Captain Landry, 3 lieutenants, 64 enlisted men, and 4 servants were present at the surrender. Of the approximately 158 men who served in the battery during the war, 16 died in battle and 20 died of disease.

BIBLIOGRAPHY
Kay, William K. "Mementoes of the Donaldsonville Artillery." *Military Collector and Historian*, VIII (1956), 21–22.
Landry, R. Prosper. "The Donaldsonville Artillery at the Battle of Fredericksburg." *Southern Historical Society Papers*, XXIII (1895), 198–202.
Levy, Eugene H. "The Donaldsonville Artillery." *Southern Bivouac*, III (March, 1885), 302–304.

Fenner's Battery

CAPTAIN. Charles E. Fenner.

This battery was organized May 16, 1862, at Jackson, Mississippi, from men of the disbanded 1st Louisiana Infantry Battalion. The battery had two 12-pounder howitzers, two 6-pounder rifled guns, and two 6-pounder smoothbores. The first duty station for the battery was Port Hudson, Louisiana. It occupied part of the fortifications there and may have fired on Union naval vessels in September, 1862. In January, 1863, the battery was assigned to General Samuel B. Maxey's brigade. With that unit, the battery moved to Jackson, Mississippi, in early May, 1863. During the Federal campaign against Jackson, July 5–25, the battery participated in several skirmishes with the enemy; at least 2 men were killed. The battery was in various camps in eastern Mississippi through the summer of 1863 and received orders to report to Mobile, Alabama, in September. From Mobile, the battery went to the Army of Tennessee at Dalton, Georgia, in December. The battery served in General John B. Hood's Corps during the Atlanta Campaign, May–July 1864, and saw action at Mill Creek Gap, Resaca, and New Hope Church. In the latter battle, the men repulsed an enemy attack that came within fifty to sixty yards of their guns. Following the battles around Atlanta, the battery went with the army on its invasion of Tennessee. When the army reached the vicinity of Nashville, General Hood detached the battery to operate with General Nathan B. Forrest's cavalry against a Federal garrison at Murfreesboro. The battery had to bury three of its cannons during the retreat from Tennessee to prevent them from falling into enemy hands. At Tupelo, Mississippi, the men apparently gave up their other guns to another command and reported for duty at Mobile. There they took over some of the large siege cannons in the city's defenses. Mobile fell to the enemy on April 12, 1865, and the men marched to Meridian, Mississippi, armed with muskets. The battery was paroled at Meridian on May 10, 1865. During the war, approximately 127 men served in the battery.

BIBLIOGRAPHY

Beers, Mrs. Fannie A. *Memories: A Record of Personal Experience and Adventure During Four Years of War.* Philadelphia, 1889, pp. 227–43.

"First Volunteers from Louisiana." *Confederate Veteran,* III (1895), 146.

[Renaud, John K.] "The Romance of a Rich Young Man." *Confederate Veteran,* XXXI (1923), 256–58.

Gibson's Battery
(Miles' Artillery)

CAPTAINS. Claude O. Gibson, resigned April, 1862; M. Brown.

This battery was organized in January, 1862, in New Orleans to serve as Company A, Miles' Legion Artillery. It had four rifled 6-pounder guns and two 12-pounder howitzers. On February 8, the battery left New Orleans for Nashville, Tennessee. When the Confederate forces evacuated that city later in the month, the battery went to Corinth, Mississippi, to join the command of General Pierre G. T. Beauregard. The battery was ordered to reinforce the 18th Louisiana Infantry at Pittsburg Landing on the Tennessee River on February 25, and it participated in a skirmish there with Federal gunboats on March 1. The battery apparently remained at Corinth during the Battle of Shiloh. The men became part of the artillery reserve of the Army of Mississippi and fell back with the army from Corinth to Tupelo in early June, 1862. On June 30, the battery was consolidated with Guibor's Missouri Battery and ceased to exist as a separate unit.

Holmes' Battery

CAPTAIN. Eugene H. Holmes, died April 9, 1865.

This battery was organized March 24, 1864, probably at Clinton, and was attached to the 1st Louisiana Cavalry. The men were members of the Crescent Regiment who had become stranded on the east side of the Mississippi River. The battery had two 12-pounder howitzers and two 6-pounder smoothbores. The men saw no real action until October 5, when they fought the enemy at Woodville, Mississippi. There the Federals captured Captain Holmes, 50 of his men, three of his guns, and most of his wagons. Though it was only a recently organized battery, one superior officer pronounced it "the most efficient arm of the [artillery] service" in eastern Louisiana and southwestern Mississippi. The remaining officers and enlisted men, with their one gun, served temporarily as part of Bradford's Mississippi Battery. In early 1865, the remnants of the battery were gathered at Mobile, Alabama, and assigned to man the cannons in Battery Missouri. They evacuated their post with the army in April, 1865, and were paroled at Meridian, Mississippi, on May 14, 1865.

King's Battery
(Bull Battery)

CAPTAINS. E. W. Fuller, died July 25, 1863; Edward T. King.

This company was organized May 14, 1862, as the St. Martin Rangers. The company converted to artillery in May, 1863, at Grand Ecore. Though formally assigned in June to the 16th Louisiana Infantry Battalion as Company D, the company remained an independent unit known as King's Battery. The men had one 30-pounder Parrott rifled gun and three 24-pounder guns, all pulled by oxen—which resulted in the nickname "Bull Battery." The battery occupied several camps near Alexandria from June to September. By early November, the battery had moved to Natchitoches but shortly received orders to report to Fort DeRussy on the Red River near Marksville. The men sent off their 30-pounder Parrott and one of their 24-pounders upon the approach of a Federal army in early March, 1864. The battery participated in the defense of Fort DeRussy on March 14, and its men became prisoners when the fort surrendered. Exchanged on June 22, the men moved to south Louisiana and served as cavalrymen or mounted infantrymen until the end of the war.

BIBLIOGRAPHY
Brasseaux, Carl A., ed. "The Glory Days: E. T. King Recalls the Civil War Years." *Attakapas Gazette*, XI (1976), 3–33.

Louisiana Guard Battery

CAPTAINS. Camille E. Girardey, resigned July, 1862; Louis D'Aquin, killed December 13, 1862; Charles Thompson, killed June 15, 1863; Charles A. Green.

The men of Company B, 1st Louisiana Infantry, were detached and assigned to duty as an independent battery on July 21, 1861. The battery saw garrison duty in southeastern Virginia and northeastern

North Carolina from the time of its formation until the spring of 1862. On August 9, the battery was in its first battle, at Cedar Mountain. It later fought in the Second Battle of Manassas under General Stonewall Jackson. In September, a report stated that the battery had one 10-pounder Parrott gun and two 3-inch rifled guns. At the Battle of Sharpsburg, September 17, 1 man was killed and 8 were wounded. The battery served with the cavalry forces on the right flank of the army during the Battle of Fredericksburg, December 13. Captain D'Aquin was killed, 1 man was wounded, and one gun became disabled in the fighting. The battery was engaged at Chancellorsville on May 2, 1863, and at Winchester on June 15. Captain Thompson received a mortal wound in the latter engagement. In the first day's fighting at Gettysburg, 1 man was killed. On July 2 and 3, the battery fought with General Wade Hampton's cavalry near Hunterstown, Pennsylvania; 1 man was killed and 5 were wounded. The battery saw some service in the Bristoe Station Campaign, October 9–22, and then occupied redoubts covering a pontoon bridge at Rappahannock Station. On November 7, Federal forces overran the battery's position and captured all four guns and 41 officers and enlisted men. The remnants of the company received orders to report to the Richmond defenses, where they manned siege batteries until the fall of 1864. Some of the men served as cavalry during the closing stages of the war. The battery participated in the retreat to Appomattox and surrendered there on April 9, 1865.

Madison Light Artillery
(Madison Tips)

CAPTAIN. George V. Moody.

Organized at New Carthage as an infantry company, this unit proceeded to Virginia and was mustered in at Lynchburg on May 23, 1861. On August 23, it was converted into an artillery company. After completing its organization at Richmond in October, the battery went to Manassas with two 12-pounder howitzers, two 3-inch rifles, and two 6-pounder smoothbores. The battery saw its first fighting during the Seven Days' Battles, engaging the enemy at Garnett's Farm, Golding's Farm, and Fair Oaks Station, June 26–29, 1862. During the 2nd Manassas Campaign, the battery served in

General James Longstreet's corps but saw no fighting. At the Battle of Sharpsburg, the battery reportedly had two 3-inch rifles and two 24-pounder howitzers. The men helped to repulse numerous enemy attacks during the battle. During the early stages of the Battle of Fredericksburg, the battery shelled the enemy-occupied city. Late in the afternoon, two guns relieved the Washington Artillery on Marye's Heights and fired until they ran out of ammunition. At Chancellorsville, the battery participated in artillery duels on May 3 and 5 near Salem Church. The battery consisted of four 24-pounder howitzers during the Gettysburg Campaign. It fought in support of elements of Longstreet's corps on July 2 and 3. The battery accompanied the corps to Georgia in September, 1863, but arrived on the battlefield of Chickamauga after the fighting had ceased. From November 4 to December 23, the battery participated in Longstreet's campaign against Knoxville. The battery went back to Virginia in time to participate in the battles of the Wilderness and Spotsylvania. The men followed the fortunes of Longstreet's corps through the Petersburg Campaign and surrendered at Appomattox on April 9, 1865—3 officers and 41 men signing paroles there.

Orleans Guard Battery

CAPTAINS. Henry Ducatel, discharged June 5, 1862; Gustave LeGardeur, Jr.

Organized March 6, 1862, at New Orleans, this battery moved to Corinth, Mississippi, with four 6-pounder guns and two 12-pounder howitzers. The battery participated in the engagement at Farmington, May 9, 1862, during which 1 man was wounded. Following the retreat of the army to Tupelo, the battery was disbanded July 21, and the men received assignments to other commands. General Braxton Bragg reorganized the battery on July 11, 1863, and assigned it to the Artillery Reserve Battalion of the Army of Tennessee. The battery saw some action at the Battle of Chickamauga, September 19–20. In November, the battery received orders to report to Charleston, South Carolina. There it was reported as having two 6-pounder bronze guns and two 12-pounder howitzers. The battery occupied various fortifications in the Charleston defenses until the evacuation of Charleston in February, 1865. On July 10, 1864, the battery helped repulse a Union barge attack on Fort Johnson and Battery Simkins. The battery served with General William B. Taliaferro's division during the Carolinas Campaign of 1865. At the Battle of Averasboro, North Carolina, March 15–16, the two howitzers engaged the enemy, and one or both guns had to be abandoned during the retreat. The battery surrendered with the army on April 26, 1865.

Robinson's Horse Artillery

COMMANDERS. Lieutenant William H. Holmes, transferred; Captain N. T. N. Robinson.

Little information on this unit exists. It originated as a company of mountain howitzers attached to the 1st Louisiana Cavalry in September, 1861. The battery followed the fortunes of the 1st Cavalry through the summer of 1863. The men played prominent roles in the engagement at Athens, Alabama, May 1, 1862, and at Big Hill, Kentucky, August 23, 1862. In the summer of 1863, former members of Wheat's Louisiana Tiger Battalion were added to the battery to make it a full company, and Captain Robinson assumed command. The battery received four 10-pounder Parrott rifled guns captured from the enemy in eastern Tennessee. Called the Louisiana Horse Artillery, the battery served with Colonel John Scott's cavalry brigade in the Chickamauga Campaign and in the operations around Chattanooga. One section delayed the crossing of the Tennessee River by part of the Union army in November, 1863, just prior to the Battle of Missionary Ridge. General Braxton Bragg ordered the consolidation of his horse artillery batteries in December, and the men of the battery received assignments to other units, ending the separate history of the battery.

BIBLIOGRAPHY
Carter, Howell. *A Cavalryman's Reminiscences of the Civil War.* New Orleans, 1900.

Watson Battery

CAPTAINS. Allen A. Bursley, resigned to become first lieutenant August, 1861; Daniel Beltzhoover, resigned April, 1862; Allen A. Bursley, transferred to ordnance duty March, 1863.

This battery was organized at New Orleans about July 1, 1861. A. C. Watson, a wealthy planter of Tensas Parish, equipped the battery, which had four 6-pounder bronze smoothbore guns and two 12-pounder howitzers. In August, the battery went to a camp on Lake Bruin near St. Joseph and drilled there for about a month. Traveling up the Mississippi River via Memphis, the battery reported for duty at Columbus, Kentucky, about October 1. At the Battle of Belmont, November 7, the men were in action for the first time. Two guns fell into Federal hands when enemy fire killed or wounded all of the horses, and casualties amounted to 2 men killed and 8 wounded and captured. In late December, the battery reported to Bowling Green, Kentucky. Assigned to the brigade of Colonel John S. Bowen, the men accompanied the brigade to Corinth, Mississippi, in February, 1862. The battery participated in the Battle of Shiloh, Tennessee, April 6–7, serving on the right flank of the army. Only one or two of the men suffered any injuries. The battery remained in northern Mississippi when General Braxton Bragg's army marched into Kentucky. On October 3 and 4, the battery participated in the Battle of Corinth. It helped cover the retreat of the Confederate forces in an engagement at Tuscumbia River Bridge on October 5. In early 1863, the battery moved to Port Hudson, Louisiana, to reinforce the garrison there. The men served at various times under Generals Albert Rust, Abraham Buford, and Samuel B. Maxey at Port Hudson. Two guns were added to the battery, and Lieutenant E. A. Toledano assumed command when Captain Bursley transferred to ordnance duty. During the siege of Port Hudson, May 23–July 9, 1863, two sections of the battery served along the Confederate center, and one section held a position on the Confederate left. Following the surrender of Port Hudson, the men reported to a parole camp at Enterprise, Mississippi. In late 1863, the men received orders to join a Mississippi battery, and the Watson Battery ceased to exist. During the war, 13 of the battery's men were killed in battle, 1 was killed in an accident, and 17 died of disease.

BIBLIOGRAPHY

Rowland, Dunbar. "Military History of Mississippi, 1803–1898." In *The Official and Statistical Register of the State of Mississippi, 1908.* Jackson, 1909, pp. 879–80.

II/Cavalry

1st Regiment

COLONEL. John S. Scott, relieved March 7, 1865.
LIEUTENANT COLONEL. J. O. Nixon.
MAJORS. Gervais Schlater, resigned November 8, 1862; J. M. Taylor, resigned September 24, 1864; Sieb W. Campbell.

COMPANIES AND THEIR COMMANDERS

Company A, Ed Moore Rangers (Iberville). Calvin W. Keep, resigned October 23, 1862; Samuel Matthews.
Company B, Baton Rouge Rangers (East Baton Rouge). J. M. Taylor, promoted major November 28, 1862; N. W. Pope.
Company C (West Feliciana). William W. Leake, resigned October 23, 1862; E. Green Davis.
Company D, Rapides Rangers (Rapides). John Routh Williams, resigned October 23, 1862; Emile Enete.
Company E, Jackson Mounted Men (East Feliciana). Gus A. Scott, killed June 21, 1863; Joseph C. Reily.
Company F (Concordia). Joseph Benjamin, resigned October 23, 1862; C. B. Wheeler.
Company G, Creole Chargers (Avoyelles). Fenelon Cannon, resigned October 23, 1862; James M. Corbin.
Company H (East Baton Rouge). John Campbell, resigned October 23, 1862; James G. McGimsey.
Company I, Morgan Rangers (Pointe Coupee). Ovide Lejeune, resigned October 23, 1862; John H. Graham.
Company K, Louisiana Dragoons (Catahoula). William L. Ditto, resigned December 10, 1862; Francis A. F. Harper, resigned July 21, 1863; William L. Ditto.

This regiment was organized at Baton Rouge on September 11, 1861. Ordered to Nashville, Tennessee, the regiment traveled by steamer to Memphis and from there by train to Nashville. From the latter place, the men rode to Bowling Green, Kentucky, to report to General Albert S. Johnston, and went into winter quarters there. When the Confederate army evacuated Bowling Green in February, 1862, the regiment accompanied it to Nashville. On March 9, a detachment of the regiment fought a skirmish near the city and drove the enemy back. The men participated in the Battle of Shiloh, April 6–7, and fought in several skirmishes in northern Alabama on May 1 and 2. After receiving orders to report to East Tennessee, the regiment took its station at Kingston; it occasionally skirmished with the enemy during the summer of 1862. Colonel Scott took command of a small cavalry brigade and led it on a raid into Kentucky in August. The brigade fought skirmishes at Loudon, Big Hill, and Richmond. Accompanying General Edmund Kirby Smith on his invasion of Kentucky, the regiment captured Frankfort on September 3 and raised its flag over the state capitol. From September 13 to 17, the men fought in the siege of Mumfordville and witnessed the surrender of the Federal garrison. The regiment held a position on the right flank of General Braxton Bragg's army during the Battle of Perryville, October 8, and retreated with the army back to middle Tennessee. After playing a minor role in the Battle of Murfreesboro, the regiment returned to East Tennessee. From March 22 to April 1, 1863, the regiment participated in a raid into Kentucky and fought in several skirmishes there. Scott again received brigade command and occupied Kingston, Tennessee, for several months. From July 25 to August 6, the brigade conducted a raid into Kentucky. The regiment lost 100 men, who were captured in a skirmish near Lancaster on July 31. Scott's brigade moved from Knoxville to join Bragg's army in northern Georgia and saw hard action in the battle of Chickamauga, September 19–20. Following this battle, the regiment served as the army's headquarters guard. The men participated in the Battle of Missionary Ridge, November 25. During the early months of 1864, the regiment was stationed at Dalton, Georgia. The men received orders to report to the District of Southwest Mississippi and East Louisiana in April, 1864. They made an unsuccessful attack on a Union stockade fort near Mount Pleasant Landing south of Port Hudson on May 15. In late June, the regiment moved to Jackson, Mississippi; and it fought with an enemy force moving toward that city from Vicksburg, July 3–7. Returning to eastern Louisiana, the regiment participated in skirmishes at Doyal's Plantation on August 5 and at Thompson's Creek on October 5. An enemy raiding party pushed the regiment out of Liberty, Mississippi on November 18 and caused severe losses. After following enemy cavalry that was raiding from Baton Rouge to Pascagoula, Mississippi, in December, the regiment moved into northern Mississippi. The men fought in several skirmishes near Columbus in early 1865. The regiment surrendered May 5, 1865, near Gainesville, Alabama.

BIBLIOGRAPHY

Carter, Howell. *A Cavalryman's Reminiscences of the Civil War.* 1900; rpr. Baton Rouge, 1979.

[Ditto, W. L.]. "Prisoners 'Charged' a Kentucky Orchard." *Confederate Veteran,* XVI (1908), 573.

Gaines, J. N. "Hard Experience by Scouts in Kentucky." *Confederate Veteran,* XVII (1909), 66.

Gremillion, Nelson. *Company G, 1st Regiment Louisiana Cavalry, C.S.A.: A Narrative.* Lafayette, 1987.

2nd Regiment
(33rd Regiment Partisan Rangers)

COLONEL. William G. Vincent.

LIEUTENANT COLONELS. James A. McWaters, killed January 14, 1863; Winter W. Breazeale, resigned January 13, 1864; James D. Blair, resigned April 10, 1865; W. Overton Breazeale.

MAJORS. Winter W. Breazeale, promoted lieutenant colonel January 14, 1863; James D. Blair, promoted lieutenant colonel January 13, 1864; W. Overton Breazeale, promoted lieutenant colonel April 10, 1865; S. C. Furman.

COMPANIES AND THEIR COMMANDERS

Company A, Independent Rangers (St. Landry). James M. Thompson, resigned (?), transferred to Reserve Corps; Louis D. Prescott.

Company B, Marion Rangers (Natchitoches). James D. Blair, promoted major January 14, 1863; W. F. Kephart, cashiered 1864.

Company C, Natchitoches Rangers (Natchitoches). W. Overton Breazeale, promoted major January 13, 1864; H. Polycarp Gallien.

Company D, Ile Breville Rangers (Natchitoches). F. A. Prudhomme.

Company E, Furman Rangers (Bienville). S. C. Furman, promoted major April 10, 1865; J. F. Scarborough.

Company F, Alligator Rangers (Bienville). A. O. P. Pickens, deserted March 30, 1865.

Company G, McWaters Rangers (Rapides). Thomas J. Stafford, resigned April 28, 1865; E. T. Lewis.

Company H (Assumption). B. S. Tappan, murdered September 10, 1862; J. B. Whittington.

Company I (Iberville). Allen Jumel, transferred to quartermaster department 1865; Alexander Hebert.

Company K (Pointe Coupee). Severin Porche, disposition unknown; Amedee C. Broussard.

This regiment was formed about September 1, 1862, near Donaldsonville by a merger of Breazeale's Battalion and five independent companies. On September 25, portions of the regiment engaged a small enemy force on Bayou Lafourche several miles below Donaldsonville and drove it back to its gunboats. The men again fought the Federals in the Battle of Labadieville, October 27, and retreated with the Confederate army to near Patterson on Bayou Teche. The men skirmished with the enemy during the closing days of 1862 and fought unsuccessfully to defend the gunboat *Cotton* on Bayou Teche, January 14, 1863. The regiment acted as a reserve force and picketed the shore of Grand Lake during the Battle of Bisland, April 12–13. On April 14, the regiment played a major role in the Battle of Irish Bend. The men helped perform rear guard duty during the retreat of General Richard Taylor's army from Franklin to Alexandria. When Taylor's army moved back into south Louisiana in June, the regiment was in the vanguard. A detachment of the regiment assisted in capturing the Union garrison at Brashear City on June 23. Through the late summer and fall of 1863, the men performed picket duty and scout duty along Bayou Teche and conducted several campaigns against Jayhawkers and deserters in the southwest Louisiana prairies. The regiment was almost constantly engaged with enemy forces during the unsuccessful Federal campaign toward Opelousas in October and November, 1863. Through the winter of 1863–64, the regiment remained near St. Martinville to watch the enemy at Brashear City and guard the lower Atchafalaya River. The Federal advance toward Alexandria in March, 1864, slowly pushed the regiment back past that town. On the night of March 21, at Henderson's Hill, the regiment and a Texas artillery battery were surprised and overrun, losing 200 prisoners. The men fought dismounted in the Battle of Mansfield, April 8. Several days later, General Taylor ordered the regiment and the 7th Louisiana Cavalry into south Louisiana to drive out small enemy garrisons and to clear the region of Jayhawkers. The regiment returned to Taylor's army in time to participate in several skirmishes at the end of the Red River Campaign. From the summer of 1864 until the end of the war, the regiment operated in south Louisiana. The men performed picket, outpost, and scout duty along the Atchafalaya River and Bayou Teche and conducted occasional raids into the Bayou Lafourche region. War's end found the remnants of the regiment in camp near Natchitoches. Some of the men received their paroles there; others surrendered at Opelousas and Washington.

BIBLIOGRAPHY

Richardson, Frank L. "War as I Saw It." *Louisiana Historical Quarterly,* VI (1923), 89–106, 223–54.

3rd (Harrison's) Regiment

COLONEL. Isaac F. Harrison.
LIEUTENANT COLONELS. Francis W. Moore, resigned(?); William R. Purvis.
MAJOR. E. S. McCall.

COMPANIES AND THEIR COMMANDERS

Company A, Tensas Cavalry (Tensas). E. S. McCall, promoted major; William Buckner.
Company B (Madison). R. G. Harper, died July 1863; H. P. Wells.
Company C, Faulkner's or Caldwell Defenders (Caldwell). Anthony W. Faulkner, captured April 4, 1864, removed; J. S. Fluitt.
Company D (Catahoula). William R. Purvis, promoted lieutenant colonel October 28, 1864; William H. Gillespie.
Company E (Catahoula). Clarence L. James.

Company F (Morehouse). E. Comer.
Company G, Red River Rangers (Caddo). R. E. Sewall.
Company H (Jackson). John G. Peck.
Company I, Lovell Scouts (St. Mary). Alexander A. Pecot.
Company K, Prairie Rangers (St. Landry). Samuel M. Todd, deserted
    April 5, 1864; Samuel Haas.

This regiment was organized in the fall of 1863 by the addition of three independent companies to the 15th Cavalry Battalion. The regiment operated in northeast Louisiana near the Mississippi River during the remainder of the year. In January, 1864, the men assisted in crossing weapons and other supplies westward over the river for use by the Confederate soldiers in the Trans-Mississippi Department. Several companies participated in skirmishes with Union gunboats on the Ouachita and Black rivers in early March, 1864. Colonel Harrison led a brigade made up of the 3rd, 4th, 5th, and 6th Cavalry regiments during the Red River Campaign, March–May, 1864. The regiment skirmished with the Union gunboats and transports as they moved up the river toward Shreveport and again as they retreated toward Alexandria. An enemy force attacked the brigade's camp near St. Maurice on Bayou Des Cedars on April 17 but were driven back. On April 24, the brigade made a rush into Pineville. An enemy cavalry force moved against the brigade, but Harrison attacked the enemy forces at Hadnot's Plantation on May 1 and drove them back. The regiment continued to harass enemy naval vessels south of Alexandria on May 8 and 9. Harrison's brigade returned to northeast Louisiana after the Red River Campaign. In September and October, the men accompanied the infantry of the Army of Western Louisiana on a campaign into southern Arkansas. By December, the brigade had returned to the Monroe area. From January, 1865, until the end of the war, the regiment occupied camps at Monroe, Harrisonburg, Columbia, and Alexandria. Frequently, the companies were divided and operated in different areas. The men saw very little combat except with small enemy raiding parties moving inland from Vidalia or Vicksburg, Mississippi. By mid-May, 1865, many of the men of the regiment had deserted and gone to their homes. Formal surrender of the regiment occurred May 26, 1865, with the rest of the troops in the Trans-Mississippi Department.

3rd (Pargoud's) Regiment

COLONEL. J. Frank Pargoud.
LIEUTENANT COLONEL. Samuel L. Chambliss.
MAJOR. Richard L. Capers.

COMPANIES AND THEIR COMMANDERS

Company A. James H. Capers.
Company B, McKoin Rangers (Morehouse). John McKoin.
Company C. W. H. Corbin.
Company D, Claiborne Partisan Rangers (Claiborne). John S. Young.
Company E. John G. Randle.
Company F. H. Gelder.
Company G (Madison). R. G. Harper.
Company H (Catahoula). William R. Purvis.
Company I, Faulkner's or Caldwell Defenders (Caldwell). Anthony W. Faulkner.
Company K (Catahoula). Clarence L. James.

This regiment was organized at Monroe about October, 1862, by the addition of four independent companies to the 13th Louisiana Cavalry Battalion. The officers and many of the enlisted men of the latter unit objected to being placed under Colonel Pargoud. The confusion created by the formation of the regiment permitted a Union raiding party to strike at Delhi and Dallas Station in December without meeting any opposition. The Confederate War Department never approved Pargoud's appointment to command, and the regiment was broken up in February, 1863. The 13th Cavalry Battalion then resumed its old organization, and the four independent companies soon became part of the 15th Louisiana Cavalry Battalion.

BIBLIOGRAPHY
Wailes, L. A. "A Perilous but Successful Scout." *Confederate Veteran*, XXII (1914), 121–22.
———. "A War Mystery." *Confederate Veteran*, XXIX (1921), 65.

3rd (Wingfield's) Regiment

COLONEL. James H. Wingfield.
LIEUTENANT COLONEL. Obadiah P. Amacker.
MAJOR. Edwin A. Scott.

COMPANIES AND THEIR COMMANDERS

Company A (Washington[?]). John J. Slocum.
Company B (Livingston[?]). Richard Bredow.
Company C (Washington[?]). J. M. Wallis.
Company D (St. Helena). Julius E. Wilson.
Company E, Beaver Creek Rifles (St. Helena). Richard M. Amacker.
Company F, Louisiana Guards(?) (East Baton Rouge). Robert W. Greenwell.
Company G (Livingston[?]). Evander S. Morgan.
Company H (St. Helena). William B. Kemp.
Company I (East Feliciana). John F. Keller.
Company K (Washington[?]). William Turner.

The 9th Louisiana Battalion Partisan Rangers was redesignated the 3rd Cavalry Regiment about September, 1864, possibly in ignorance of the existence of Colonel Isaac F. Harrison's regiment with the same number. Through the fall of that year, the regiment operated in eastern Louisiana and southwestern Mississippi. The men helped oppose an enemy raid on Clinton in October and later skirmished with the Federals between Bayou Sara and Woodville, Mississippi. A Federal force overran the regiment's camp near Jackson, Louisiana, on November 15. As part of Colonel John S. Scott's cavalry brigade, the regiment followed an enemy raiding force from Baton Rouge to Pascagoula, Mississippi, in December. The regiment accompanied the brigade to northern Mississippi late that month. Most of the regiment remained there until the end of the war, but detachments came back into eastern Louisiana to collect absentees and deserters and to oppose small enemy raids. The regiment surrendered at Gainesville, Alabama, on May 8, 1865.

4th Regiment

COLONEL. A. J. McNeill.
LIEUTENANT COLONEL. Matt. F. Johnson.
MAJOR. Name unknown.

COMPANIES AND THEIR COMMANDERS

Company A. John McNeill.
Company B. Robert I. Ward.

Company C (Madison[?]). Charlie Collins, killed January 1864;
   H. C. Edrington.
Company D. W. B. Chambliss.
Company E (Union). R. E. Amis.
Company F (Tensas[?]). John D. Stokes Newell.
Company G. W. B. Keene.
Company H. Johnson P. Sale, resigned February 25, 1865.
Company I. H. C. Edrington.
Company K. Sylvester York.

This regiment was organized about January, 1864, by the addition of
four companies to Lieutenant Colonel A. J. McNeill's Cavalry Battalion, probably in the Monroe area. The regiment served in Colonel
Isaac F. Harrison's cavalry brigade, which made up part of the Sub-
District of North Louisiana. This brigade operated in the parishes
along the Mississippi River in northeast Louisiana during the early
months of 1864. During the opening stages of the Red River Campaign, in March, the regiment followed the progress of the Union
gunboats and transports up the river from Alexandria toward Shreveport. On April 4, an enemy cavalry and infantry force attacked the
regiment at Campti and drove it away from the town. The regiment
again helped to harass the Union vessels during their retreat down
the river. Federal soldiers attacked the brigade's camp at Bayou Des
Cedars near St. Maurice on April 17, but Harrison's men drove the
enemy back. On April 24, the brigade made a quick raid into Pineville. The men fought in the engagement at Hadnot's Plantation on
May 1, defeating a large enemy force. At the end of the Red River
Campaign, the regiment established its headquarters at Oak Ridge.
For several months, the men performed outpost and picket duty in
that vicinity. They fought in a skirmish at Goodrich's Landing on
July 25. The regiment accompanied Harrison's brigade into southern
Arkansas in September. On October 9, an enemy force attacked the
regiment at Mt. Elba and drove it back toward Warren. By November,
the regiment had returned to its camp at Oak Ridge. From that time
until the end of the war, the men mostly did picket duty near Bayou
Bartholomew and near Floyd on Bayou Macon. On February 2, 1865,
a Union raiding party scattered the 60 men of the regiment who occupied the camp at Oak Ridge. By April, a portion of the regiment
had moved to Columbia to assist in the defense of that area. Most of
the men dispersed to their homes in late April and early May, 1865,

when surrender of the Confederate armies west of the Mississippi River became imminent. Some of the men received their official paroles at Monroe.

BIBLIOGRAPHY

Anderson, John Q. "Joseph Carson, Louisiana Confederate Soldier." *Louisiana History*, I (1960), 44–69.

Fowler, Donald M. "'Mules Won't Do!': The Troubles of a Downsville Soldier in the Civil War, 1864–1865." *North Louisiana Historical Association Journal*, XIV (1983), 61–81.

5th Regiment

COLONEL. Richard L. Capers.

LIEUTENANT COLONELS. James Hixon Capers, resigned August 1, 1864; John S. Young.

MAJORS. John S. Young, promoted lieutenant colonel August 1, 1864; W. H. Corbin.

COMPANIES AND THEIR COMMANDERS

Company A. S. J. Adams.

Company B. W. H. Corbin, promoted major August 1, 1864; J. J. Holden.

Company C, McKoin Rangers (Morehouse). John McKoin.

Company D. John G. Randle, resigned August 2, 1864; Augustus G. Cobb.

Company E. Thomas B. Thompkins.

Company F, Claiborne Partisan Rangers (Claiborne). G. A. Gordon.

Company G (Claiborne and Union, Arkansas). D. S. Arnold, resigned May 4, 1864; H. A. Sledge.

Company H (Jackson[?]). John A. B. Williams.

Company I (Union[?]). James E. Woodward.

Company K. William T. Hall.

This regiment was organized February 20, 1864, by the addition of four companies to the 13th Louisiana Cavalry Battalion. The regiment became part of Colonel Isaac F. Harrison's cavalry brigade in the Sub-District of North Louisiana. Most of the men's early service consisted of scouting and picket duty between the Ouachita and Mississippi rivers. A portion of the regiment participated in skirmishes with Union gunboats on the Black River in March, 1864. During the Red River Campaign, March–May, the men saw some skirmishing on the north bank of the river as they harassed enemy gunboats and transports. The regiment helped defeat an enemy attack on the brigade camp at Bayou Des Cedars near St. Maurice on April 17 and participated in a raid into Pineville on April 24. On May 1, the regiment fought in a skirmish at Hadnot's Plantation. Several companies of the regiment acted as support for the 2nd Louisiana Heavy Artillery Battalion during the closing stages of the Red River Campaign. Following that campaign, the regiment returned to northeast Louisiana. Again, the men did scouting and picket duty for several months. In September, the regiment went with Harrison's brigade into southern Arkansas but apparently saw no fighting. The regiment had returned to Louisiana by the end of the year. After more tedious outpost duty, the regiment moved to Alexandria about March or April, 1865. Several companies did outpost and courier duty near the Atchafalaya River. Most of the men of the regiment remained in service as other units disbanded in late April. Eventually, some of the men began drifting to their homes, and a portion of the regiment surrendered near Mansfield in May.

BIBLIOGRAPHY
Harris, D.W., and B. M. Hulse, comps. *The History of Claiborne Parish, Louisiana.* New Orleans, 1886.

6th Regiment

COLONEL. William Harrison.
LIEUTENANT COLONEL. William B. Denson.
MAJORS. —— Delacy; William J. Scott(?).

COMPANIES AND THEIR COMMANDERS

Company A, Caddo Light Horse (Caddo). William B. Denson, promoted lieutenant colonel; William J. Scott.
Company B. G. M. Sandidge.
Company C, Bossier Cavalry (Bossier). Nathan W. Sentell.
Company D (Caddo[?]). James H. Hecox.
Company E (Bossier[?]). John H. Nattin.
Company F. A. M. Alford.
Company G. William S. Lewis.

Company H (Bienville). R. B. Love.
Company I, Calcasieu Rangers (Rapides). William E. Ivey.
Company K, Martin Scouts (Rapides). Robert W. Martin.

The exact date and place of organization of this regiment remain a mystery. Several companies were added to Lieutenant Colonel William Harrison's Cavalry Battalion, possibly as late as January, 1865, to make it a regiment. Some records indicate that the regiment existed as early as September, 1864. Whatever the case may be, the regiment saw little, if any, fighting during the war. Most of its service consisted of courier and guard duty around Shreveport and Alexandria. Individual companies of the regiment may have conducted independent campaigns against deserters, draft dodgers, and Jayhawkers in northern and western Louisiana. At various times, Harrison's regiment composed part of the cavalry brigades commanded by Colonel William G. Vincent and Colonel Isaac F. Harrison. Toward the end of the war, the regiment was dismounted and attached to an infantry brigade. The regiment appears to have disbanded with other units near Mansfield in May, 1865.

7th Regiment

COLONELS. Louis Bush, appointed presiding officer of military court in Shreveport January 7, 1865; Louis A. Bringier.
LIEUTENANT COLONEL. Louis A. Bringier, promoted colonel January 7, 1865.
MAJOR. Gabriel L. Fusilier, assigned major April 1865.

COMPANIES AND THEIR COMMANDERS

Company A. James C. Murphy.
Company B. William Ira Hargroder.
Company C. William A. Whitaker.
Company D. Francois Feray.
Company E. E. B. Trinidad.
Company F. Agricole Grivemberg.
Company G. Eugene B. Olivier.
Company H (St. Martin[?]). Louis Ranson.
Company I, Chasseurs du Teche. Charles A. Tertrou.
Company K. G. W. Hudspeth.

Major General Richard Taylor authorized the formation of this regiment to operate against Jayhawkers in southwestern Louisiana. Many of the men who joined it were deserters from infantry units, principally the 10th Louisiana (Yellow Jackets) Infantry Battalion. Colonel Louis Bush mustered in the regiment as the 4th Louisiana Cavalry on March 13, 1864, at Moundville, though its organization remained incomplete. The men retreated to Natchitoches in advance of General Nathaniel Banks's Union army, which had started its Red River Campaign. The regiment did picket duty between Natchitoches and Alexandria and participated in skirmishes at Crump's Hill, April 2, and at Wilson's Farm, April 7. About April 11, the regiment accompanied the 2nd Louisiana Cavalry on a raid into the Opelousas and Attakapas region to clear out small bands of enemy soldiers and groups of Jayhawkers. The men had returned to the Red River area by April 22, when they fired on a Union transport about fourteen miles southeast of Alexandria. After a few days in that area, the regiment returned to south Louisiana to recruit and perform outpost duty. From June, 1864, until the end of the war, the men remained on the latter duty, occasionally engaging in campaigns against Jayhawkers or in picket duty near the Atchafalaya River. In October, 1864, the regiment reorganized and changed its designation to the 7th Louisiana Cavalry. Small parties of the regiment, particularly from Companies A and C, made raids into the Bayou Lafourche region in late 1864 and early 1865. These raids had as their objective the acquisition of horses and supplies as well as the harassment of the enemy. The majority of the regiment occupied a camp near Alexandria in May, 1865, when the Trans-Mississippi Department surrendered; but some men received their paroles at Franklin.

8th Regiment

COLONEL. Benjamin W. Clark.
LIEUTENANT COLONEL. Samuel McCutcheon.
MAJOR. Thomas J. Caldwell.

COMPANIES AND THEIR COMMANDERS

Company A, Rapides Minute Company (Rapides). J. W. Texada.
Company B. J. W. Creagh.

Company C, Young Greys (DeSoto). John W. Stuart.
Company D. William H. Terrell.
Company E, Jackson Volunteers(?) (Jackson). M. B. Kidd.
Company F, Franklin Rangers (Franklin). W. M. Guice.
Company G, Murdock Guards (Rapides and Avoyelles). R. W. Heath.
Company H, Bossier Rangers (Bossier). Thomas Player.
Company I. R. H. Turner.
Company K. W. W. Gahagan(?).

This regiment was organized October 27, 1864, probably in south Louisiana, by the combining of the 1st and 2nd Louisiana State Guards Cavalry battalions. The men performed picket and outpost duty along lower Bayou Teche and the upper Atchafalaya River during most of their service. They made up part of a cavalry brigade commanded by General Joseph L. Brent while on those duties. Portions of the regiment participated in brief campaigns against Jayhawkers and deserters in western St. Landry Parish in the early months of 1865. Confederate authorities may have dismounted the regiment late in the war. The regiment appears to have been near Natchitoches or Mansfield at the surrender, in May, 1865.

Gober's Regiment Mounted Infantry

COLONEL. Daniel C. Gober.
LIEUTENANT COLONEL. Haley M. Carter(?).
MAJORS. Thomas Bynum; James T. Coleman.

COMPANIES AND THEIR COMMANDERS

Company A, Skipwith Guards (East Feliciana). Joseph A. Norwood.
Company B, Spencer Guards (St. Helena[?]). Thaddeus C. S. Robertson.
Company C, formerly members of Miles' Louisiana Legion. John T. Nolan.
Company D, formerly members of 9th Louisiana Infantry Battalion. T. Winthrop Brown.
Company E (St. Helena and East Baton Rouge). Robert E. Corcoran.
Company F (St. James, Ascension, and East Baton Rouge). Robert E. Ambrose.
Company G (East Feliciana). John C. McKowen.
Company H. Composition and commander unknown.

Company I (Livingston, East Baton Rouge, and Ascension). Henry L.
  Daigre.
Company K. Composition and commander unknown.

This unit was organized in June, 1864, probably at Clinton, by the
joining and mounting of fragments of infantry units serving in the
area. Colonel John S. Scott, commanding the area, had requested formation of the regiment as support for his artillery batteries operat-
ing along the Mississippi River. Some records erroneously refer to
the unit as the 5th Louisiana Cavalry. The men participated in a
skirmish at Doyal's Plantation below Baton Rouge on August 5,
1864. With Powers' Regiment, Gober's men helped drive an enemy
force from Thompson's Creek near Jackson to St. Francisville on October 5. Later in the day, the two regiments moved toward Woodville, Mississippi, to intercept another enemy raid. On the morning of October 6, the enemy attacked them and drove them back.
Toward the end of October, the six Louisiana companies serving in
Powers' Regiment, which was disbanded, received orders to report
to Gober to give him a full regiment. During a Federal raid on Liberty, Mississippi, portions of the regiment fought in skirmishes at
Merritt's Plantation, November 15, and at Liberty, November 18. As
part of Scott's cavalry brigade, the regiment followed an enemy raiding party from Baton Rouge to Pascagoula, Mississippi, in early December. After a short rest near Mobile, Alabama, the brigade moved
to northern Mississippi. A small portion of the regiment fought in a
skirmish at Franklin, Mississippi, on January 2, 1865. In late December, 1864, or January, 1865, the five companies that had originally composed part of the 18th Louisiana Cavalry Battalion were
ordered back into that organization. Gober soon assumed command
of Scott's brigade, and the remaining companies of the regiment became part of Colonel Fred N. Ogden's new cavalry regiment.

Ogden's Regiment

COLONEL. Fred N. Ogden.

COMPANIES AND THEIR COMMANDERS

Company A, New River Rangers (Ascension). Joseph Gonzales.
*Company B, Skipwith Guards (East Feliciana), formerly Company
  A, 27th Infantry.* Joseph A. Norwood.

Company C, Plains Store Rangers (East Baton Rouge). Gilbert C. Mills.

Company D, Spencer Guards (St. Helena[?], formerly Company H, 27th Infantry. Thaddeus C. S. Robertson.

Company E, Mullen's Scouts and Sharpshooters (Orleans). Louis S. Greenlee.

Company F (East Feliciana). Tully R. Brady.

Company G (Ascension). H. R. Doyal.

Company H (Iberville). Joseph U. Babin.

Company I (East Baton Rouge). Joseph Hinson.

Company K (East Baton Rouge). B. F. Burnett.

This regiment was probably organized in January, 1865, possibly in Mississippi. Ogden received under his command three or four companies from Gober's Regiment Mounted Infantry, three companies formerly with the 14th Confederate Cavalry Regiment, one company from his own temporary battalion, and two recently organized companies. These two new companies, G and H, and possibly one or more of the others, because of their familiarity with the countryside, operated along the lower Amite River and near the Mississippi River south of Baton Rouge until about April, 1865. The other companies participated in the marches and engagements of Colonel John Scott's cavalry brigade in northern and central Mississippi. In April, the companies all united near Meridian; they were surrendered at Gainesville, Alabama, on May 12, 1865.

Powers' Regiment

COLONEL. Frank Powers.
LIEUTENANT COLONEL. John C. McKowen.
MAJOR. Robert A. Owens.

COMPANIES AND THEIR COMMANDERS

Company A, Clay Dragoons (Mississippi). Joseph S. Terry.

Company B (St. James, Ascension, and East Baton Rouge). Robert E. Ambrose.

Company C (St. Helena and East Baton Rouge). R. Emmet Corcoran.

Company D (St. Tammany and Washington). James E. Randolph.

Company E (Mississippi). I. F. Sessions.

Company F (East Feliciana). John C. McKowen, promoted lieuten-
ant colonel June 1, 1864; Tully R. Brady.
Company G (Mississippi). Robert A. Owens, promoted major June 1,
1864.
Company H (Washington and Pike County, Mississippi). James M.
Bates.
Company I (Livingston, East Baton Rouge, and Ascension). Henry L.
Daigre.
Company K (St. Tammany and Washington). John J. Wheat.

Colonel Powers began trying to organize a regiment in December,
1863. About March, 1864, six companies of the 18th Louisiana Cavalry Battalion, one independent Louisiana company, and three Mississippi companies were placed under Powers' command. The new
regiment is attributed to both Louisiana and the regular Confederate
army. Some sources erroneously call the unit the 4th Louisiana Cavalry Regiment. On April 7, the regiment defeated an enemy force
near Port Hudson and captured an artillery piece. The men performed picket and outpost duty between Clinton, Louisiana, and
Woodville, Mississippi, during the remainder of the spring. In June,
the regiment moved to Jackson, Mississippi, as part of Colonel John
Scott's cavalry brigade. The men skirmished with an enemy force
moving against the city from Vicksburg, July 5–7, and pursued the
enemy on their retreat back to Vicksburg. In late July or early August, the regiment returned to the Clinton area. For the next several
months, the men performed picket and outpost duty again. On October 5, they helped drive an enemy force from near Jackson, Louisiana, to St. Francisville. The next day, the regiment moved toward
Woodville to oppose another enemy raid. Later in the month, the six
Louisiana companies in the regiment were transferred to Gober's
Regiment Mounted Infantry. The Mississippi companies went into
another command. Powers eventually commanded a Mississippi
cavalry regiment that Union sources confused with this mixed unit.

1st State Guards Battalion

LIEUTENANT COLONEL. Benjamin W. Clark.
MAJORS. R. E. Wyche; Thomas J. Caldwell.

COMPANIES AND THEIR COMMANDERS

Company A, Bossier Rangers (Bossier). R. E. Wyche, promoted major
July 4, 1863; Thomas J. Caldwell, promoted major April 7, 1864;
Thomas Player.

Company B, Franklin Rangers (Franklin). W. M. Guice.

*Company C, Avoyelles Rangers or Murdock Guards (Avoyelles and
Rapides).* W. H. Murdock, died September 5, 1863; George B.
Marshall; R. W. Heath.

Organized as part of the Louisiana State Army in March, 1863, this
battalion was officially mustered in on June 12 at Shreveport. The
men performed picket duty near Simmesport in April and May and
fell back to Shreveport when Federal forces marched against Alexandria in early May. By the fall of that year, the battalion had moved
to the area of the Black and Little rivers to protect it from raids out
of Vidalia. A Union force skirmished with part of the battalion at
Trinity on November 15, surprising and capturing about 14 men. In
early February, 1864, the battalion moved to Holloway's Prairie to
participate in a campaign against Jayhawkers in that area. The campaign lasted until the latter part of the month. On March 10, the battalion was transferred to Confederate service as part of the newly
designated Louisiana State Guard. One source states that the battalion was present at but did not participate in the Battle of Mansfield,
April 8. Later in the month, the men were attached to Colonel
George W. Baylor's Texas cavalry brigade and fought in the Battle of
Monett's Ferry, April 23. In June, the battalion moved to south Louisiana and performed picket and outpost duty along Bayou Teche.
The men continued their service in south Louisiana until Octo-
ber 27. On that day, the battalion was consolidated with the 2nd
Louisiana State Guard Battalion to form the 8th Louisiana Cavalry
Regiment.

BIBLIOGRAPHY

Appendix to Sliger, J. E. "How General Taylor Fought the Battle of
Mansfield, La." *Confederate Veteran,* XXXI (1923), 456–58.

1st Trans-Mississippi Battalion

MAJOR. Thompson J. Bird.

COMPANIES AND THEIR COMMANDERS

Company A (Louisiana). John A. Hawkins; Edwin S. Crawford.
Company B (Louisiana). T. B. Gray.
Company C (Arkansas, Louisiana, and Texas). George W. Buckner.
Company D (Arkansas, Louisiana, and Texas). James E. Haden.
Company E (Arkansas, Louisiana, and Texas). Benjamin Turner.

This battalion was organized at Shreveport on March 19, 1864, with four companies. Company E joined the battalion in June. At times, the unit was called the 1st Arkansas and Louisiana Cavalry Battalion or the 1st Battalion Mounted Cadets. The members of the unit were men and boys over or under conscript age and men who had received disability discharges from other units. Throughout its entire service, the battalion performed courier duty under the direct supervision of the headquarters of the Trans-Mississippi Department. The men carried messages to and from a number of cities and towns, including Shreveport, Alexandria, and Monroe, Louisiana; Houston, Texas; and Camden and Washington, Arkansas. At the end of the war, many men simply went home; others signed paroles at the cities nearest their duty stations.

2nd State Guards Battalion

LIEUTENANT COLONEL. Henry M. Favrot.
MAJOR. Samuel McCutcheon.

COMPANIES AND THEIR COMMANDERS

Company A, Rapides Minute Company (Rapides). J. W. Texada.
Company B. J. W. Creagh.
Company C, Young Greys (DeSoto). John W. Stuart.
Company D. William H. Terrell.
Company E. W. W. Gahagan; resigned August 3, 1864.
Company (?). E. C. (M. B.[?]) Kidd.
Company (?). Organization and commander unknown.

This battalion was formed about February 15, 1864, by the mounting of the 1st Louisiana State Troops Infantry Battalion and the addition to it of four newly organized State Guard cavalry companies. Formal transfer to the Louisiana State Guard occurred March 10. The battalion joined General Richard Taylor's army in late March. At the Battle of Mansfield, April 8, the battalion remained in reserve and did not participate in the fighting. The battalion received orders on April 24 to report to a camp of instruction at Shreveport. After a brief period of drilling, the battalion moved to Opelousas in early May to participate in a campaign against Jayhawkers and to recruit new soldiers. By the end of May, the battalion had moved to a camp near Franklin. For the next few months, the men performed outpost and picket duty along lower Bayou Teche. On June 22, Company C fought a skirmish with the enemy near Berwick Bay. By mid-September the battalion had relocated to Monterey on the Black River, probably to guard that area against enemy raids. On October 27, 1864, the battalion was consolidated with the 1st Louisiana State Guard Cavalry Battalion to form the 8th Louisiana Cavalry Regiment.

3rd State Guards Battalion

MAJOR. James B. Corkern.

COMPANIES AND THEIR COMMANDERS

Company A. Daniel B. Gorham.
Company B. Edward D. Cheatham.

No precise data exist on the date of formation of this unit. Efforts to raise men for it may have begun as early as April, 1864. Governor Henry W. Allen appointed the battalion and company officers on June 25. The governor originally intended the battalion to serve in eastern Louisiana, where it was raised; and by early July, the men had gone into active service with Colonel John S. Scott's cavalry brigade near Clinton. Confederate authorities did not want to accept the battalion, because it did not have the required four companies. A report dated August 4 placed the battalion at Stony Point and gave its strength as 96 men. The men had few weapons and equipment. Governor Allen on September 28 ordered the battalion to cross the Mississippi River and report to General Simon B. Buckner at Alexandria. Some of the men may have reached Alexandria by early December. It appears the battalion was disbanded shortly afterwards.

9th Battalion Partisan Rangers

LIEUTENANT COLONEL. James H. Wingfield.
MAJORS. James DeBaun; Fred N. Ogden (temporarily).

COMPANIES AND THEIR COMMANDERS

Company A (Washington[?]). John J. Slocum.
Company B (Livingston[?]). Richard Bredow.
Company C (Washington[?]). A. C. Bickham, resigned November 1, 1862; George W. Lewis, died in prison December 4, 1863; J. M. Wallis.
Company D (St. Helena). Julius E. Wilson.
Company E, Beaver Creek Rifles (St. Helena). Obadiah P. Amacker.
Company F, Louisiana Guards(?) (East Baton Rouge). Wilson Tate, resigned February, 1864; Robert W. Greenwell.
Company G (Livingston and East Baton Rouge). Evander S. Morgan.
Company H (St. Helena). William B. Kemp; Richard V. McMichael (temporarily).
Company I (East Feliciana). Edwin A. Scott.
Company K (1st), disbanded. Richard V. McMichael.
Company K (2nd). William Turner.

Organized as the 1st Louisiana Regiment Partisan Rangers about May 28, 1862, at Camp Moore, this unit had its designation changed to the 9th Battalion Partisan Rangers in August. The battalion performed picket duty along the Amite River and the north shore of Lake Pontchartrain during June and July. Federal forces attacked and defeated four companies near Benton's Ferry on the Amite on July 25. On July 27, some of the men stationed near Madison-ville skirmished with a Federal force that landed near there from an armed transport steamer. During the Battle of Baton Rouge, August 5, the men acted as pickets on the various roads leading into the town. They occupied Baton Rouge when the Federals evacuated it on August 21. General Daniel Ruggles disbanded several companies on August 30. The battalion did picket duty near Baton Rouge and along the north shore of Lake Pontchartrain for the remainder of the year. A detachment of the battalion attacked and drove back the steamer *G. Brown* on Bayou Bonfouca on November 21. When the Federals reoccupied Baton Rouge, in December, the men near the town withdrew their picket posts to the Amite River. Early in 1863, the Confederate War Department rescinded Ruggles' orders disbanding the companies and authorized their reorganization. This reorganization appears to have occurred at Camp Moore. General Franklin Gardner ordered the battalion to Port Hudson to perform duty there. During the Federal feint attack on the Port Hudson land defenses on March 14 and 15, the battalion skirmished with and drove back portions of the enemy army. Part of the battalion attempted to intercept Colonel Benjamin Grierson's cavalry raiders as they made their way toward Baton Rouge in late April. The men skirmished with Grierson's force on May 1 at Wall's Bridge near Osyka, Mississippi. The battalion picketed the roads leading toward Port Hudson when General Nathaniel P. Banks's army began marching toward that place in mid-May. The men fought in several skirmishes near Thompson's and Sandy creeks on May 23 and 25. During the siege of Port Hudson, May 23–July 9, the majority of the battalion acted as infantrymen on the left wing of the Confederate defenses. A small detachment helped stop the attack of the black Louisiana Native Guards on May 27. The battalion was surrendered with the Port Hudson garrison, and most of the officers went into Federal prisons. Throughout the fall and winter of 1863 and the early spring of 1864, the remnants of the battalion remained demoralized and scattered. Major Fred N. Ogden assumed temporary command in March, 1864, and brought the battalion back into a disciplined and organized state. In June, the battalion accompanied Colonel John Scott's cavalry brigade to Jackson, Mississippi, and fought in skirmishes near there on July 5 to 7. By late July, the battalion had returned to the Clinton area. In September, the battalion was redesignated the 3rd Louisiana (Wingfield's) Cavalry.

13th Battalion Partisan Rangers

LIEUTENANT COLONELS. Samuel L. Chambliss, resigned April 30, 1863; Richard L. Capers.

MAJORS. Richard L. Capers, promoted lieutenant colonel April 30, 1863; James H. Capers.

COMPANIES AND THEIR COMMANDERS

Company A. James H. Capers, promoted major April 30, 1863; S. J. Adams.

Company B. W. H. Corbin.
Company C, McKoin Rangers (Morehouse). John McKoin.
Company D. John G. Randle.
Company E (Caddo[?]). Hiram Gibbs, resigned October 26, 1863;
Thomas B. Thompkins.
Company F, Claiborne Partisan Rangers (Claiborne). John S. Young.
Company G (Union, Arkansas, and Claiborne). D. S. Arnold.

This battalion was organized on August 26, 1862, at Monroe; Companies E and F came from Bayliss' Louisiana Battalion Partisan Rangers. The men did picket duty in East Carroll Parish near Lake Providence for several months. In November, four independent companies were added to the battalion to create the 3rd Louisiana Cavalry. Colonel J. Frank Pargoud received a commission to command the new regiment. Many of the officers and enlisted men of the former battalion protested the appointment of Pargoud over Chambliss. During the confusion created by this consolidation of units, a Federal raid struck Delhi and Dallas Station without opposition from any Confederate forces. As a result of this raid, the 13th Battalion was restored as a separate organization. The battalion returned to its duty in East Carroll Parish and fought in a skirmish at Lake Providence on February 10, 1863. The men helped in attempts to oppose the march of General Ulysses S. Grant's Union army through northeastern Louisiana in April. On May 10, several companies fought skirmishes at Caledonia and Pin Hook. Colonel Frank Bartlett led the battalion and a Texas cavalry unit in an attack on the Federal garrison in the town of Lake Providence on June 9. By early July, the battalion had moved to Delhi. The men soon became part of Colonel Isaac F. Harrison's cavalry brigade. Lieutenant Colonel Capers received permission in October to recruit new companies and raise the battalion to a regiment. He had succeeded in his task by early the next year; and on February 20, 1864, the new unit was organized as the 5th Louisiana Cavalry Regiment.

BIBLIOGRAPHY

Durham, Ken. "'Dear Rebecca': The Civil War Letters of William Edwards Paxton, 1861–1863." *Louisiana History,* XX (1979), 169–96.
Harris, D. W., and B. M. Hulse. *The History of Claiborne Parish, Louisiana.* New Orleans, 1886.

15th Battalion

LIEUTENANT COLONEL. Isaac F. Harrison.

MAJORS. Isaac F. Harrison, promoted lieutenant colonel July 8, 1863; E. S. McCall.

COMPANIES AND THEIR COMMANDERS

Company A, Tensas Cavalry (Tensas). Albert Bondurant, resigned February 28, 1863; E. S. McCall, promoted major July 8, 1863; William Buckner.

Company B (Madison). R. G. Harper.

Company C, Faulkner's Defenders (Caldwell). Anthony W. Faulkner.

Company D (Catahoula). William R. Purvis.

Company E (Catahoula). Clarence L. James.

Company F (Morehouse). E. Comer.

Company G, Red River Rangers (Caddo). R. Sewell.

This battalion was organized about January, 1863, probably at Monroe. The battalion appears to have operated in Madison Parish near the Mississippi River during its first few months in service. On April 4, the men fought in skirmishes near Richmond and Bayou Vidal. The battalion unsuccessfully opposed the march of General Ulysses S. Grant's army through Tensas Parish later in the month, fighting one sizable engagement at Choctaw Bayou on April 28. Portions of the battalion participated in the defense of Fort Beauregard near Harrisonburg, May 10–11. During the siege of Vicksburg, Mississippi, the battalion fought to protect Madison and Tensas parishes from enemy raiding parties. On June 3, a portion of the battalion drove an enemy force out of Richmond. The next day, Company A captured an enemy camp located on Lake St. Joseph. Part of the battalion defeated a larger enemy force at Richmond on June 6. Major Harrison furnished some of his men to General John G. Walker's Texas infantry division to act as scouts and guides during Walker's operations around Milliken's Bend and Young's Bend. These men probably participated in the attacks on those Union garrisons. Harrison's successes against the enemy so impressed General Richard Taylor that the latter began an effort to raise the battalion to a regiment. Possibly by November, 1863, three new companies had joined the battalion and made it the 3rd Louisiana Cavalry Regiment.

18th Battalion

LIEUTENANT COLONEL. Haley M. Carter.
MAJOR. H. Newton Sherburne.

COMPANIES AND THEIR COMMANDERS

Company A (St. Tammany, Livingston, and St. Helena). Thomas C. W. Ellis.

Company B (St. Helena and East Baton Rouge). Robert Emmet Corcoran.

Company C (St. James, Ascension, and East Baton Rouge). Robert E. Ambrose.

Company D (St. Tammany and Washington). James E. Randolph.

Company E (Pike County, Mississippi, and Washington). James M. Bates (did not rejoin battalion at reorganization).

Company F (Mississippi[?]). J. Doyle (did not rejoin battalion at reorganization).

Company G (Livingston, Ascension, and East Baton Rouge), paroled as Company E. Henry L. Daigre.

Company H (Livingston), paroled as Company F. Hannibal Carter.

Company I (Livingston and St. Helena), paroled as Company G. John J. Wheat.

This battalion, organized at Clinton about January 25, 1864, was originally called the 10th Louisiana Cavalry Battalion. The battalion performed picket duty between Clinton and Baton Rouge and toward Springfield. On several occasions, the men fought small skirmishes with enemy troops. In March, six companies were transferred to Powers' Regiment and two others went into a temporary battalion commanded by Lieutenant Colonel Fred N. Ogden. On November 21, orders were issued reorganizing the 18th Battalion. This did not take place until December, 1864, or January, 1865, while the men were on duty in central Mississippi with Colonel John S. Scott's cavalry brigade. The battalion remained in that area and had problems with men deserting to go back to eastern Louisiana. On April 6, the battalion participated in a skirmish in Pickens County, Alabama.

The battalion was surrendered and paroled at Gainesville, Alabama, on May 12, 1865.

19th Battalion

LIEUTENANT COLONEL. A. J. McNeill.
MAJOR. Matt. F. Johnson.

COMPANIES AND THEIR COMMANDERS (probable)

Company A. John McNeill.
Company B. Robert I. Ward.
Company C (Madison[?]). Charlie Collins.
Company D. W. B. Chambliss.
Company E. R. E. Amis.
Company F (Tensas[?]). John D. Stokes Newell.

No substantive information on this unit exists. The battalion appears to have been formed around Companies A and B about September, 1863. Its number probably was assigned by the Confederate War Department but never used by the battalion, which went by the name McNeill's Battalion. In early 1864, four new companies joined the battalion to form the 4th Louisiana Cavalry Regiment.

Bayliss' Battalion Partisan Rangers

MAJOR. W H. Bayliss.

COMPANIES AND THEIR COMMANDERS

Company A, Claiborne Rangers (Claiborne). Richard L. Capers.
Company B (Caddo[?]). Hiram Gibbs.

This battalion was organized June 27, 1862, with 158 men. Governor Thomas O. Moore authorized Major Bayliss to raise two companies under the provisions of the partisan ranger act passed by the Confederate Congress. The battalion did not exist for long. The two companies became part of the 13th Louisiana Battalion Partisan Rangers on August 26, 1862.

Breazeale's Battalion Partisan Rangers

MAJOR. Winter W. Breazeale.

COMPANIES AND THEIR COMMANDERS

Company A, Marion Rangers (Natchitoches). James D. Blair.
Company B, Natchitoches Rangers (Natchitoches). W. Overton Breazeale.
Company C, Ile de Breville Rangers (Natchitoches). F. A. Prudhomme.
Company D, Du Lac Espagnol (Bienville[?]). J. F. Scarborough.
Company E, Furman Rangers (Bienville). S. C. Furman.
Company F, Alligator Rangers (Bienville). A. O. P. Pickens.

This battalion was organized at Natchitoches about July 27, 1862. Governor Thomas O. Moore ordered the battalion to move to Moreauville via Alexandria. The men may not have made this move, since a report dated August 21 placed them in Natchitoches. On that day, the battalion was transferred to Confederate service. In early September, General Richard Taylor ordered the battalion to Opelousas. Shortly after their arrival in south Louisiana, the five companies that made the move were joined with five independent companies to form the 2nd Louisiana Cavalry Regiment.

Cage's Battalion

MAJOR. John B. Cage (acting).

COMPANIES AND THEIR COMMANDERS

Company A (East Baton Rouge). B. F. Bryan.
Company B, New River Rangers (Ascension). Joseph Gonzales.
Company C, Plains Store Rangers (East Baton Rouge). Gilbert C. Mills.

This temporary organization consisted of three companies assigned at various times to Miles' Louisiana Legion and is sometimes called Miles' Legion Cavalry. The battalion is also referred to as the 10th Louisiana Cavalry Battalion, but probably erroneously. John B. Cage, the senior captain, assumed command of the battalion as acting major, probably at Clinton in mid-May, 1863. At that time, the battalion had about 250 men. The battalion operated under Colonel John L. Logan's command and harassed the rear outposts of General Nathaniel P. Banks's army as it laid siege to Port Hudson. On June 3, the men participated in a skirmish at Pretty Creek west of Clinton and helped defeat the enemy force commanded by Colonel Benjamin Grierson. After the surrender of Port Hudson, Logan's cavalry fell back to Crystal Springs, Mississippi. The battalion returned to eastern Louisiana and fought in a skirmish at Jackson on August 3. On September 14, 1863, the battalion was consolidated with six Mississippi companies and another Louisiana company to form the 14th Confederate Cavalry Regiment.

BIBLIOGRAPHY
Pascoe, W. H. "Confederate Cavalry Around Port Hudson." *Southern Historical Society Papers*, XXXIII (1905), 83–96.

Harrison's Battalion

LIEUTENANT COLONEL. William Harrison.
MAJOR. William B. Denson(?).

COMPANIES AND THEIR COMMANDERS

Company A, Caddo Light Horse (Caddo). William B. Denson, promoted; William J. Scott.
Company B. G. M. Sandidge.
Company C, Bossier Cavalry (Bossier). Nathan W. Sentell.
Company D (Caddo[?]). James H. Hecox.
Company E (Bossier[?]). John H. Nattin.
Company F. A. M. Alford.

This battalion was organized about December, 1863, probably at Shreveport. No substantive information on the battalion exists. As early as January, 1864, General Richard Taylor sought to find unattached companies so he could increase the battalion to a regiment. The men apparently did guard and courier duty for the headquarters of the Trans-Mississippi Department in Shreveport. On April 9, 1864, General Edmund Kirby Smith ordered the battalion to report for duty at Mansfield, but no record indicates that the men participated in any of the closing stages of the Red River Campaign. About January, 1865, four new companies were added to the battalion to create the 6th Louisiana Cavalry Regiment.

Ogden's Battalion

LIEUTENANT COLONEL. Fred N. Ogden.
MAJOR. B. F. Bryan.

COMPANIES AND THEIR COMMANDERS

Company A (East Baton Rouge). B. F. Bryan, promoted major June 6, 1864; Joseph Hinson.
Company B. Composition and commander unknown.
Company C. Composition and commander unknown.
Company D. Composition and commander unknown.
Company E. Composition and commander unknown.
Company F (St. Helena). Hannibal Carter.
Company G. Composition and commander unknown.
Company H (St. Tammany, Livingston, and St. Helena). Thomas C. W. Ellis.

This was a temporary battalion organized at Clinton on June 6, 1864, with three Louisiana and three Mississippi companies. Two other Louisiana companies may have served with the battalion for brief periods of time. The men did picket duty in the area until late in the month. At that time, they accompanied Colonel John Scott's cavalry brigade to Jackson, Mississippi. The battalion skirmished with the enemy near that city on July 5 to 7. Returning to Clinton later in the month, the battalion again did picket and outpost duty in the area during the remainder of the summer. In October, efforts were made to fill the battalion to regimental size and place it under Colonel Duncan S. Cage, but the plan never reached fruition. Enemy troops overran the battalion's camp at Clinton on November 16 and scattered the men. Ogden gathered 60 to 70 men in time to participate with Scott's brigade in an engagement at Liberty, Mississippi, on November 18. In early December, the brigade pursued an enemy raiding force from Baton Rouge to Pascagoula, Mississippi. The brigade rested near Mobile, Alabama, and then moved into central Mississippi. In January, 1865, the battalion was broken up. Two Louisiana companies went into the 18th Louisiana Cavalry Battalion, and one went into a new regiment placed under Ogden's command.

Red River Scouts Battalion

COMPANIES AND THEIR COMMANDERS

Company A. Willis A. Stewart.
Company B. James Cassidy.
Company C. Norman White.

This battalion is sometimes referred to as the Red River Sharpshooters, or the Steamboat Battalion. Companies A and B were formed at Shreveport in 1863, possibly as early as the summer, by the mounting of men who had served as crewmen on steamboats. No information exists on the date of the formation of Company C. General Edmund Kirby Smith formed the companies to act as rangers or pickets along the Red River. No field officer was ever appointed to command the battalion. On November 3, Companies A and B received orders to report to General Richard Taylor at Alexandria. Taylor apparently stationed Company A on the south side of the Red River and Company B on the north side to help scout in the vicinity of the lower Black and Ouachita rivers. By early March, 1864, both companies were near Marksville. Most of Company B again moved across the Red River, but a small detachment made up part of the garrison of Fort DeRussy when Federal forces captured it March 14. Company A fell back through Alexandria and Natchitoches to Shreveport as the Federal army advanced up the river. Company B continued scouting and picket duty on the north side of the river during the early stages of the Red River Campaign. The sources do not mention the battalion again until April, 1865. At that time, according to reports, Companies A and C were in southern Rapides and Avoyelles parishes doing picket duty and breaking up the illegal cotton trade with the enemy. The battalion probably disbanded in that area in May, 1865, but one source places Company B at Shreveport at the surrender of the Trans-Mississippi Department.

III/Infantry

1st Regiment Regulars

COLONELS. Adley H. Gladden, promoted brigadier general September 10, 1861; Daniel W. Adams, promoted brigadier general May 23, 1862; John A. Jacques, cashiered February 13, 1863; James Strawbridge.

LIEUTENANT COLONELS. Daniel W. Adams, promoted colonel September 10, 1861; John A. Jacques, promoted colonel May 23, 1862; Fred H. Farrar, Jr., died January 3, 1863; James Strawbridge, promoted colonel February 13, 1863; F. M. Kent, died April 2, 1864; S. S. Batchelor.

MAJORS. Charles M. Bradford, resigned July 23, 1861; John A. Jacques, promoted lieutenant colonel September 10, 1861; Fred H. Farrar, Jr., promoted lieutenant colonel May 23, 1862; James Strawbridge, promoted lieutenant colonel January 3, 1863; F. M. Kent, promoted lieutenant colonel February 16, 1863; S. S. Batchelor, promoted lieutenant colonel April 2, 1864; Douglas West.

COMPANIES AND THEIR COMMANDERS

Company A. Fred H. Farrar, Jr., promoted major September 10, 1861; Taylor Beatty, resigned February 13, 1863; W. A. Reid.

Company B. John A. Jacques, transferred to Company D; Thomas Overton, resigned May 21, 1861; P. H. Thompson, resigned February 24, 1862; James Cooper.

Company C. F. M. Kent, promoted major January 6, 1863; Charles H. Tew.

Company D. John A. Jacques, promoted major August 23, 1861; James H. Trezevant.

Company E. William H. Scott, died December 18, 1861; Edward C. Preston, absent; Thomas Butler.

Company F. James Strawbridge, promoted major May 23, 1862; James W. Stringfellow.

Company G. J. Thomas Wheat, killed April 6, 1862; William H. Sparks, killed July 28, 1864; J. C. Stafford(?).

Company H. S. S. Batchelor, promoted major February 16, 1863; Charles H. Tew.

Company I. Douglas West, promoted major April 2, 1864; J. C. Stafford.

Company K. Charles Taylor, died May 8, 1863; Robert C. Kennedy.

This regiment was organized February 5, 1861, as part of the Louisiana State Army and transferred to Confederate service on March 13 with about 860 men. The regiment received orders in early April to report for duty at Pensacola, Florida. Only three companies—A, B, and C—had completed recruiting at that time, so the governor called upon volunteer units to fill out the regiment's organization. Five companies responded and went to Pensacola with the three companies already mentioned. There the men spent the next several weeks drilling. By late May, the remainder of the 1st Regulars' companies had reported to Pensacola. The five volunteer companies formed themselves into the 1st Louisiana Infantry Battalion and left under orders for Virginia. During the summer and fall of 1861, the regiment continued to drill. The companies took turns manning the heavy artillery batteries around Pensacola. Two companies participated in the action on Santa Rosa Island, October 8–9. The regiment took part in the defense of Fort McRae and Fort Barrancas, November 22–23, when the Federals bombarded them from Fort Pickens. On February 26, 1862, the regiment received orders to go to Corinth, Mississippi. The men occupied Purdy, Tennessee, during a Federal expedition toward that town, March 9–14. A detachment of the regiment pushed back an enemy force marching toward the Memphis and Charleston Railroad near Yellow Creek, March 14–15. The regiment suffered heavy casualties during the opening attack at the Battle of Shiloh, April 6. By the end of the day, the regiment had only 101 men remaining present for duty. The regiment participated in the operations around Corinth from April 29 to June 11 and retreated with the army to Tupelo. When General Braxton Bragg led the army by rail via Mobile to Chattanooga in July, the regiment marched with the army's wagon trains overland to the Tennessee city. The regiment made up part of General Jones Withers' division during the invasion of Kentucky, August 28–October 19. Withers' Division marched to support other Confederate troops near Lexington on October 7 and missed the Battle of Perryville the next day. Retreating with the army, the regiment went into camp at Tullahoma, Tennessee. The men participated in attacks at the Battle of Murfreesboro on December 31, 1862, and January 2, 1863; 102 men were killed, wounded, or missing. During the spring and summer of 1863, the regiment acted as support for the army's reserve artillery. The regiment was consolidated with the 8th Arkansas Infantry and fought in the Battle of Chickamauga, September 19–20. With fewer than 100 men present for duty, the regiment was assigned as headquarters guard for the army during the Chattanooga Campaign. The men remained on this duty at Dalton, Georgia, during the early spring of 1864. Assigned to General Randall L. Gibson's Louisiana brigade in April, the regiment participated in the various marches of the Atlanta Campaign, May–July, but saw very little fighting until the Battle of Ezra Church on July 28. The men marched with the army on its invasion of Tennessee and fought at Nashville, December 15–16. Following the Tennessee Campaign, Gibson's brigade went to Mobile, Alabama, in February, 1865. There the regiment was consolidated with the 16th and 20th Louisiana regiments and 4th Louisiana Battalion and fought at Spanish Fort, March 27–April 8. The men surrendered at Gainesville, Alabama, on May 12, 1865. The regiment lost 176 men in battle—52 by disease, 2 by accident, 1 by murder, and 2 by execution.

BIBLIOGRAPHY
Moore, Waldo W., ed. "Infantry Captain Describes Confederate Invasion of Kentucky in Autumn of 1862." *North Louisiana Historical Association Newsletter*, VII (1967), 7–15.

1st Regiment

COLONELS. Albert G. Blanchard, promoted brigadier general September 21, 1861; William G. Vincent, dropped April 28, 1862; William R. Shivers, retired 1864[?]); Samuel R. Harrison, resigned June 8, 1862; James Nelligan.
LIEUTENANT COLONELS. William G. Vincent, promoted colo-

nel September 21, 1861; William R. Shivers, promoted colonel; Michael Nolan, killed July 3, 1863; James Nelligan, promoted colonel.

MAJORS. William R. Shivers, promoted lieutenant colonel September 27, 1861; Samuel R. Harrison, promoted colonel; Michael Nolan, promoted lieutenant colonel April 28, 1862; James Nelligan, promoted lieutenant colonel July 3, 1863; Charles E. Cormier.

COMPANIES AND THEIR COMMANDERS

Company A, Caddo Rifles (Caddo). Charles Dailee, dropped April 28, 1862; Alex Boarman, detached September, 1864.

Company B (1st), Louisiana Guards Company B (Orleans), detached as artillery at Richmond July 5, 1861. Camille E. Girardey.

Company B (2nd), Red River Rebels (Rapides). James C. Wise, dropped April 28, 1862; J. P. Groves, died July 18, 1864, of wounds received July 9.

Company C (1st), Louisiana Guards Company C (Orleans), transferred to 1st Battalion July 16, 1861. Francis Rawle.

Company C (2nd), Slocumb Rifles (Orleans). Robert W. Armistead, died September 8, 1862; James E. Armorer.

Company D, Emmet Guards (Orleans). James Nelligan, promoted major June 16, 1862; Albert N. Cummings.

Company E, Montgomery Guards (Orleans). Michael Nolan, promoted major April 28, 1862; Michael B. Gilmore, killed June 25, 1862; Thomas Rice.

Company F, Orleans Light Guards Company D (Orleans). P. R. O'Rorke, dropped April 28, 1862; Samuel H. Snowden, promoted assistant quartermaster January, 1864; James Dillon, resigned January, 1865.

Company G, Orleans Light Guards Company B (Orleans). Thomas M. Deane, dropped April 28, 1862; Edward D. Willett.

Company H (1st), Davis Guards (Orleans), became Company I, 1st Kentucky Infantry. Ben M. Anderson.

Company H (2nd), Askew Guards Company B (Orleans), assigned March 6, 1862, transferred to 15th Regiment May 22, 1862. Andrew Brady.

Company H (3rd), Shreveport Greys (Caddo), assigned June 27, 1862; disbanded September 5, 1862. William E. Moore.

Company I, Orleans Light Guards Company A (Orleans). Charles E. Cormier, promoted major July 3, 1863; Joseph Taylor.

Company K, Orleans Light Guards Company C (Orleans). John M. Galt, resigned April 28, 1861; Charles N. Frost, resigned November 11, 1861; William L. Randall, resigned January 30, 1863; Louis W. McLaughlin.

This regiment was organized in New Orleans on April 28, 1861, and received orders to go to Richmond, Virginia. From that city, the regiment went to Norfolk. The men remained in the area until early 1862, when they moved into North Carolina. They arrived on the field too late to participate in the skirmish at South Mills on April 19. The regiment remained at Weldon until late May, when it returned to Richmond. During the Seven Days' Battles, the regiment fought at King's Schoolhouse, June 25, and at Malvern Hill, July 1; 214 men were killed, wounded, or missing in those battles. On July 26, the regiment was placed in the 2nd Louisiana Brigade with the 2nd, 9th, 10th, and 15th regiments and the 1st Zouave Battalion. The men fought in the Battle of 2nd Manassas, August 29–30, and in the Battle of Sharpsburg, September 17. At the Battle of Fredericksburg, December 13, the regiment was only lightly engaged and only a few men were wounded. The men participated in the attack by General Stonewall Jackson on the Union army's right flank in the Battle of Chancellorsville, May 2, 1863. Thrown into the attack again the next day, the regiment lost about 46 of the 125 men engaged during the two days. At the Battle of Winchester, June 15, the regiment remained in reserve and only 1 man was wounded. The regiment fought in the attack on Culp's Hill, July 2–3, during the Battle of Gettysburg. Returning to Virginia, the regiment participated in the Bristoe Station Campaign, October 9–22, and the Mine Run Campaign, November 26–December 2. At the Battle of Payne's Farm, November 27, the regiment lost about 28 of the 112 men engaged. The regiment fought at the Wilderness, May 5, and at Spotsylvania, May 7–20. In the latter battle, the enemy overran the brigade's position on May 12 and captured most of the men of the regiment. As part of General John B. Gordon's division, the remnants of the regiment participated in General Jubal Early's campaigns in the Shenandoah Valley during the summer and fall. So heavy had the casualties been that the regiment was consolidated with the 14th Louisiana Infantry Regiment during this time period. By late December, the brigade had rejoined General Robert E. Lee's army at Petersburg. The men served in the trenches around that city until it was evacuated, on April 2, 1865. When Lee surrendered at Appomattox on April 9, the regiment had only 1 officer and 18 enlisted men present for duty. Of the approximately 960 men enrolled during the war, approximately 162 were killed in battle, 74 died of disease, and 1 was killed by accident. Some 88 men deserted the regiment.

2nd Regiment

COLONELS. Lewis G. DeRussy, resigned July 19, 1861; William M. Levy, dropped April 30, 1862; Isiah T. Norwood, mortally wounded July 1, 1862; Jesse M. Williams, killed May 12, 1864; Ross E. Burke.

LIEUTENANT COLONELS. John Young, dropped April 30, 1862; Jesse M. Williams, promoted colonel June 26, 1862; Ross E. Burke, promoted colonel May 12, 1864; Michael A. Grogan.

MAJORS. Isiah T. Norwood, promoted colonel May 1, 1862; Richard W. Ashton, killed July 1, 1862; Ross E. Burke, promoted lieutenant colonel July 1, 1862; Michael A. Grogan, promoted lieutenant colonel May 12, 1864; Martin C. Redwine, killed September 17, 1864.

COMPANIES AND THEIR COMMANDERS

Company A, Lecompte Guards (Natchitoches). William M. Levy, promoted colonel July 19, 1861; Ross E. Burke, promoted major June 26, 1862; John W. Brown, killed July 22, 1864; William H. Noel.

Company B, Moore Guards (Rapides). John Kelso, dropped April 30, 1862; Michael A. Grogan, promoted major July 1, 1862; James F. Utz.

Company C, Pelican Greys (Ouachita). Arthur H. Martin, dropped April 30, 1862; Bernard B. Hemken, died July 28, 1862; Robert Roberts, resigned October 10, 1862; Dennis L. Griffin, killed June 15, 1863; N. L. Handy.

Company D, Pelican Rifles (DeSoto). Jesse M. Williams, promoted lieutenant colonel May 1, 1862; James S. Ashton, resigned June 17, 1863; Thomas S. Crump, killed June 15, 1863; William N. Cunningham.

Company E, Vernon Guards (Jackson). Oscar M. Watkins, dropped April 30, 1862; Martin C. Redwine, promoted major May 12, 1864; Eugene M. Kidd.

Company F, Claiborne Guards (Claiborne). John W. Andrews, dropped April 30, 1862; A. S. Blythe.

Company G, Floyd Guards (Carroll). John W. Dunn, dropped April 30, 1862; William C. Dixon, resigned January 13, 1863; James M. Jones, dropped April 18, 1864; John Elliott.

Company H, Atchafalaya Guards (Pointe Coupee). Richard M. Boone, resigned July 1, 1861; Thomas L. Harmanson, dropped April 30, 1862; L. G. Picou, killed June 15, 1863; James M. Batchelor.

Company I, Greenwood Guards (Caddo). William Flournoy, dropped April 30, 1862; J. L. Fortson.

Company K, Vienna Rifles (Jackson). H. W. Perrin, resigned February 20, 1862; John J. Neilson, dropped April 30, 1862; William A. Mayfield, resigned January 20, 1864; J. W. McCullough, killed June 4, 1864; C. M. Farris.

This regiment was organized May 11, 1861, at Camp Walker, New Orleans, with 1,013 men. Ordered to Richmond, Virginia, the regiment moved from there to Yorktown and helped to build earthwork defenses near the town. After several months at Yorktown, the men went to Williamsburg and again erected fortifications. The regiment spent the winter in the Yorktown area. On April 16, 1862, the enemy attacked the regiment's position at Dam No. 1, or Lee's Mill, and drove part of the regiment from its rifle pits. Companies A and C participated in a bayonet charge, which drove the enemy back. The regiment served in General Howell Cobb's brigade during the Seven Days' Battles near Richmond but saw no fighting until July 1 at Malvern Hill. In that battle, the colonel and major both fell, and the regiment's casualties totaled 182 men killed or wounded. On July 26, the regiment joined a brigade that included the 1st, 9th, 10th, and 15th Louisiana regiments and Coppens' Zouave Battalion. After being lightly engaged at Cedar Mountain, August 9, the regiment saw heavy fighting at the Battle of 2nd Manassas, August 28–30; nearly 130 men were killed or wounded. The men participated in the capture of Harper's Ferry, September 14, and fought in the Battle of Sharpsburg, September 17. At the Battle of Fredericksburg, December 13, the regiment saw only light skirmishing. With its brigade, the regiment participated in General Stonewall Jackson's famous assault at Chancellorsville, May 2, 1863, and lost more than 100 men. The regiment fought in the Battle of Winchester, June 15, and, with the 10th Louisiana Infantry, captured about 1,000 enemy prisoners. On July 2 and 3, the regiment participated in the attack on Culp's Hill during the Battle of Gettysburg. The men fought in the Bristoe Station Campaign, October 9–22, and the Mine Run Campaign, November 26–December 2, but suffered few casualties. After the regiment fought in the Battle of the Wilderness, May 5, 1864, its position was overrun at Spotsylvania, May 12, and its flag fell into enemy hands. From Spotsylvania, the regiment went with its brigade into the Shenandoah Valley. During General Jubal Early's advance toward Washington, D.C., the regiment fought in the Battle of Monocacy, July 9. Later, the men participated in the battles of Winchester, September 19; Fisher's Hill, September 21–22; and Cedar Creek, October 19. Returning to the Army of Northern Virginia at Petersburg, the regiment served through the siege of that place during the winter of 1864 and early spring of 1865. When the regiment surrendered at Appomattox Court House, only 3 officers and 41 men were present to sign paroles. Approximately 1,297 men served in the regiment. During the war, 218 men were killed, 181 died of disease, and 4 died in accidents. Approximately 88 men deserted during the war.

BIBLIOGRAPHY

Harris, D. W., and B. M. Hulse. *The History of Claiborne Parish, Louisiana.* New Orleans, 1886.

[Hurst, Lewis M.]. "In the Early Days of War." *Confederate Veteran,* XXXVI (1928), 329.

[Loyd, W. G.]. "Second Louisiana at Gettysburg." *Confederate Veteran,* VI (1898), 417.

Slack, A. L. "A War Waif in the Army." *Confederate Veteran,* II (1894), 12–13.

3rd Regiment

COLONELS. Louis Hebert, dropped May 8, 1862; Frank C. Armstrong, resigned November 5, 1862; Jerome B. Gilmore, resigned August 20, 1863; Samuel D. Russell.

LIEUTENANT COLONELS. Samuel M. Hyams, dropped May 8, 1862; Jerome B. Gilmore, promoted colonel November 5, 1862; Samuel D. Russell, promoted colonel August 22, 1863; David Pierson.

MAJOR. William F. Tunnard, dropped May 8, 1862; Samuel D. Russell, promoted lieutenant colonel November 5, 1862; David Pierson, promoted lieutenant colonel August 22, 1863; John S. Richards.

COMPANIES AND THEIR COMMANDERS

Company A, Iberville Greys (Iberville). Charles A. Brusle, dropped May 8, 1862; John Kinney, died July 9, 1863, of wounds received July 1, 1863; Thomas Gourrier.

Company B, Morehouse Guards (Morehouse). R. M. Hinson, killed August 10, 1861; W. T. Hall, resigned May 8, 1862; D. C. Morgan.

Company C, Winn Rifles (Winn). David Pierson, promoted major November 5, 1862; N. M. Middlebrook.

Company D, Pelican Rifles No. 2 (Natchitoches). James D. Blair, dropped May 8, 1862; William E. Russell.

Company E, Morehouse Fencibles (Morehouse). James F. Harris, dropped May 8, 1862; Charles H. Brashear, became captain of Company H, 22nd Consolidated Infantry.

Company F, Shreveport Rangers (Caddo). Jerome B. Gilmore, promoted lieutenant colonel May 8, 1862; William Kinney.

Company G, Pelican Rifles No. 1 (Natchitoches). Winter W. Breazeale, resigned September 24, 1861; L. Caspari, dropped May 8, 1862; William B. Butler.

Company H, Monticello Rifles (Carroll). John S. Richards, promoted major August 22, 1863; A. W. Currie.

Company I, Caldwell Guards (Caldwell). William L. Gunnels, dropped May 8, 1862; Joseph E. Johnson, died of wounds received July 1, 1863; T. McB. Meredith.

Company K, Pelican Rifles (East Baton Rouge). John B. Viglini, dropped May 8, 1862; Henry H. Gentles.

This regiment was organized at Camp Walker, New Orleans, on May 11, 1861, with 1,037 men. On May 20, the regiment left for Fort Smith, Arkansas. The men fought in the Battle of Wilson's Creek, August 10, and helped win the battle by driving back the Federal left flank and capturing a five-gun battery. Colonel Hebert led a brigade, which included the 3rd Louisiana, in the Battle of Pea Ridge, March 6–8, 1862; and again the regiment distinguished itself in the fighting. In April, the regiment accompanied the Army of the West across the Mississippi River to Corinth, Mississippi. The men fought in the Battle of Farmington, May 9. After the evacuation of Corinth, the regiment remained in northern Mississippi as the main army began its invasion of Kentucky. The regiment was heavily engaged at Iuka, September 19, losing more than 100 men. On October 3 and 4, the men participated in the Battle of Corinth. The men reported for duty at Snyder's Bluff north of Vicksburg, January 2, 1863. In late March, the regiment marched to oppose the enemy's Steele's Bayou Expedition. The men were entrenched along the lower part of Deer Creek but did not engage the enemy. During the Federal demonstrations against Haynes' Bluff and Snyder's Bluff, April 29–May 1, the men skirmished with the enemy soldiers. The regiment participated in the Siege of Vicksburg, May 19–July 4. On June 25, the Federals blew up the regiment's redan and made an unsuccessful attempt to overrun the position. In the explosion and subsequent fighting, 6 of the regiment's men were killed and 21 were wounded. The enemy exploded another mine at the regiment's position on July 1; 1 man was killed and 21 were wounded. After the surrender of Vicksburg, most of the men went home on parole. A small number went into a parole camp at Enterprise, Mississippi, and eventually became Company H, 22nd Louisiana Consolidated Infantry. In September, 1863, the men were declared exchanged and ordered into camp at Alexandria. Few men reported to camp at that time; not until July, 1864, did the regiment reunite in a camp at Pineville. The regiment moved to Camp Boggs at Shreveport in August and remained there doing guard duty until the end of the war. Anticipating the surrender of the Trans-Mississippi Department, the regiment dispersed on May 19 and 20, 1865. Of approximately 1,136 men enrolled in the regiment during the war, 123 were killed in battle, 74 died of disease, 3 died in accidents, 2 were murdered, and 1 drowned.

BIBLIOGRAPHY
"Maj. Gen. Will H. Tunnard." *Confederate Veteran*, VII (1899), 22.
[Morrison, W. L.]. "Honor to the Third Louisiana Regiment." *Confederate Veteran*, II (1894), 341.
Tunnard, Willie H. *A Southern Record: The Story of the 3rd Louisi-*

ana Infantry, C.S.A. Edited by Edwin C. Bearss. 1866; rpr. Dayton, Ohio, 1970.

Watson, William. *Life in the Confederate Army.* New York, 1888.

4th Regiment

COLONELS. Robert J. Barrow, resigned March 21, 1862; Henry W. Allen, promoted brigadier general January 19, 1863; Samuel E. Hunter.

LIEUTENANT COLONELS. Henry W. Allen, promoted colonel March 21, 1862; Samuel E. Hunter, promoted colonel January 19, 1863; William F. Pennington.

MAJORS. Samuel E. Hunter, promoted lieutenant colonel March 21, 1862; Thomas E. Vick, dropped May 19, 1862; William F. Pennington, promoted lieutenant colonel January 19, 1863; Edward J. Pullen.

COMPANIES AND THEIR COMMANDERS

Company A (formerly K), Hunter Rifles Company A (East Feliciana). Edward J. Pullen, promoted major January 19, 1863; A. T. Feister, killed August 31, 1864.

Company B (formerly A), National Guards (East Baton Rouge). Henry A. Rauhman, resigned December 31, 1861; Charles Betz, dropped May 19, 1862; Robert L. Pruyn, dropped May 19, 1864; David Devall.

Company C (formerly B), Lake Providence Cadets (Carroll). Franc Whicher, died of disease January 7, 1862; William F. Pennington, promoted major May 19, 1862; Charles R. Purdy, killed June 26, 1863.

Company D (formerly E), West Feliciana Rifles (West Feliciana). Charles Tooraen, killed April 6, 1862; Resin B. Turner, resigned November 6, 1862; James Reid.

Company E (formerly H), Lafourche Guards (Lafourche). Thomas E. Vick, promoted major March 21, 1862; Peter E. Lorio.

Company F (formerly C), Delta Rifles (West Baton Rouge). H. M. Favrot, resigned May 19, 1862; O. P. Skolfield.

Company G (1st), Beaver Creek Rifles (St. Helena), became Company E, 9th Battalion Partisan Rangers May, 1862. James H. Wingfield.

Company G (2nd) (formerly I), Hunter Rifles Company B (East Feli-

ciana). John T. Hilliard, killed April 6, 1862; Cader R. Cornelius.
Company H (formerly D), West Baton Rouge Tirailleurs (West Baton Rouge). F. A. Williams, dropped May 19, 1862; Sosthene Aillet, resigned November 1, 1862; Trasimond Landry.
Company I (formerly F), St. Helena Rifles (St. Helena). John B. Taylor, killed April 6, 1862; J. K. Womack, dropped May 25, 1864; C. E. Kennon.
Company K, Packwood Guards (St. Helena), added May 29, 1862. George H. Packwood.

This regiment was organized at Camp Moore on May 25, 1861, with 862 men. It received orders to report to the Mississippi Gulf Coast. Through the summer, the companies were divided up between camps at Pascagoula, Biloxi, Pass Christian, Mississippi City, and Ship Island. After the evacuation of Ship Island in September, the regiment moved to Franklin and Brashear City to protect the lower Atchafalaya River and Bayou Teche. In February, 1862, the regiment was ordered to Jackson, Tennessee, to reinforce General Pierre G. T. Beauregard's army. The regiment fought in the Battle of Shiloh, April 6–7, and lost 209 of the 575 men engaged. On May 2, the regiment was ordered to Edward's Station, Mississippi. During the first Federal campaign against Vicksburg, May 18–July 27, the regiment performed picket duty around the city. The regiment moved to Camp Moore with General John C. Breckinridge's army in July. On August 5, the regiment fought in the Battle of Baton Rouge; 42 men were killed, wounded, or missing. The regiment was the first to occupy Port Hudson and helped erect the fortifications there during the fall and winter. The men remained at Port Hudson through the spring of 1863. On May 1, they received orders to try to intercept Colonel Benjamin Grierson's raiders, and then they marched on to Jackson, Mississippi. A detachment of the regiment, mostly men from Company C, remained behind and participated in the Siege of Port Hudson, May 23–July 9. The regiment joined General William W. Loring's division at Jackson but soon transferred to General Samuel G. French's division. The men saw some fighting during the Jackson Campaign, July 5–25, and retreated with the army to Morton. During the fall and early winter, the regiment made up part of the garrison at Mobile, Alabama. In December, the regiment moved to Dalton, Georgia, and joined the Army of Tennessee. The men returned to Mobile in February, 1864, but joined the Army of Tennessee again in May. On May 27, the regiment fought in the Battle of New Hope Church. The regiment was transferred to General Randall L. Gibson's Louisiana brigade on July 19. The next day, the brigade participated in the Battle of Peachtree Creek. On July 28, the men fought in the Battle of Ezra Church. The regiment made a gallant but futile attack on the enemy at Jonesboro on August 31. In that battle, the regiment was decimated, losing 64 of the 104 men engaged. The regiment was consolidated with the 30th Louisiana Infantry for the invasion of Tennessee. The men fought in a skirmish at Florence, Alabama, but were in reserve during the Battle of Franklin, Tennessee, November 30. Most of the men remaining in the regiment were captured at Nashville, December 16–17. By March, 1865, only 1 lieutenant and 18 enlisted men of the regiment still remained. This remnant was consolidated with the 13th and 30th Louisiana regiments and 14th Louisiana Battalion Sharpshooters and was stationed again at Mobile. The men fought at Spanish Fort, March 27–April 8. After evacuating Mobile, the men reached Meridian, Mississippi, and surrendered there May 12, 1865. During the war, some 1,045 men served in the regiment. Of that number, 155 died in battle, 60 died of disease, 2 died in accidents, 2 were murdered, and 1 drowned.

BIBLIOGRAPHY

Campbell, W. R. "Fourth Louisiana Infantry." *Confederate Veteran*, XVI (1908), 299.

Kendall, John S., ed. "The Diary of Surgeon Craig, Fourth Louisiana Regiment, C.S.A., 1864–1865." *Louisiana Historical Quarterly*, VIII (1925), 53–70.

———. "Recollections of a Confederate Officer." *Louisiana Historical Quarterly*, XXIX (1946), 1041–1228.

Lambert, Samuel. *A Record of the Late Fourth Louisiana Reg't, C.S.A.* Clinton, n.d.

Richards, A. P. *The Saint Helena Rifles.* Edited by Randall Shoemaker. Houston, 1968.

Rowe, John S. "Fourth Louisiana Infantry." *Confederate Veteran*, XVI (1908), 261.

"Sketches of Veterans—Louisiana Division." *Confederate Veteran*, VI (1898), 574–78.

Stephenson, Wendell H., and E. A. Davis, eds. "The Civil War Diary

of William Micajah Barrow, September 23, 1861–July 13, 1862."
Louisiana Historical Quarterly, XVII (1934), 436–51, 712–31.

Taylor, F. Jay, ed. *Reluctant Rebel: The Secret Diary of Robert
Patrick, 1861–1865*. Baton Rouge, 1959.

5th Regiment

COLONELS. Theodore G. Hunt, resigned July 31, 1862; Henry Forno,
retired April 29, 1864.

LIEUTENANT COLONELS. Henro Forno, promoted colonel July 31,
1862; William T. Dean, resigned January 3, 1863; Bruce Menger,
killed May 13, 1864.

MAJORS. William T. Dean, promoted lieutenant colonel July 31,
1862; Bruce Menger, promoted lieutenant colonel January 3,
1863; Alexander Hart, retired March 20, 1865.

COMPANIES AND THEIR COMMANDERS

Company A, Crescent City Guards (Orleans). John A. Hall, resigned
December 21, 1861; John G. Angell.

Company B, Chalmette Rifle Guards (Orleans). A. E. Shaw, resigned August 23, 1861; Alex. Riouffe, resigned August 4, 1862;
John McGurk.

Company C, Bienville Guards (Orleans). Mark L. Moore, died December 14, 1861; James M. Coffey, dropped April 1, 1863; Philip J.
Rabenau, died January 31, 1864; John A. Russell, resigned January 19, 1865.

Company D, DeSoto Rifles (Orleans). W. B. Koontz, resigned October 3, 1861; George Seymour, resigned October 4, 1862; Frank L.
Moore.

Company E, Orleans Cadet Company B (Orleans). Charles Hobday,
resigned August 5, 1861; Alexander Hart, promoted major January 3, 1863; Leonce P. Guyol, resigned March 25, 1863; James
Garrity.

Company F, Orleans Southrons (Orleans). Ossian F. Peck, resigned
June 28, 1862; Frederick Richardson, killed July 1, 1863; James
Gubbins, killed October 19, 1864.

Company G, Louisiana Swamp Rangers (St. Helena). Edward J.
Jones, resigned October 30, 1862; George Headler, cashiered February 4, 1863; St. Clair Johns.

Company H, Perret Guards (Orleans). Arthur Connor, died August 4, 1862; Thomas Dixon, resigned February 24, 1863; John W. Taylor, killed May 5, 1864.

Company I, Carondelet Invincibles (Orleans). Bruce Menger, promoted major July 31, 1862; James S. Charles, resigned February 4, 1863; Jerome Patterson, retired February 2, 1865.

Company K, Monroe Guards (Orleans). Thomas Dolan, resigned December 21, 1861; Thomas H. Biscoe, killed May 5, 1864.

This regiment was organized at Camp Moore on June 4, 1861, with 863 men. The regiment went to Virginia and took its station near Warwick Court House as part of the Army of the Peninsula. During the winter of 1861, the men did some duty at Williamsburg and learned how to operate field artillery pieces. The men played a minor role in the engagement at Dam No. 1, or Lee's Mill, April 16, 1862, and in a skirmish at Williamsburg, May 4. At New Bridge on the Chickahominy River near Richmond, the regiment was driven back in a fight with the 4th Michigan Infantry on May 24. In the engagement, 75 men of the regiment were killed, wounded, or missing. The regiment saw little fighting in the Seven Days' Battles except in a successful engagement at White Oak Swamp on June 29. On July 26, the regiment was brigaded with the 6th, 7th, 8th, and 14th Louisiana regiments and Wheat's Battalion. The men were only lightly engaged at Cedar Mountain on August 9. During the 2nd Manassas Campaign, the regiment fought at Bristoe Station, August 26; at Kettle Run, August 27; and at 2nd Manassas, August 29–30. On September 1, the men participated in the Battle of Chantilly. The regiment was heavily engaged at the Battle of Sharpsburg, September 17; 49 men were killed or wounded. At Fredericksburg, on December 13, the regiment was in reserve at Hamilton's Crossing. On April 29, 1863, the regiment and the 6th Louisiana Infantry disputed the construction of pontoon bridges and the crossing of the Rappahannock River by the Federals south of Fredericksburg. The regiment participated in the Battle of Salem Church, May 4. At the Battle of Winchester, June 13–15, the regiment acted as the brigade reserve and saw little fighting. The men helped attack and rout part of the Union army at Gettysburg on July 1 and participated in the attack on Cemetery Hill late on July 2. A small detachment of the regiment and of men from the 9th Louisiana Infantry conducted a raid across the

Rapidan River at Raccoon Ford on September 16 and captured 42 men of the 5th New York Cavalry. When the Federals overran the brigade at Rappahannock Station, November 7, practically the entire regiment (123 officers and enlisted men) fell into enemy hands. The remnants of the regiment fought in the Battle of the Wilderness, May 5, 1864, and at Spotsylvania, May 9–19. The men helped stop the Federal attack at the Mule Shoe on May 12 during the latter battle. In June, the men marched into the Shenandoah Valley and participated in all the battles fought there during that summer and fall. The 5th, 6th, and 7th Louisiana regiments suffered a large number of casualties. Therefore, by late October, its remnants had been consolidated into one company. The men saw duty in the trenches at Petersburg. They surrendered at Appomattox on April 9, 1865. Only 1 officer and 18 enlisted men were still on duty at the surrender. Of the 1,074 men who served in the regiment, 161 died in battle, 66 died of disease, 2 died in accidents, 1 was murdered, and 1 was executed. About 118 men deserted.

BIBLIOGRAPHY
[Chisolm, B. B.]. "Forward, the Louisiana Brigade!" *Confederate Veteran*, XXVII (1919), 449.
Compton, James. "Memoirs of . . . Lieutenant, Co. A, Jackson Railroad Rifles." *Illinois Central Magazine*, II (September, 1913), 13–18; II (October, 1913), 13–18.
Souby, Eddie. "Bravery Honored by a Foe," in *Camp Fires of the Confederacy*, edited by Ben La Bree. Louisville, Ky., 1898, pp. 180–84.

6th Regiment

COLONELS. Isaac G. Seymour, killed June 27, 1862; Henry B. Strong, killed September 17, 1862; Nathaniel G. Offutt, resigned November 7, 1862; William Monaghan, killed August 28, 1864.

LIEUTENANT COLONELS. Louis Lay, resigned February 13, 1862; Henry B. Strong, promoted colonel June 27, 1862; Nathaniel G. Offutt, promoted colonel September 17, 1862; William Monaghan, promoted colonel November 7, 1862; Joseph Hanlon.

MAJORS. Samuel L. James, resigned December 1, 1861; George W. Christy, dropped May 9, 1862; Arthur McArthur, killed May 25, 1862; Nathaniel G. Offutt, promoted lieutenant colonel June 27, 1862; William Monaghan, promoted lieutenant colonel September 17, 1862; Joseph Hanlon, promoted lieutenant colonel November 7, 1862; William H. Manning.

COMPANIES AND THEIR COMMANDERS

Company A, Union and Sabine Rifles (Union and Sabine). Arthur McArthur, promoted major May 9, 1862; Allen M. Callaway, killed September 17, 1862; Joseph F. Phillips, retired December 7, 1864.

Company B, Calhoun Guards (Orleans). Henry B. Strong, promoted lieutenant colonel May 9, 1862; Thomas Redmond.

Company C, St. Landry Light Guards (St. Landry). Nathaniel G. Offutt, promoted major May 26, 1862; H. Bain Ritchie, killed September 17, 1862; Louis A. Cormier, killed July 2, 1863; Parnell Scott.

Company D, Tensas Rifles (Tensas). Charles B. Tenney, died October 3, 1861; David F. Buckner.

Company E, Mercer Guards (Orleans). Thomas F. Walker, resigned October 4, 1861; John J. Rivera.

Company F, Irish Brigade Company B (Orleans). William Monaghan, promoted major June 27, 1862; Michael O'Connor.

Company G, Pemberton Rangers (Orleans). Isaac A. Smith, killed June 9, 1862; Frank Clarke, detached and promoted major in Provisional Army of the Confederate States March 11, 1864; Jeff. D. Van Benthuysen.

Company H, Orleans Rifles (Orleans). Thomas F. Fisher, transferred to quartermaster department August 24, 1861; William H. Buttrick, resigned July 17, 1862; Charles M. Pilcher.

Company I, Irish Brigade Company A (Orleans). Joseph Hanlon, promoted major September 17, 1862; Blayney T. Walshe, retired March 4, 1865.

Company K, Violet Guards (Orleans). William H. Manning, promoted major November 7, 1862; George P. Ring.

This regiment, which was organized June 4, 1861, at Camp Moore with 916 men, went to Virginia. The regiment was guarding supplies and did not participate in the Battle of 1st Manassas, July 21. Several days later, the regiment was brigaded with the 7th, 8th, and 9th Louisiana regiments and the 1st Louisiana Special Battalion. After spending the winter near Centerville and Orange Court House, the brigade joined General Stonewall Jackson's army in the Shenandoah Valley in the spring of 1862. The regiment was in reserve at Front Royal on May 23 but skirmished with the enemy at Middletown the next day, capturing two enemy flags. At the Battle of Winchester, May 25, the regiment helped drive back the Federals. The regiment fought in the Battle of Port Republic, June 9; 66 of its men were killed or wounded. The men skirmished with the enemy at Hundley's Corner on the night of June 26 and participated in the Battle of Gaines' Mill on June 27. Marching with Jackson's Corps into northern Virginia, the regiment fought at Bristoe Station, August 26; at Kettle Run, August 27; at 2nd Manassas, August 29–30; and at Chantilly, September 1. The men saw heavy fighting in the Battle of Sharpsburg, September 17; 52 were killed or wounded. In the Battle of Fredericksburg, December 13, the regiment was in reserve and suffered only a few casualties from enemy artillery fire. With the 5th Louisiana Infantry, the men disputed the Federal crossing of the Rappahannock River below Fredericksburg on April 29, 1863. On May 3, the regiment was driven from Marye's Heights and had 27 men captured. The regiment participated in the Battle of Salem Church, May 4. On June 14, the regiment helped drive the enemy back from Winchester. The men assisted in the attack that routed the Federal XI Corps at Gettysburg on July 1. The next afternoon they participated in an attack on Cemetery Hill; 53 of them were killed, wounded, or missing. Returning to Virginia, the regiment fought in the Bristoe Station Campaign, October 9–22. The Federals overran the brigade at Rappahannock Station on November 7 and captured 89 men of the regiment. In the spring of 1864 campaign, the remnants of the regiment fought at the Wilderness, May 5, and at Spotsylvania, May 9–19. On May 12, the brigade helped repulse the Federal attack at the Mule Shoe that had overrun the army's other Louisiana brigade. The brigade accompanied General Jubal Early's army to the Shenandoah Valley and participated in all of the battles fought there from June to October. By November, the regiment's strength was so low that the regiment was consolidated into one company with the remnants of the 5th and 7th Louisiana regiments. The men rejoined the Army of Northern Virginia at Petersburg and saw action at Hatcher's Run, February 6, 1865, and at Fort Steadman, March 25. When the army surrendered at Appomattox, on April 9, only 4 officers and 48 enlisted men remained on duty. Approximately 1,146 men served in the regiment during the war; 219 were killed in battle, 104 died of disease, 5 were killed in accidents, 1 drowned, and 1 was executed for desertion. At least 232 men deserted during the war.

BIBLIOGRAPHY

"Sketches of Veterans—Louisiana Division." *Confederate Veteran*, VI (1898), 574–78.

Vandiver, Frank E., ed. "A Collection of Louisiana Confederate Letters." *Louisiana Historical Quarterly*, XXVI (1943), 937–74.

[Walshe, B. F.]. "Recollections of Gaines's Mill." *Confederate Veteran*, VII (1899), 54–55.

———. "Sixth Louisiana Regiment." *Confederate Veteran*, XIX (1911), 300–301.

7th Regiment

COLONELS. Harry T. Hays, promoted brigadier general July 25, 1862; Davidson B. Penn.

LIEUTENANT COLONELS. Charles DeChoiseul, died of wounds June 22, 1862; Davidson B. Penn, promoted colonel July 25, 1862; Thomas M. Terry.

MAJORS. Davidson B. Penn, promoted lieutenant colonel June 22, 1862; Thomas M. Terry, promoted lieutenant colonel July 25, 1862; J. Moore Wilson.

COMPANIES AND THEIR COMMANDERS

Company A, Continental Guards (Orleans). George Clark, resigned October 28, 1861; Edwin McFarland, died of wounds September 19, 1862; William P. Thompson, died of wounds July 21, 1863; Lawrence Pendergast.

Company B, Baton Rouge Fencibles (East Baton Rouge). Andrew S. Herron, promoted colonel of cavalry and appointed to military court May, 1863; William A. Martin.

Company C, Sarsfield Rangers (Orleans). J. Moore Wilson, promoted major July 25, 1862; Charles Cameron, retired September 21, 1864.

Company D, Virginia Guards (Orleans). Robert P. Scott, resigned October 1, 1862; Louis H. Malarcher.

Company E, Crescent City Rifles Company B (Orleans). Samuel H. Gilman, resigned January 3, 1862; Conrad Green.

Company F, Irish Volunteers (Assumption). William B. Ratliff, resigned September 18, 1861; Thomas Gibbs Morgan, died January 21, 1864; Thomas W. Kerrigan, retired July 20, 1864.

Company G, American Rifles (Orleans). William D. Rickarby, re-signed April 2, 1863; Samuel Flower.

Company H, Crescent City Rifles Company C (Orleans). Henry T. Jett, resigned August 23, 1861; William P. Harper, retired October 8, 1864.

Company I, Virginia Blues (Orleans). Daniel A. Wilson, Jr., appointed judge advocate, 2nd Corps, Army of Northern Virginia, January 1, 1863; Charles E. Bellinger.

Company K, Livingston Rifles (Livingston). Thomas M. Terry, promoted major June 22, 1862; Alpheus G. Tucker, resigned February 4, 1863; William F. Ogden.

This regiment was organized June 5, 1861, at Camp Moore with 944 men. Ordered to Virginia, the regiment went into camp near Manassas. The men participated in a skirmish at Blackburn's Ford on July 18. In the Battle of 1st Manassas, July 21, the regiment helped attack and rout the Union army's right flank but suffered only light casualties. Later in the month, the regiment, along with the 6th, 8th, and 9th Louisiana regiments and Wheat's Tiger Battalion, joined what came to be known as the 1st Louisiana Brigade. In the spring of 1862, the brigade joined General Stonewall Jackson's army in the Shenandoah Valley and played a major role in its victories there. The regiment was in reserve at Front Royal on May 23 but suffered two casualties. At the Battle of Winchester, May 25, the men participated in the assault by the brigade, which drove the enemy from the field. The regiment played a small part in the Battle of Cross Keys, June 8. At the Battle of Port Republic, June 9, the regiment was separated from the brigade and suffered casualties of nearly 50 percent. During the Seven Days' Battles, the regiment fought at Gaines' Mill, June 27, and at Malvern Hill, July 1. The men saw limited action at Cedar Mountain, August 9, but did much fighting in the battles of the 2nd Manassas Campaign, August 26–30, and in the Battle of Chantilly, September 1. The regiment was present at the capture of Harper's Ferry, September 14. In the Battle of Sharpsburg, September 17, 69 men were killed, wounded, or missing. The men were in reserve near Hamilton's Crossing during the Battle of Fredericksburg, December 13. When the Federals crossed the Rappahannock River in May, 1863, the regiment skirmished with them on May 2 before falling back to Marye's Heights. The men fought the Federals again on May 3 and 4 in that area. After skirmishing with the enemy at Winchester on June 13, the regiment was heavily engaged there the next day and captured two cannons in a small redoubt. The men were in the first day's fight at Gettysburg, July 1, and received praise for their conduct during the night attack on Cemetery Hill, July 2. In the Bristoe Station Campaign, October 9–22, the regiment saw little fighting. On November 7, the enemy overran the entrenchments at Rappahannock Station held by the brigade, and 180 men of the regiment fell into enemy hands. The brigade fought in the Battle of the Wilderness, May 5, 1864, and helped blunt the enemy attack at the Mule Shoe, May 12, during the Spotsylvania Campaign. After skirmishing with the Federals near Cold Harbor, June 2–3, the brigade marched into the Shenandoah Valley and stopped an enemy advance there. The regiment fought in the Battle of Monocacy, July 9, during General Jubal Early's advance on Washington, D.C. In the battles against General Phil Sheridan's army, the brigade fought at Winchester, September 19; at Fisher's Hill, September 22; and at Cedar Creek, October 19. So reduced in numbers had the regiment become by late November that it was consolidated with the 5th and 6th Louisiana regiments into a single company. The brigade saw duty in the trenches at Petersburg during the winter of 1864–65. When the army surrendered at Appomattox, on April 9, 1865, only 42 men remained to sign paroles. The regiment had approximately 1,077 men on its rolls during the war. Of that number, 190 died in battle, 68 died of disease, 2 died in accidents, 1 was murdered, and 1 was executed. About 53 men deserted the regiment.

BIBLIOGRAPHY

[Belcher, Alexander]. "A Pair of Mittens." *Southern Bivouac*, II (April, 1884), 378.
Hawn, William. *All Around the Civil War*. New York, [1908?].
Leahy, Mrs. D. W. "Colonel Davidson Bradfute Penn." *Louisiana Genealogical Register*, XXIV (1977), 247–52.
Roden, J. B. "Trip from New Orleans to Louisville in 1861." *Confederate Veteran*, XVIII (1910), 236–37.

8th Regiment

COLONELS. Henry B. Kelly, appointed judge of military court April 6, 1863; Trevanian D. Lewis, killed July 2, 1863; Alcibiades DeBlanc, retired August 15, 1864.

LIEUTENANT COLONELS. Francis R. T. Nicholls, promoted brigadier general October 15, 1862; Trevanian D. Lewis, promoted colonel April 6, 1863; Alcibiades DeBlanc, promoted colonel July 2, 1863; German A. Lester, killed June 2, 1864.

MAJORS. John B. Prados, dropped May 7, 1862; Trevanian D. Lewis, promoted lieutenant colonel July 2, 1862; Alcibiades DeBlanc, promoted lieutenant colonel April 6, 1863; German A. Lester, promoted lieutenant colonel July 2, 1863.

COMPANIES AND THEIR COMMANDERS

Company A, Creole Guards (East Baton Rouge). Leon J. Fremaux, resigned March 19, 1862; Antoine L. Gusman.

Company B, Bienville Rifles (Orleans). Augustin Larose, dropped April 24, 1862; Robert Current, killed September 17, 1862; Louis Prados.

Company C, Attakapas Guards (St. Martin). Alcibiades DeBlanc, promoted major October 15, 1862; Charles Duchamp.

Company D, Sumter Guards (Orleans). Francis Newman, resigned September 17, 1861; Frank M. Harney, promoted assistant quartermaster May 19, 1863; John B. Hereford, resigned November 3, 1863; William Cooper.

Company E, Franklin Sharpshooters (Franklin). German A. Lester, promoted major April 6, 1863; Newton Z. Guice, killed July 24, 1864.

Company F, Opelousas Guards (St. Landry). James C. Pratt, dropped April 24, 1862; Albert Dejean, killed June 14, 1863; E. Sumter Taylor.

Company G, Minden Blues (Claiborne). John Langdon Lewis, resigned December 9, 1861; Benjamin F. Sims, died August 24, 1862; Samuel Y. Webb.

Company H, Cheneyville Rifles (Rapides). Patrick F. Keary.

Company I, Rapides Invincibles (Rapides). Lee Crandall, promoted major in an Arkansas unit February 26, 1863; William K. Johnson.

Company K, Phoenix Company (Ascension). Lawrence D. Nicholls, killed June 27, 1862; Victor St. Martin, killed July 2, 1863; William Sims.

This regiment was organized at Camp Moore on June 15, 1861, with 889 men. Six companies of the regiment reached Manassas, Virginia, on July 17. During the battle there on July 21, the regiment was in reserve guarding supplies and was not engaged. Soon afterwards, the regiment became part of what was known as the 1st Louisiana Brigade, along with the 6th, 7th, and 9th Louisiana regiments and the 1st Louisiana Special Battalion. The brigade wintered in northern Virginia and in the spring joined General Stonewall Jackson's army in the Shenandoah Valley. On May 23, 1862, the regiment participated in the capture of Front Royal. The men fought in the Battle of Winchester, May 25, but suffered few casualties. Federal troops captured a portion of the regiment on May 30 at Front Royal while the men were guarding supplies. The regiment saw limited action at Cross Keys, June 8, and was heavily engaged at Port Republic, June 9. During the Seven Days' Battles near Richmond, the regiment fought at Gaines' Mill, June 27, and at Malvern Hill, July 1. The regiment skirmished with the enemy at Bristoe Station and Kettle Run, August 27–28. In the first day's fighting at 2nd Manassas, August 29, the men helped drive back an enemy attack. The men fought again at Chantilly, September 1. In the bloody Battle of Sharpsburg, September 17, 103 men were killed or wounded. The regiment was held in reserve during the Battle of Fredericksburg, December 13. On May 3 and 4, 1863, the regiment fought in the actions at Marye's Heights and Salem Church. The men remained in reserve during the skirmishing at Winchester, June 13–14. On July 1, the brigade helped rout part of the Federal army near Gettysburg. The regiment participated in the attack on Cemetery Hill, July 2, and lost its flag in the fighting. After the army returned to Virginia, the regiment took part in the Bristoe Station Campaign, October 9–22. The enemy overran the brigade at Rappahannock Station on November 7 and captured 162 officers and enlisted men of the regiment. The brigade attacked the Federals on May 5, 1864, during the Battle of the Wilderness. On May 12, the brigade helped stop the Federal attack that overran most of the entrenchments known as the Mule Shoe. After seeing some fighting at Cold Harbor, June 1–3, the remnants of the regiment accompanied the brigade to the Shenandoah Valley. The men fought in the battles of Monocacy, July 9; Winchester, July 24; Shepherdstown, August 25; Winchester, September 19; Fisher's Hill, September 21–22; and Cedar Creek, October 19. In December, the brigade rejoined the army at Petersburg and saw some fighting there in February and March, 1865. At Appomattox on April 9, 3 officers and 54 enlisted men surrendered. Of the total of 1,321 men enrolled in the regiment during the war, 252 were killed, 171 died of disease, 2 were murdered, and 1 died in an accident. About 80 men deserted from the regiment.

BIBLIOGRAPHY
"Cheneyville (La.) Rifles' Flag Returned." *Confederate Veteran*, XIX (1911), 373–74.
Davis, Edwin A., ed. "A Louisiana Volunteer, Letters of William J. Walter, 1861–1862." *Southwest Review*, XIX (1933), 78–88.
Harris, D. W., and B. M. Hulse. *The History of Claiborne Parish, Louisiana.* New Orleans, 1886.
Thomas, William, III. "The Minden Blues: Bull Run to Appomattox Court House." *North Louisiana Historical Association Journal*, VIII (1977), 65–75.

9th Regiment

COLONELS. Richard Taylor, promoted brigadier general October 21, 1861; Edward G. Randolph, dropped April 24, 1862; Leroy A. Stafford, promoted brigadier general October 8, 1863; William R. Peck, promoted brigadier general February 18, 1865.

LIEUTENANT COLONELS. Edward G. Randolph, promoted colonel October 21, 1861; N. J. Walker, dropped April 24, 1862; William R. Peck, promoted colonel October 8, 1863; John J. Hodges.

MAJORS. N. J. Walker, promoted lieutenant colonel October 21, 1861; James R. Kavanaugh, dropped April 24, 1862; Henry L. N. Williams, killed July 3, 1863; John J. Hodges, promoted lieutenant colonel October 8, 1863; Alfred A. Singletary.

COMPANIES AND THEIR COMMANDERS

Company A, Moore Fencibles (Claiborne). Richard L. Capers, dropped April 24, 1862; Rhydon Grigsby, killed September 17, 1862; Francis J. Montgomery.

Company B, Stafford Guards (Rapides). Leroy A. Stafford, promoted colonel April 24, 1862; W. T. Cummings, killed May 4, 1863; A. C. Bringhurst, died November 29, 1863; J. D. Workman, killed September 22, 1864.

Company C, Bienville Blues (Bienville). Benjamin W. Pearce, dropped April 24, 1862; R. Allen Pierson, killed July 18, 1864.

Company D, Bossier Volunteers (Bossier). John J. Hodges, promoted major July 3, 1863; Richard J. Hancock.

Company E, Milliken Bend Guards (Madison). William R. Peck, promoted lieutenant colonel April 24, 1862; George D. Shadburne, resigned October 1, 1862; Edward Owens.

Company F, DeSoto Blues (DeSoto). Henry L. N. Williams, promoted major April 24, 1862; William F. T. Bennett, killed July 9, 1864.

Company G, Colyell Guards (Livingston). John S. Gardner, dropped April 24, 1862; Alfred A. Singletary, promoted major October 8, 1863; William E. O'Reilly, retired February, 1865.

Company H, Brush Valley Guards (Bienville). W. F. Gray, dropped April 24, 1862; Grove Cook, mortally wounded May 3, 1863; Cornelius Shively.

Company I, Washington Rifles (Washington). Hardy Richardson, dropped April 24, 1862; Martin G. Williams.

Company K, Jackson Greys (Jackson), became Company M, 12th Louisiana Infantry Regiment, October, 1862. James R. Kavanaugh, promoted major October 21, 1861; George W. McCranie.

One of the most distinguished Louisiana units in the war, this regiment was organized at Camp Moore on July 6, 1861, with 949 men. Proceeding to Virginia, the regiment arrived at Manassas too late on July 21 to participate in the battle fought there. Assigned to the 1st Louisiana Brigade with the 6th, 7th, and 8th Louisiana regiments and Wheat's Tiger Battalion, the regiment went into the Shenandoah Valley to join General Stonewall Jackson's army in May, 1862. Company A participated in the capture of Front Royal on May 23. The regiment fought at Middletown, May 24; at Winchester, May 25; at Strasburg, June 1; and at Port Republic, June 9. At the Battle of Gaines' Mill, June 27, the men suffered fewer than 20 casualties. The regiment saw limited fighting at Malvern Hill on July 1. On July 26, the 2nd Louisiana Brigade was formed with the 1st, 2nd, 9th,

10th, and 15th Louisiana regiments and Coppens' Zouave Battalion. The regiment was lightly engaged at the end of the Battle of Cedar Mountain, August 9. During the 2nd Manassas Campaign, August 28–30, the regiment suffered nearly 100 casualties. When the regiment ran out of ammunition on August 30, the men threw rocks at the attacking enemy soldiers until new ammunition could be brought up. A private of Company D was said to have killed Union general Philip Kearney during the Battle of Chantilly, September 1. The regiment was heavily engaged in the Battle of Sharpsburg, September 17, and suffered 82 casualties. On October 5, the regiment transferred back to the 1st Louisiana Brigade in exchange for the 14th Louisiana Regiment and was thereafter always associated with the brigade. Though the regiment was held in reserve at the Battle of Fredericksburg, December 13, 12 of its men were killed or wounded by enemy artilley fire. The men again saw heavy fighting at Chancellorsville, May 3–4, while defending Marye's Heights and attacking the enemy at Salem Church. At the Battle of Winchester, June 14, the regiment participated in the main attack, which overran the enemy. The regiment was in the attack at Gettysburg, July 1, which routed the Federal XI Corps. In the night attack on Cemetery Hill, July 2, the regiment temporarily captured several enemy cannons but had to retreat because of lack of support. A small detachment of the regiment joined a similar group from the 5th Louisiana Regiment on September 16 to make a quick raid across the Rappahannock River at Raccoon Ford. The raiders killed several men and captured 42 others of the 5th New York Cavalry. In the Battle of Rappahannock Station, November 7, the regiment was at first in reserve. The men made a counterattack to try to recover the cannons of the Louisiana Guard Artillery, but 130 officers and enlisted men were captured by the enemy in the attempt. The remnants of the regiment fought in the Battle of the Wilderness, May 5, 1864, and at the Mule Shoe in the Battle of Spotsylvania, May 12. In June, the brigade went to the Shenandoah Valley and participated in all of the battles fought there during the summer and fall of that year. The men rejoined the main army in December and served in the trenches at Petersburg until the evacuation of that place on April 2, 1865. When the army surrendered at Appomattox, on April 9, the regiment was the strongest of all the Louisiana units, with 4 officers and 64 enlisted men. In the course of the war, approximately 1,474 men served in the regiment. Of that number, 233 were killed, 349 died of disease, and 4 died in accidents; this was the highest death rate of all Louisiana units in Virginia. At least 115 men deserted the regiment. Three of the regiment's 4 colonels became generals during the war.

BIBLIOGRAPHY

Hancock, Capt. R. J. "William Singleton." *Confederate Veteran*, XIV (1906), 498–99.

Handerson, Henry E. *Yankee in Gray: The Civil War Memoirs of Henry E. Handerson with a Selection of His Wartime Letters.* Cleveland, 1962.

Harris, D. W., and B. M. Hulse. *The History of Claiborne Parish, Louisiana.* New Orleans, 1886.

Moore, Waldo W., ed. "First Hand Account of Life in the II Corps of Lee's Army." *North Louisiana Historical Association Newsletter*, VIII (1968), 8–12.

Reed, Thomas Benton. *A Private in Gray.* Camden, Ark., 1905.

Rice, Joe M. "An Account of the Battle of Fredericksburg, 1863, Written by J. R. Williams." *North Louisiana Historical Association Journal*, XVII (1986), 39–42.

[Roby, T. K.]. "Reminiscences of a Private." *Confederate Veteran*, XXIII (1915), 548–50.

10th Regiment

COLONELS. Mandeville Marigny, resigned July 23, 1862; Eugene Waggaman.

LIEUTENANT COLONELS. Jules C. Denis, resigned December 28, 1861; Eugene Waggaman, promoted colonel July 23, 1862; William H. Spencer, killed August 30, 1862; John M. Leggett, killed May 3, 1863; Henry D. Monier.

MAJORS. Felix Dumonteil, resigned January 4, 1862; William H. Spencer, promoted lieutenant colonel July 23, 1862; John M. Leggett, promoted lieutenant colonel August 30, 1862; Henry D. Monier, promoted lieutenant colonel May 3, 1863; Thomas N. Powell, killed April 3, 1865.

COMPANIES AND THEIR COMMANDERS

Company A, Shepherd Guards (Orleans). Alfred Philips, resigned December 28, 1861; Jacob A. Cohen, killed August 30, 1862; Isaac L. Lyons.

Company B, Derbigny Guards (Orleans). Lea F. Bakewell, resigned August 26, 1861; Edward W. Huntington, resigned December 28, 1861; Henry C. Marks, killed July 1, 1862; James Buckner, promoted assistant quartermaster October 6, 1862; Charles Knowlton, retired October 31, 1864.

Company C, Hewitt Guards (Orleans). Richard M. Hewitt, resigned December 28, 1861; Thomas N. Powell, promoted major May 3, 1864; James Scott.

Company D, Hawkins Guards (Orleans). Charles F. White, resigned December 21, 1861; Jacob H. Williams, resigned November 8, 1862; Ernest Webre, retired January 10, 1865.

Company E, Louisiana Swamp Rifles (Pointe Coupee). David N. Dickey, resigned April 15, 1862; Sainville Cucullu, dropped January 5, 1863; Samuel H. Faulkner.

Company F, Louisiana Rebels (Orleans). John M. Leggett, promoted major July 28, 1862; Albert F. Pagnier, retired November 8, 1864.

Company G, Orleans Rangers (Orleans). Edward Crevon, resigned December 21, 1861; M. A. Guerin, resigned May 28, 1862; Michael A. Becnel, resigned June 23, 1862; Charles B. Marmillion.

Company H, Orleans Blues (Orleans). William B. Barnett, resigned January 13, 1863; Leon Jastremski.

Company I, Tirailleurs d'Orleans (Orleans). Eugene Waggaman, promoted lieutenant colonel December 28, 1861; Henry D. Monier, promoted major January 29, 1863; Alphonse Jonte, killed May 3, 1863; P. Leclaire, killed May 12, 1864.

Company K, Confederate States Rangers (St. Landry). William H. Spencer, promoted major January 16, 1862; Auguste Perrodin.

This regiment was organized at Camp Moore on July 22, 1861, with 796 men, by the addition of five companies to the 2nd Louisiana Special Battalion. The regiment went to Virginia and received orders to report to the Army of the Peninsula at Yorktown. On April 16, 1862, the regiment moved to support units engaged with the enemy at Dam No. 1, or Lee's Mills. The men skirmished with the enemy on May 4 at Williamsburg. During the Seven Days' Battles, the men saw no fighting until July 1 at Malvern Hill. In that battle, the regiment was the only Confederate unit to penetrate the Federal lines; 87 of its men were killed, wounded, or missing. On July 26, the regiment was brigaded with the 1st, 2nd, 9th, and 15th Louisiana regiments and with Coppens' Zouave Battalion. The men participated in the Battle of Cedar Mountain, August 9, and in the 2nd Manassas Campaign, August 28–30. After witnessing the capture of Harper's Ferry, the regiment fought in the Battle of Sharpsburg, September 17; 57 of its men were killed, wounded, or missing. The men were in reserve during the Battle of Fredericksburg, December 13. On May 2, 1863, the brigade participated in General Stonewall Jackson's attack on the Federal right flank at Chancellorsville. The next day, the men again attacked the enemy; and in the two days of fighting, approximately 94 men became casualties. On June 15, the regiment and the 2nd Louisiana Regiment captured 1,000 Federals near Winchester. The men participated in the attacks on Culp's Hill at Gettysburg, July 2–3, and suffered 116 casualties. By July 17, only 109 officers and enlisted men were still present for duty. The regiment fought in the Bristoe Station Campaign, October 9–22, and in the Mine Run Campaign, November 26–December 2. On May 5, 1864, the regiment was engaged in the Battle of the Wilderness. The enemy overran the brigade at the Mule Shoe during the Battle of Spotsylvania, May 12, and 56 men of the regiment were captured. On June 3, the Federals captured the regiment's flag during the Battle of Cold Harbor. The few remaining men accompanied the brigade to the Shenandoah Valley in mid-June. There they fought in the following battles and engagements: Monocacy, July 9; Cedar Creek, August 12; Leetown, August 25; Winchester, September 19; Fisher's Hill, September 21–22; and Cedar Creek, October 19. Following these battles, the remnants of the regiment were consolidated with the remnants of the 15th Louisiana into a single company. The brigade rejoined General Robert E. Lee's army at Petersburg in December. The regiment participated in the attack on Fort Steadman on March 25, 1865. When Lee surrendered at Appomattox Court House, on April 9, Colonel Waggaman commanded the remnants of the two Louisiana brigades in the army. Three officers and 13 enlisted men of the regiment were paroled. The regiment had a total enrollment of 845 men.

During the war, 142 men were killed, 58 died of disease, 3 were murdered, and 2 died in accidents.

BIBLIOGRAPHY

Buckley, Cornelius M., S. J., trans. *A Frenchman, a Chaplain, a Rebel: The War Letters of Pere Louis-Hippolyte Gache, S. J.* Chicago, 1981.

"Colonel Eugene Waggaman, Who Led the Tenth Louisiana Regiment in the Famous Charge at Malvern Hill." *Southern Historical Society Papers*, XVI (1888), 446–51.

"Eugene Waggaman." *Southern Historical Society Papers*, XXV (1897), 180–86.

Pinkowski, Edward. *Pills, Pen and Politics: The Story of General Leon Jastremski.* Wilmington, Del., 1974.

11th Regiment

COLONEL. Samuel F. Marks.

LIEUTENANT COLONEL. Robert H. Barrow.

MAJORS. E. G. W. Butler, mortally wounded November 7, 1861; James A. Ventress, Jr., resigned December 30, 1861; Alexander Mason.

COMPANIES AND THEIR COMMANDERS

Company A, Dillon Guards (Orleans). M. W. Murphy, resigned March 31, 1862; Joseph H. Miller.

Company B, Labauve Guards (Iberville). James A. Ventress, Jr., promoted major November 7, 1861; Joseph Warro, resigned June 4, 1862; John C. Kleinpeter.

Company C, Holmes Light Guards (Orleans). James H. McCann; James G. White.

Company D, Cannon Guards (Orleans). John E. Austin.

Company E, Westbrook Guards (Rapides). Uriah Westbrook, resigned March 31, 1862; Benjamin Turner.

Company F, Continental Guards (Orleans). John G. Fleming.

Company G, Catahoula Greys (Catahoula). Alexander Mason, promoted major December 30, 1861; Richard H. Harris.

Company H, Pointe Coupee Volunteers (Pointe Coupee). Wylie Barrow, resigned February 7, 1862; Thompson J. Bird.

Company I, Rosale Guards (West Feliciana). John J. Barrow, resigned May 8, 1862; G. Merrick Miller.
Company K, Shreveport Rebels (Caddo). A. Schaffner; Laurence L. Butler.
Company L (Orleans), transferred to 20th Louisiana Regiment. Albert A. Lipscomb.

This regiment was organized at Camp Moore on August 13, 1861, with 857 men. Ordered to Kentucky, the regiment became part of the garrison at Columbus. On November 7, the men fought in the Battle of Belmont, Missouri; 12 were killed and 42 were wounded. The regiment moved to Island No. 10 after the evacuation of Columbus and remained there until March 17, 1862, when it went to Fort Pillow. The regiment took 550 men into the Battle of Shiloh, April 6, and suffered heavily in a bayonet charge against an enemy artillery battery. Lieutenant John Cowley, who had lost his right arm at Belmont, lost his left arm in the battle. On May 9, the regiment participated in the Battle of Farmington, Mississippi; 12 of its men were killed, wounded, or missing. General Braxton Bragg ordered the regiment disbanded on August 19 because of its decline in numbers caused by battle casualties and illness. The men of Companies C, D, E, F, and G went into the 13th Louisiana Regiment; and those of Companies A, B, H, I, and K went into the 20th Louisiana Regiment. Some picked men were organized as part of the 14th Louisiana Battalion Sharpshooters.

12th Regiment

COLONELS. Thomas M. Scott, promoted brigadier general May 10, 1864; Noel L. Nelson, killed November 30, 1864; Thomas C. Standifer.
LIEUTENANT COLONELS. Wade H. Hough, resigned May 4, 1862; James A. Boyd, resigned January 5, 1863; Noel L. Nelson, promoted colonel May 10, 1864; Thomas C. Standifer, promoted colonel; Evander McN. Graham.
MAJORS. John C. Knott, dropped May 11, 1862; Noel L. Nelson, promoted lieutenant colonel January 5, 1863; Thomas C. Standifer, promoted lieutenant colonel May 10, 1864; Henry V. McCain; John A. Dixon.

COMPANIES AND THEIR COMMANDERS

Company A, North Louisiana Cadets (DeSoto). John T. Jordan, resigned October 14, 1864.

Company B, Arcadia Invincibles (Bienville). Thomas C. Standifer, promoted major January 5, 1863; Joseph A. Bivin, killed July 20, 1864; Jonathan Anders.

Company C, Southern Sentinels (Winn). John A. Dixon, promoted major; Angus C. Alexander.

Company D, Beauregard Fencibles (Winn). Henry V. McCain, promoted major May 10, 1864.

Company E, Independent Rangers (Union). D. L. Hicks; Evander McN. Graham, promoted lieutenant colonel.

Company F, Morehouse Stars (Morehouse). James H. Stevens, resigned April 30, 1863; Christopher C. Davenport, resigned January 24, 1865; William N. Potts(?).

Company G (Claiborne), added April 1, 1862. Thomas J. Hightower, resigned August 5, 1862; Thomas Price.

Company H, Jackson Sharpshooters (Jackson). James H. Seale, resigned April 22, 1862; James T. Davis.

Company I, Farmer Guards (Union). Charles W. Hodge, resigned(?); John E. Woodward, resigned March 7, 1863; John W. McBride.

Company K, Caldwell Invincibles (Caldwell). James A. Boyd, promoted lieutenant colonel May 4, 1862; Jones Meredith, resigned October 31, 1862; Andrew J. Braden.

Company L, Claiborne Guards or Rangers (Claiborne). Isaac L. Leonard, resigned(?); Noel L. Nelson, promoted major May 11, 1862; Robert A. Crow, died September 13, 1863; Benjamin F. Hargrove, reduced in rank December 17, 1863; James J. Crow.

Company M (1st), Farmer Rangers (Natchitoches), consolidated into Company C August 1, 1862. Banajah D. Owen, dropped May 11, 1862; Angus C. Alexander.

Company M (2nd), Jackson Greys (Jackson), formerly Company K, 9th Louisiana Regiment, added October, 1862. George W. McCranie, resigned January 16, 1865; Joseph L. Bond.

This regiment was organized at Camp Moore on August 13, 1861, with 704 men, and was the only Louisiana infantry regiment with twelve companies. The regiment went to Kentucky and became part of the garrison at Columbus. On November 7, the men crossed the Mississippi River to participate in the Battle of Belmont but arrived too late to fight. When the Confederates evacuated Columbus, the regiment went to New Madrid and Island No. 10. The men helped repulse an enemy attack on the latter place on the night of March 4 and 5, 1862. On March 17, the regiment moved to Fort Pillow. There it withstood a nearly six-week bombardment by Federal gunboats. After the evacuation of Fort Pillow, the regiment marched to Grenada, Mississippi. The men did duty there and at Holly Springs until mid-August, when they went to Port Hudson, Louisiana. They remained there only about ten days and then returned to Grenada. On October 3 and 4, the regiment fought in the Battle of Corinth. The men spent the winter at Grenada, Holly Springs, and Canton. In February, 1863, the regiment returned to Port Hudson and witnessed the Union naval attack there on March 14. In early April, the regiment left to join the Army of Tennessee. The men got to Atlanta, Georgia, but received orders to return to Mississippi to intercept Colonel Benjamin Grierson's Union cavalry raid. Failing to catch Grierson, the regiment took its station at Port Gibson. On May 16, the regiment fought in the Battle of Baker's Creek and performed ably in covering the retreat of the Confederate army. The men made up part of General Joseph E. Johnston's army at Jackson during the summer of 1863. A detachment of 160 men under Captain John A. Dixon served in General John C. Vaughn's brigade during the siege of Vicksburg, May 19–July 4, 1863, and were paroled at the surrender of that place. During that fall and winter, the regiment occupied camps at Morton and Canton. The men moved around during the early months of 1864, being stationed at Meridian, Mississippi, and Demopolis and Montevallo, Alabama. In May, the regiment joined the Army of Tennessee at Resaca, Georgia. During the retreat to Atlanta, the men fought at Marietta, Kennesaw Mountain, Lost Mountain, and Bethel Church. The regiment participated in the Battle of Peachtree Creek on July 20; 73 of its men were killed, wounded, or missing, and its flag was captured. On July 22, the men fought in the Battle of Atlanta. Following the evacuation of that city, the regiment accompanied the army on its invasion of Tennessee. The regiment participated in the bloody attack at Franklin, November 30; nearly 80 of its men were killed or wounded. The regiment fought in the Battle of Nashville, December 15–16, and retreated with the army to

Tupelo, Mississippi. In February, 1865, the regiment went to North Carolina and joined the army of General Joe Johnston. The men fought their last battle at Bentonville on March 19. On April 26, the regiment surrendered at Greensboro. Some 1,457 men served in the regiment during the war; 304 died in battle and 302 died of disease.

BIBLIOGRAPHY
Bond, J. L. "Col. T. C. Standifer." *Confederate Veteran*, V (1897), 462–63.
Eakin, Sue Lyles, and Morgan Peoples, eds. *"In Defense of My Country . . .": The Letters of a Shiloh Confederate Soldier, Sergeant George Washington Bolton, and His Union Parish Neighbors of the Twelfth Regiment of Louisiana Volunteers (1861–1864)*. Bernice, 1983.
Greif, J. V. "Baker's Creek and Champion Hill." *Confederate Veteran*, IV (1896), 350–52.
Harris, D. W., and B. M. Hulse. *The History of Claiborne Parish, Louisiana*. New Orleans, 1886.
[Merrill, C. E.]. "Battle of Franklin Recalled." *Confederate Veteran*, V (1897), 600.
Nicholson, James W. *Stories of Dixie*. 1915; rpr. Baton Rouge, 1966.
Thompson, William Y. *E. M. Graham: North Louisianian*. Lafayette, 1984.

13th Regiment

COLONELS. Randall L. Gibson, promoted brigadier general January 11, 1864; Aristide Gerard, dropped August 22, 1864; Francis L. Campbell.

LIEUTENANT COLONELS. Aristide Gerard, promoted colonel January 11, 1864; Francis L. Campbell, promoted colonel August 22, 1864; Edgar M. Dubroca.

MAJORS. Anatole P. Avegno, mortally wounded April 7, 1862; Stephen O'Leary, resigned December 5, 1862; Francis L. Campbell, promoted lieutenant colonel January 11, 1864; Edgar M. Dubroca, promoted lieutenant colonel August 22, 1864; M. O. Tracy.

COMPANIES AND THEIR COMMANDERS

Company A, Southern Celts (Orleans). Stephen O'Leary, promoted major April 7, 1862; Francis L. Campbell, promoted major December 5, 1862; Edgar M. Dubroca, promoted major January 11, 1864; John W. Labouisse(?); William A. Metcalfe, died April 2, 1864; Eugene J. Blasco, killed May 15, 1864; M. O. Tracy, promoted major August 22, 1864; John M. King, transferred to Company B; John McGrath.

Company B, 5th Company Governor's Guards (Orleans). Francis L. Campbell, transferred to Company A April 7, 1862; Edgar M. Dubroca, transferred to Company A December 5, 1862; M. O. Tracy, transferred to Company A May 15, 1864; George Norton, transferred to Company E November 1864(?); John M. King, retired January 20, 1865.

Company C, 6th Company Governor's Guards (Orleans). Edgar M. Dubroca, transferred to Company B April, 1862(?); William A. Metcalfe, transferred to Company A January, 1864(?); John Daly(?); J. B. Lallande.

Company D, 3rd Company Governor's Guards (Orleans). Bernard Avegno, resigned May 1, 1862; George Norton, transferred to Company B January, 1864(?); John McGrath.

Company E, 2nd Company Governor's Guards (Orleans). Justin Fremaux, resigned May 17, 1862; John Daly, transferred to Company C(?); J. W. Labouisse (temporarily, November and December, 1862[?]); Britton Bennett, transferred to Company I August, 1864(?); George Norton.

Company F, 1st Company Governor's Guards (Orleans). Auguste Cassard, wounded April 6, 1862, and did not return, dropped November 24, 1864; John M. King, transferred to Company A; John McGrath; Eugene J. Blasco, killed May 15, 1864; John McGrath.

Company G, St. Mary Volunteers (St. Mary). James C. Murphy, resigned July 19, 1862; John McGrath, transferred to Company D January, 1864(?); Arthur L. Stuart.

Company H, Gladden Rifles (Orleans). William A. Metcalfe, transferred to Company C July, 1862(?); Britton Bennett, absent sick, transferred to Company E January, 1864(?); John W. Labouisse (temporarily, until October 1862[?]); Charles S. Luzenberg (temporarily), resigned July 1, 1864, in Company K; John McGrath.

Company I, 4th Company Governor's Guards (Orleans). M. O. Tracy, transferred to Company B December, 1862(?); Jean A. Dumartrait, transferred to Company K(?), absent from November, 1862, dropped November 24, 1864; Arthur L. Stuart, transferred to Company G January, 1864; J. B. Lallande, transferred to Company C April 8, 1864; Britton Bennett.

Company K, Norton Guards (Orleans). George Norton, transferred to Company D May 1, 1862; John W. Labouisse, transferred to Company E November, 1862; Britton Bennett, transferred to Company H; Arthur L. Stuart(?); Charles S. Luzenberg, transferred to Company H January, 1864, resigned July 1, 1864, in Company K; Eugene J. Blasco, killed May 15, 1864; Charles Jeffreys.

Four independent companies were added to the Battalion of Governor's Guards, or Avegno Zouaves, to create this regiment, which was organized September 11, 1861, at Camp Moore with 830 men. After several months at Camp Chalmette near New Orleans, the regiment left by steamer for Columbus, Kentucky, and arrived in late November. From Columbus, the men went to Corinth, Mississippi. On April 6 and 7, 1862, the regiment fought in the battle of Shiloh and suffered severe casualties. The men participated in the Battle of Farmington, May 9, and received praise for an attack on the enemy. After the evacuation of Corinth, the regiment camped for a time at Tupelo. The men accompanied the Army of Tennessee on its invasion of Kentucky in August. On October 8, the regiment performed gallantly in the Battle of Perryville. Returning to central Tennessee, the regiment went into winter quarters at Tullahoma. On November 30, 1862, General Braxton Bragg ordered the consolidation of the regiment into five companies. These companies joined five companies of the 20th Louisiana Regiment to form the 13th and 20th Louisiana Consolidated Regiment. Despite the merger, promotions of officers continued as though the regiments were still separate. In February, 1865, this consolidated regiment was broken up. The remnants of the 13th Louisiana Regiment were then merged with the 4th and 30th Louisiana regiments and the 14th Louisiana Battalion Sharpshooters. This new unit fought in the Siege of Spanish Fort east of Mobile, Alabama, March 27–April 8, 1865. After the evacuation of Mobile, the men of the 13th Louisiana were placed in a new consolidated unit called the Chalmette Regiment, which surrendered at Gainesville on May 8, 1865. One source says the 13th Louisiana had only 22 men remaining on duty at the surrender.

BIBLIOGRAPHY

McGrath, John. "In a Louisiana Regiment." *Southern Historical Society Papers,* XXXI (1903), 103–20.

Richardson, Frank L. "War as I Saw It." *Louisiana Historical Quarterly,* VI (1923), 89–106, 223–54.

13th and 20th Consolidated Regiment

COLONELS. Randall L. Gibson, brigade commander from September 20, 1863, promoted brigadier general January 11, 1864; Leon Von Zinken, retired November, 1864; Francis L. Campbell.

LIEUTENANT COLONELS. Leon Von Zinken, promoted colonel September 20, 1863; Francis L. Campbell, promoted colonel November, 1864; Edgar M. Dubroca(?).

MAJORS. Charles Guillett, mortally wounded January 2, 1863; Francis L. Campbell, promoted lieutenant colonel January 11, 1864(?); Samuel L. Bishop.

COMPANIES AND THEIR COMMANDERS

Company A (20th Louisiana). Albert A. Lipscomb.

Company B (13th Louisiana). Edgar M. Dubroca, promoted major(?); E. J. Blasco, killed May 15, 1864.

Company C (13th Louisiana). George Norton, detached as brigade assistant adjutant general February, 1864; J. B. Lallande.

Company D (20th Louisiana). Samuel L. Bishop, promoted major January 11, 1864(?); Theodore Eichholtz, died of wounds December 1, 1863; Samuel Sutter.

Company E (13th Louisiana). John McGrath.

Company F (20th Louisiana). Robert L. Keene, captured January 10, 1863, exchanged May 4, 1863; Gebhard Kehrwald, deserted December 16, 1863; Robert L. Keene.

Company G (20th Louisiana). H. Brummerstadt, killed January 2, 1863; Theodore Schneider, killed September 20, 1863; Alexander Dresel.

Company H (20th Louisiana). Thomas M. Ryan, died of wounds

January 20, 1863; Adolphus P. Webre, killed July 28, 1864; John D. Caulfield.

Company I (13th Louisiana). John M. King, wounded and captured January 2, 1863; Britton Bennett, absent from November 15, 1863; John M. King, retired January 2, 1865; William P. Richardson.

Company K (13th Louisiana). John W. Labouisse; Arthur L. Stuart.

This regiment was formed at Shelbyville, Tennessee, on November 30, 1862, with an aggregate strength of 1,075 men. The regiment was heavily involved in the Battle of Murfreesboro; 187 of its men were killed, wounded, or missing on December 31, 1862, and 129 on January 2, 1863. The names of 22 men were placed on the government's Roll of Honor for gallant conduct in the battle. The regiment spent the winter and spring near Tullahoma. In late May, the regiment went to Jackson, Mississippi, to join General Joseph E. Johnston's army. The men saw some fighting in the Siege of Jackson, July 5–25, and retreated with the army to Morton. Returning to the Army of Tennessee in late August, the regiment participated in the Battle of Chickamauga, September 19–20, and captured an enemy battery during one attack. On November 25, the regiment fought in the Battle of Missionary Ridge. During the winter and early spring, the men occupied camps near Dalton, Georgia. They fought at Resaca, May 14–15, and at New Hope Church, May 25, during the Atlanta Campaign. On July 28, the regiment lost heavily in the Battle of Ezra Church. The regiment accompanied the army on its invasion of Tennessee and fought in the Battle of Nashville, December 15–16. In February, 1865, at Mobile, Alabama, the regiment was broken up. The men of the 13th Louisiana were consolidated with those of the 4th and 30th Louisiana regiments and the 14th Louisiana Battalion Sharpshooters; the men of the 20th Louisiana were combined with the remnants of the 1st Louisiana Regulars and the 16th Louisiana.

14th Regiment

COLONELS. Valery Sulakowski, resigned February 19, 1862; Richard W. Jones, resigned August 15, 1862; Zebulon York, promoted brigadier general May 31, 1864; David Zable.

LIEUTENANT COLONELS. Richard W. Jones, promoted colonel February 19, 1862; Zebulon York, promoted colonel August 15, 1862; David Zable, promoted colonel May 31, 1864.

MAJORS. Zebulon York, promoted lieutenant colonel February 19, 1862; David Zable, promoted lieutenant colonel August 15, 1862; William H. Toler, dropped November 24, 1864.

COMPANIES AND THEIR COMMANDERS

Company A, Armstrong Guards (Tensas). Thomas P. Farrar, resigned March 12, 1862; Robert King, died June 7, 1862; Prosper King, resigned January 14, 1863; Stephen O. Cotton.

Company B (1st), Franko Rifles (Orleans), disbanded after August, 1861. Robert Dalton, resigned September 12, 1861.

Company B (2nd), Jefferson Cadets (Orleans). W. H. Zimmerman, resigned February 7, 1863; John B. Hood, dropped November 24, 1864.

Company C, Askew Guards (Orleans). John W. T. Leech.

Company D (1st), Empire Rangers (Plaquemine), transferred to 3rd Louisiana Battalion. Robert A. Wilkinson.

Company D (2nd), McClure Guards (Orleans). Robert M. Austin, resigned November 27, 1861; Royal O. Smith, resigned June 2, 1862; Randolph Bradley, killed June 27, 1862; James R. Norment, dropped April 6, 1864; Benjamin R. Hyatt.

Company E, Nixon Rifles (Pointe Coupee). William H. Cooley, resigned September 20, 1861; Benjamin C. Cooley, dropped May 2, 1864; William Hoffman.

Company F, Concordia Rifles (Concordia). William H. Toler, promoted major August 15, 1862; William K. Penny.

Company G, Avengo Rifles (Orleans). P. F. Mancosas, resigned October 5, 1861; A. F. Mallett, resigned May 26, 1862; W. W. Scott, killed June 27, 1862; Ladislas Wankowicz, resigned December 22, 1862; Morton C. Macmisball, died July 26, 1863; John L. Lemon.

Company H, Quitman Rangers (Orleans). Henry Gillum, resigned June 12, 1862; Thomas A. McDannold.

Company I, Tiger Bayou Rifles. Field F. Montgomery, promoted assistant quartermaster October 8, 1862; Charles R. Martin, resigned February 19, 1863; George H. Pouncey, dropped May 24, 1864.

Company K, Lafayette Rifle Cadets (Orleans). David Zable, promoted major February 19, 1862; Henry M. Verlander, deserted December 13, 1862; Henry B. Myatt, resigned November 9, 1863; John Mooney.

This regiment was organized June 16, 1861, as the 1st Regiment, Polish Brigade. It was mustered into Confederate service as the 13th Louisiana Regiment at Camp Pulaski, near Amite, on August 24. The regiment received orders to go to Virginia. While en route, some of the men got drunk and rioted at Grand Junction, Tennessee. Five men died before the officers could quell the mutiny. One company was disbanded as a result of the affair. The regiment went to Yorktown in September. On September 21, the War Department changed the regiment's designation to the 14th Louisiana Regiment. The men served in the trenches during the Siege of Yorktown, in April, 1862, and fought in the Battle of Williamsburg, May 5. During the second day's fighting at the Battle of Seven Pines, June 1, the regiment saw limited action. The regiment participated in the battles of Mechanicsville, June 26; Gaines' Mill, June 27; and Frayser's Farm, June 30. During these engagements, 243 men were killed or wounded. On July 26, the regiment joined the 1st Louisiana Brigade, which included the 5th, 6th, 7th, and 8th regiments. The men saw only light skirmishing in the Battle of Cedar Mountain, August 9. During the 2nd Manassas Campaign, the regiment fought at Bristoe Station, August 26; at Kettle Run, August 27; at 2nd Manassas, August 29–30; and at Chantilly, September 1. The losses for those battles amounted to 49 men killed, wounded, or missing. In the Battle of Sharpsburg, September 17, the regiment suffered 53 casualties. The regiment transferred to the 2nd Louisiana Brigade on October 5 in exchange for the 9th Louisiana Regiment. From that time on, it served with the 1st, 2nd, 10th, and 15th Louisiana regiments. At the Battle of Fredericksburg, December 13, the regiment remained in reserve; but it did some skirmishing with the enemy the next day. The brigade participated in General Stonewall Jackson's attacks on the Federal flank in the Battle of Chancellorsville, May 2–3, 1863. In the Battle of Winchester, June 15, the regiment captured 300 to 400 men of the 67th Pennsylvania Infantry Regiment. The brigade made assaults against Culp's Hill, July 2–3, during the Battle of Gettysburg; 65 of its men were killed or wounded. When the army returned to Virginia, the brigade participated in the Bristoe Station Campaign, October 9–22. At the Battle of Payne's Farm, November 27, the regiment suffered 28 casualties. The brigade fought in the battles of the Wilderness, May 5, and Spotsylvania, May 9–20. The enemy overran the brigade's trenches on May 12 and captured most of the men engaged. After skirmishing with the enemy at Cold Harbor, June 1–3, the brigade joined General Jubal Early's army in the Shenandoah Valley. There the men fought in all the battles of the army from July to October. The regiment had suffered so many casualties by late October that it and the remnants of the 1st Louisiana Regiment were consolidated into a single company. The brigade rejoined the Army of Northern Virginia at Petersburg in December and served in the trenches there until the army evacuated the town in April, 1865. By the surrender at Appomattox, on April 9, only 2 officers and 25 enlisted men remained to sign paroles. Some 1,026 men served in the regiment during the war; 184 were killed, 85 died of disease, 1 died in an accident, 1 drowned, 1 was shot by court martial, and 5 were shot in the riot. The unit was the only Louisiana regiment in the Army of Northern Virginia that had no field officers die during the war.

BIBLIOGRAPHY

Connor, Forrest P., ed. "Letters of Lieutenant Robert H. Miller to His Family, 1861–1862." *Virginia Magazine of History and Biography*, LXX (1962), 62–91.

Dodd, William H. "A Confederate War Journal." *Historical Records and Studies, U.S. Catholic Historical Society*, XXXII (1941), 94–103.

Hewitt, Lawrence L., ed. "The Civil War Memoirs of Private W. P. Snakenberg, Company K, 14th Louisiana Infantry Regiment." Amite (La.) *News Digest*, August 29, September 5, 12, October 3, 10, 17, 1984.

Kajencki, Col. Francis C. "The Louisiana Tiger." *Louisiana History*, XV (1974), 49–58.

Leech, J. W. T. "The Battle of Frayser's Farm." *Southern Historical Society Papers*, XXI (1893), 160–65.

Sheeran, James B. *Confederate Chaplain: A War Journal*. Edited by Joseph T. Durkin. Milwaukee, [1960].

15th Regiment

COLONEL. Edmund Pendleton.
LIEUTENANT COLONELS. Robert A. Wilkinson, killed August 30, 1862; McGavock Goodwyn.
MAJORS. McGavock Goodwyn, promoted lieutenant colonel August 30, 1862; Andrew Brady.

COMPANIES AND THEIR COMMANDERS

Company A, Askew Guards Company B (Orleans). Andrew Brady, promoted major August 30, 1862; David T. Merrick, relieved November 15, 1864.
Company B, Empire Rangers (Orleans). Henry J. Egan.
Company C, Grosse Tete Creoles (Iberville). William Bowman.
Company D, St. Ceran Rifles (Orleans). Levi T. Jennings.
Company E, Grivot Rifles (Orleans). Samuel D. McChesney, died December 2, 1863.
Company F, St. James Rifles (Orleans). Charles W. McClellan, killed June 1, 1864.
Company G, Davenport Rebels (Morehouse). William C. Michie.
Company H, Bogart Guards (Orleans). Joseph F. Wetherup.
Company I, Catahoula Guerrillas (Catahoula). Samuel W. Spencer, killed August 28, 1862; William Guss, dropped April 18, 1864; Joseph H. Dale.
Company K, Crescent City Blues Company B (Orleans). A. M. Ashbridge, relieved September 10, 1864.

This regiment was organized near Richmond, Virginia, on July 25, 1862, by the addition of two companies of the 7th Louisiana Battalion to the 3rd Louisiana Battalion. The next day, the new regiment was brigaded with the 1st, 2nd, 9th, and 10th Louisiana regiments and Coppens' Zouave Battalion. On August 9, the regiment played a minor role in the Battle of Cedar Mountain. The men fought in the battles of Groveton, August 28, and 2nd Manassas, August 29–30; 21 men were killed, 41 were wounded, and 3 were missing. At the Battle of Sharpsburg, September 17, the regiment suffered only light casualties in the fighting around the Dunkard Church. The regiment was in reserve and did not engage in the Battle of Fredericksburg, December 13. On May 2, 1863, the regiment took part in the attack of General Stonewall Jackson's corps on the Union flank at Chancellorsville. The men were in the continued fighting with General Joseph Hooker's army the next day. During the Battle of Winchester, June 13–15, the regiment acted as the brigade reserve. The regiment participated in the attacks against Culp's Hill at Gettysburg, July 2–3. By July 17, the regiment had only 17 officers and 101 enlisted men present for duty. When the army returned to Virginia, the regiment took part in the Bristoe Station Campaign, October 9–22. During the Mine Run Campaign, the men fought in the Battle of Payne's Farm, November 27, suffering 15 casualties. The brigade fought in the Battle of the Wilderness, May 5, 1864. Federal soldiers overran the brigade's position at Spotsylvania, May 12, capturing a number of men of the regiment and its flag. After skirmishing with the enemy near Cold Harbor, June 1–3, the brigade marched to the Shenandoah Valley. There the men participated in all the battles fought during the summer and fall—Monocacy, July 9; Winchester, July 24; Shepherdstown, August 25; Winchester, September 19; Fisher's Hill, September 21–22; and Cedar Creek, October 19. By the end of the valley campaigns, the regiment had so few men remaining that it was consolidated with the 10th Louisiana Regiment into a single company. The men rejoined the Army of Northern Virginia at Petersburg in December. They served in the trenches there and saw action in early 1865 at Hatcher's Run, February 6, and Fort Stedman, March 25. When the army evacuated Richmond and Petersburg, the men accompanied it on the long march to Appomattox. At the surrender on April 9, only 2 officers and 17 enlisted men were left to sign paroles. The regiment carried 901 men on its rolls during the war; 143 were killed, 98 died of disease, and 1 was executed. Approximately 130 men deserted.

BIBLIOGRAPHY

Hicks, E. M. "Stories of Service in Virginia." *Confederate Veteran,* XX (1912), 561–62.

Laurence, Debra Nance. "Letters from a North Louisiana Tiger." *North Louisiana Historical Association Journal,* X (1979), 130–47.

[McChesney, Wallace H.]. "Captain Charles McLellan." *Confederate Veteran,* VI (1898), 506–507.

16th Regiment

COLONELS. Preston Pond, resigned May 2, 1862; Daniel Gober, detached April 17, 1864.

LIEUTENANT COLONELS. Enoch Mason, dropped May 2, 1862; William E. Walker, died November 30, 1862; Robert H. Lindsay.

MAJORS. Daniel Gober, promoted colonel May 2, 1862; Robert H. Lindsay, promoted lieutenant colonel November 30, 1862; Frank M. Raxsdale.

COMPANIES AND THEIR COMMANDERS

Company A, East Feliciana Guards (East Feliciana). James O. Fuqua, dropped May 8, 1862; Lewellyn G. Chapman, resigned(?) November 6, 1863; B. F. Brown, sent on conscript duty.

Company B, Edwards Guards (St. Tammany). Nicholas S. Edwards, dropped May 8, 1862; Samuel A. Hayden.

Company C, Caddo Fencibles (Caddo). Robert H. Lindsay, promoted major May 8, 1862; Chauncey Ford.

Company D, Walker Roughs (Livingston). William E. Walker, promoted lieutenant colonel May 8, 1862; John W. Addison.

Company E, Rapides Tigers (Rapides). Frank M. Raxsdale, promoted major November 30, 1862; James McFeely.

Company F, St. Helena Rebels (St. Helena). D. W. Thompson, dropped May 8, 1862; Ezekiel John Ellis.

Company G, Pine Woods Sharpshooters (Rapides). Calvin E. Hosea, resigned June 31, 1862; Lewis M. Pipkin.

Company H, Evergreen Invincibles (Avoyelles). Frederic White, resigned November 28, 1861; Robert L. Oliver, killed August 31, 1864.

Company I, Castor Guards (Bienville). W. T. Mabry, dropped May 8, 1862, died of wounds May 15; James M. Houston.

Company K, Big Cane Rifles (St. Landry). William G. Ellerbee, killed April 6, 1862; Louis Stagg.

This regiment was organized at Camp Moore on September 29, 1861, with 851 men. The regiment moved to New Orleans and spent the winter at Camp Benjamin. In February, 1862, the regiment went to Corinth, Mississippi, as part of General Daniel Ruggles' brigade. The regiment took 330 men into the Battle of Shiloh, April 6, and suffered 90 casualties during the attack. On May 9, the men fought in an engagement at Farmington, Mississippi; 14 men were killed or wounded. The regiment was part of General Daniel W. Adams' Louisiana brigade during the invasion of Kentucky, August–October. On October 8, the men participated in the Battle of Perryville and apparently had few casualties. The army went into winter quarters at Tullahoma, Tennessee. Near there, General Braxton Bragg consolidated the regiment into five companies and merged it with the 25th Louisiana Regiment on November 30, 1862. Even though the officers of both regiments were part of a new unit, they received promotions as though they were still in their original regiments. On February 3, 1865, the consolidated unit was broken up, and the remnants of the 16th Louisiana were combined with those of the 1st Louisiana Regulars and 20th Louisiana Regiment. The men fought in the Siege of Spanish Fort, Alabama, March 27–April 8. Following the evacuation of Mobile, the men of the 16th Louisiana were placed in a new consolidated unit called the Chalmette Regiment; they surrendered with it at Gainesville on May 8.

BIBLIOGRAPHY

"Inquiry for and about Veterans." *Confederate Veteran*, XVI (1908), 347–48.

[Lindsay, R. H.]. "Capture of Florence, Ala., Under Hood." *Confederate Veteran*, V (1897), 423.

———. "Trick to Learn Position of the Enemy." *Confederate Veteran*, VIII (1900), 75.

[Thompson, William L.]. "Capt. S. A. Hayden as a Spy." *Confederate Veteran*, V (1897), 559.

16th and 25th Consolidated Regiment

COLONELS. Stuart W. Fisk, killed December 31, 1862; Daniel Gober, detached April 17, 1864; J. C. Lewis, mortally wounded August 31, 1864; Frank C. Zacharie.

LIEUTENANT COLONELS. Robert H. Lindsay(?); Frank C. Zacharie, promoted colonel August 31, 1864; Robert H. Lindsay; Calvin H. Moore(?).

MAJORS. Frank C. Zacharie, promoted lieutenant colonel March 16, 1863(?); Calvin H. Moore, promoted lieutenant colonel(?).

Companies and Their Commanders

Company A (Companies D and H, 16th Louisiana). Robert P. Oliver; Lewellyn G. Chapman, March–May, 1863; Robert P. Oliver, killed August 31, 1864.

Company B (Companies A and I, 25th Louisiana). C. F. Rabenhorst; Charles W. Lewis, ordered to Trans-Mississippi Department June, 1864; Clement H. Watson, promoted brigade adjutant and inspector general.

Company C (Companies B and E, 16th Louisiana). Calvin H. Moore, promoted major March 16, 1863; Clement H. Watson, transferred to Company B.

Company D (Companies D and F, 25th Louisiana). W. T. Miller, resigned January 8, 1864; George L. Walton.

Company E (Companies C and H, 25th Louisiana). William F. Mellen, retired August 22, 1864; John M. Clayton.

Company F (Companies B and E, 16th Louisiana). Samuel A. Hayden.

Company G (Companies I and K, 16th Louisiana). Louis Stagg.

Company H (Companies F and G, 16th Louisiana). Ezekiel John Ellis; Louis M. Pipkin, April–August, 1863; Ezekiel John Ellis, captured November 25, 1863; James McFeely.

Company I (Companies A and C, 16th Louisiana). Chauncey Ford, captured September 20, 1863; B. F. Brown, on leave from May 4, 1864; Chauncey Ford.

Company K (Companies G and K, 25th Louisiana). W. R. C. Lyons; Seaborne Aycock, killed August 31, 1864; W. R. C. Lyons.

This regiment was formed at Shelbyville, Tennessee, on November 30, 1862, with an aggregate strength of 1,078 men. The regiment participated in the attacks on December 31, 1862, and January 2, 1863, during the Battle of Murfreesboro and suffered 438 casualties. With its brigade, the regiment joined General Joseph E. Johnston's army at Jackson, Mississippi, in May, 1863. At Jackson, the men played a part in the siege of July 5 to 25 and suffered a small number of casualties. The brigade returned to the Army of Tennessee in time to fight in the Battle of Chickamauga, September 19–20. There the regiment lost nearly one-third of its men as prisoners to the enemy. The men fought in the Battle of Missionary Ridge, November 25, and spent the winter at Dalton, Georgia. During the Atlanta Campaign, the regiment fought at Mill Creek Gap, May 7; Resaca, May 14–15; and New Hope Church, May 25–28. In those engagements, 63 men were killed, wounded, or missing. The men participated in the battles of Atlanta, July 22; Ezra Church, July 28; and Jonesboro, August 31. On October 30, the regiment captured the Federal garrison at Florence, Alabama. The men fought in the Battle of Nashville, December 15–16, during the army's invasion of Tennessee. In February, 1865, while at Mobile, Alabama, the regiment was broken up. The remnants of the 16th Louisiana were consolidated with the 1st Louisiana Regulars and 20th Louisiana as a new unit. The men of the 25th Louisiana were merged with those of the 4th Louisiana Battalion.

17th Regiment

COLONELS. S. S. Heard, dropped May 23, 1862; Robert Richardson.
LIEUTENANT COLONELS. Charles Jones, dropped May 23, 1862; Madison Rogers, killed May 20, 1863; William Antoine Redditt.
MAJORS. Robert B. Jones, resigned March 14, 1862; W. A. Maddox, resigned August 28, 1862; William Antoine Redditt, promoted lieutenant colonel May 20, 1863; David W. Self.

COMPANIES AND THEIR COMMANDERS

Company A, Ouachita Southrons (Ouachita), later Company E. Madison Rogers, promoted lieutenant colonel May 23, 1862; Samuel S. Adams.
Company B, Sabine Rifles (Sabine). David W. Self, promoted major May 20, 1863.
Company C, Catahoula Rebels (Catahoula), later Company K. R. H. Cuny, dropped May 23, 1862; Robert Michael.
Company D, Phoenix Rifles (Union), later Company C. Jordan Gray Taylor.
Company E, Landrum Guards (Caddo), later Company I. Thomas A. Sharp, dropped May 23, 1862; S. M. Chapman.
Company F, Caddo Lake Boys (Caddo). James A. Jeter, dropped May 23, 1862; F. G. Spearman.
Company G, Simmons Stars (Catahoula), later Company A. W. A. Simmons, dropped May 23, 1862; B. F. Street.

Company H, Morehouse Southrons (Morehouse), later Company G.
William M. Otterson, dropped May 23, 1862; Samuel M. Steven-
son, resigned March 30, 1863.
Company I, Catahoula Guards (Catahoula), later Company A.
William Antoine Redditt, promoted major August 28, 1862;
William A. Scott.
Company K, Claiborne Invincibles (Claiborne), later Company H.
W. A. Maddox, promoted major May 23, 1862; Gabriel M. Killgore.

This regiment was organized at Camp Moore on September 29, 1861,
with 832 men. From Camp Moore, the regiment went to New Orleans. As part of General Daniel Ruggles' brigade, the regiment occupied Camp Chalmette and later Camp Benjamin. The brigade
went to Corinth, Mississippi, in February, 1862. On April 6 and 7,
the men fought in the Battle of Shiloh. Ordered to Vicksburg in May,
the men saw only picket duty during the first Union attack on that
place, May 18–July 27. The regiment helped repulse the enemy attacks on Chickasaw Bluffs north of Vicksburg, December 26–29.
Remaining near Vicksburg through the winter, the regiment was assigned to General William E. Baldwin's brigade. On May 1, 1863, the
regiment fought in the Battle of Port Gibson and bore the brunt of
the fighting during the Confederate retreat. The men fell back to
Vicksburg and participated in the siege there, May 19–July 4. Paroled
at the surrender of Vicksburg, the men returned to their homes. In
January, 1864, the regiment reported to a parole camp near Shreveport
for a short time. The men reassembled at Minden in May and soon
went to Pineville. As part of General Allen Thomas' brigade, the
regiment remained in garrison at Pineville until May, 1865. In that
month, the men camped at Cotile briefly and then marched to Mansfield. There the men disbanded about May 19. One report states that
Company C was the only company in the regiment's division to remain on duty until discharged and that the company guarded the
brigade's ammunition supply against the soldiers who were disbanding and going home.

BIBLIOGRAPHY
Cooper, William W., and Donald M. Fowler. "'Your Affectionate
Husband': Letters from a Catahoula Parish Confederate Soldier,
September 1861–May 1862." *North Louisiana Historical Asso-
ciation Journal*, XIV (1983), 21–40.

Gaskell, J. E. "Battle of Chickasaw Bayou." *Confederate Veteran*, XXIII (1915), 128.

———. "Surrendered at Vicksburg." *Confederate Veteran*, XXXIII (1925), 286.

Harris, D. W., and B. M. Hulse. *The History of Claiborne Parish, Louisiana.* New Orleans, 1886.

Maynard, Douglas, ed. "Vicksburg Diary: The Journal of Gabriel M. Killgore." *Civil War History*, X (1964), 33–53.

Small, J. A. *Memories of the Civil War as Experienced by an Old Veteran.* N.p., n.d.

Vandiver, Frank E., ed. "A Collection of Louisiana Confederate Letters." *Louisiana Historical Quarterly*, XXVI (1943), 937–74.

18th Regiment

COLONELS. J. J. A. Alfred Mouton, promoted brigadier general April 16, 1862; Alfred Roman, dropped May 10, 1862; Leopold L. Armant.

LIEUTENANT COLONELS. Alfred Roman, promoted colonel April 16, 1862; Louis Bush, dropped May 10, 1862; Joseph Collins.

MAJORS. Louis Bush, promoted lieutenant colonel April 16, 1862; Leopold L. Armant, promoted colonel May 10, 1862; William Mouton.

COMPANIES AND THEIR COMMANDERS

Company A, St. James Rifles (St. James). Jules A. Druilhet, dropped May 10, 1862; William Sanchez.

Company B, St. Landry Volunteers (St. Landry). Henry L. Garland, dropped May 10, 1862; C. M. Shepherd.

Company C, Natchitoches Rebels (Natchitoches). John D. Wood, killed April 6, 1862; Emile Cloutier, Jr.

Company D, Hayes Champions (St. Mary). James D. Hayes, dropped May 10, 1862; Benjamin S. Story.

Company E, Chasseurs St. Jacques (St. James). E. Camille Mire, dropped May 10, 1862; Alexander S. Poche.

Company F, Arcadian Guards (Lafayette). William Mouton, promoted major May 10, 1862; A. Pope Bailey.

Company G, Lafourche Creoles (Lafourche). J. Kleber Gourdain.

Company H, Confederate Guards (Orleans). Henry Huntington, mortally wounded April 6, 1862; Paul B. Leeds.

Company I, Orleans Cadet Company C (Orleans). Joseph Collins, promoted lieutenant colonel May 10, 1862; John T. Lavery.

Company K, Opelousas Volunteers (St. Landry). Louis Lastrapes, killed April 6, 1862; James G. Hayes.

This regiment was partially organized at Camp Moore on October 5, 1861, with seven companies. On October 8, the regiment moved to Camp Roman near Carrollton, where an eighth company joined it. The regiment transferred to Camp Benjamin on January 3, 1862. Two additional companies joined the regiment there to complete its organization. On February 16, the men traveled by railroad to Corinth, Mississippi. They were assigned to picket Pittsburg Landing on the Tennessee River. There they engaged and repulsed a landing party from two enemy gunboats and drove away the gunboats on March 1. The regiment fought in the Battle of Shiloh, April 6–7; in one attack, 200 men were killed or wounded. Falling back to Corinth, the regiment served in the trenches there until the evacuation of the town on May 29. After remaining in camp at Tupelo for two months, the regiment received orders to report for duty at Mobile, Alabama. The men were assigned to a camp at Pollard to guard the approaches to Mobile from Pensacola, Florida. On October 2, the regiment left for western Louisiana; it reached New Iberia on October 12. The men fought in the Battle of Labadieville, October 27, and retreated with the army to Fort Bisland on Bayou Teche. They spent the winter and early spring at Camp Qui Vive at Fausse Point and returned to Bisland in mid-March, 1863. On April 12 and 13, the regiment participated in the Battle of Bisland but suffered few casualties. The army retreated through Opelousas and Alexandria to Natchitoches. In June, the regiment returned to south Louisiana and participated in the operations around Bayou Lafourche in July. During August, September, and October, the regiment marched back and forth between Vermilionville, Simmesport, and Moundville. On November 14, the regiment merged with the 10th Louisiana Battalion at Simmesport to form the 18th Louisiana Consolidated Infantry Regiment.

BIBLIOGRAPHY

Bergeron, Arthur W., Jr., ed. *Reminiscences of Uncle Silas: The History of the Eighteenth Louisiana Infantry Regiment.* Baton Rouge, 1981.

[Cantzon, Charles E.]. "'Record of a Confederate Soldier,'" *Confederate Veteran*, XVII (1909), 23.

18th Consolidated Regiment

COLONELS. Leopold L. Armant, killed April 8, 1864; Joseph Collins.
LIEUTENANT COLONELS. Joseph Collins, promoted colonel April 8, 1864; William Mouton.
MAJORS. William Mouton, promoted lieutenant colonel April 8, 1864; J. Kleber Gourdain.

COMPANIES AND THEIR COMMANDERS

Company A. Louis Becnel.
Company B. S. Alexander Poche.
Company C. William Sanchez.
Company D. Arthur W. Hyatt, promoted lieutenant colonel in Consolidated Crescent Regiment April 24, 1864; F. F. Perrodin.
Company E. Benjamin S. Story.
Company F. C. M. Shepherd, promoted assistant quartermaster April 16, 1864; Levi M. Hargis.
Company G. Henry B. Stevens, transferred to Company O, Consolidated Crescent Regiment; H. Crawford.
Company H. John T. Lavery, mortally wounded April 8, 1864; Horatio N. Jenkins.
Company I. A. Pope Bailey.
Company K. Arthur F. Simon, promoted major 10th Louisiana Battalion; Alex. Castille.

This regiment was formed at Simmesport on November 14, 1863, by a merger of the 18th Louisiana Regiment and the 10th Louisiana Battalion. With General Alfred Mouton's (later Henry Gray's) infantry brigade, the regiment marched to Monroe. The brigade started for Pineville on January 31, 1864, and reached it ten days later. When the Federal Red River Campaign began in mid-March, the brigade traveled to Lecompte and then retreated with General Richard Taylor's army toward Shreveport. The regiment participated in the Battle of Mansfield, April 8; nearly 100 men were killed or wounded. During the Battle of Pleasant Hill, April 9, the regiment was only lightly engaged late in the day. With Taylor's army, the regiment pursued the Federals down the Red River and fought in the Battle of Yellow

Bayou, May 18. The regiment camped at Marksville, McNutt's Hill, and Beaver Creek during the next two months. In August, the brigade marched to Monroe; and in September, it accompanied the army into southern Arkansas. The men spent the next two months at Camden and Walnut's Hill. By late November, the brigade had encamped at Minden. In late January, 1865, the brigade marched to Pineville. The men remained there until February, when they moved to Bayou Cotile. In May, the brigade marched to Mansfield; it disbanded there on May 19 after hearing of the imminent surrender of the Trans-Mississippi Department.

19th Regiment

COLONELS. Benjamin L. Hodge, resigned July 15, 1862; Wesley P. Winans, killed November 25, 1863; Richard W. Turner.

LIEUTENANT COLONELS. James M. Hollingsworth, dropped May 8, 1862; Wesley P. Winans, promoted colonel July 15, 1862; Richard W. Turner, promoted colonel November 25, 1863; Hyder A. Kennedy.

MAJORS. Wesley P. Winans, promoted lieutenant colonel May 8, 1862; Richard W. Turner, promoted lieutenant colonel July 15, 1862; Loudon Butler, killed September 20, 1863; Hyder A. Kennedy, promoted lieutenant colonel November 25, 1863; Winfrey B. Scott, killed May 27, 1864; Camp Flournoy.

COMPANIES AND THEIR COMMANDERS

Company A, Vance Guards (Bossier). Richard W. Turner, promoted major May 8, 1862; B. B. Matlock.

Company B, Robins Greys (Bossier). Loudon Butler, promoted major July 15, 1862; John A. Bruton, killed September 20, 1863; Henry J. James, mortally wounded March 27, 1865.

Company C, Claiborne Volunteers (Claiborne). Hyder A. Kennedy, promoted major September 20, 1863; S. A. Hightower.

Company D, Claiborne Greys (Claiborne). Winfrey B. Scott, promoted major November 25, 1863; Morris Miller.

Company E, Stars of Equality (Union). Hillory H. Ham, resigned January 9, 1862; James B. Landers, resigned November 13, 1863; William R. Roberts.

Company F, Henry Marshall Guards (DeSoto). A. J. Fortson, dropped

May 8, 1862; Andrew J. Handly, killed November 25, 1863; John W. Pitts.

Company G, Caddo 10th (Caddo). J. P. Bridges, dropped May 8, 1862; Camp Flournoy, promoted major May 27, 1864; Joseph A. Harrison.

Company H, DeSoto Creoles (DeSoto). John H. Sutherlin, resigned January 10, 1862; Joshua L. Logan, resigned April 25, 1862; Michael G. Pearson, killed May 26, 1864; William H. Farmer.

Company I, Keachi Warriors (Caddo). D. S. Wells, dropped June 20, 1862; J. F. Smith.

Company K, Anacoco Rangers (Sabine and Rapides). William W. Smart, discharged for ill health June 27, 1862; John W. Jones.

This regiment was organized at Camp Moore on November 19, 1861, with eight companies. On December 11, two more companies joined the regiment, giving it a total of 873 men. The regiment spent the winter in New Orleans. In February, 1862, it went to Corinth, Mississippi. The men fought in the Battle of Shiloh, April 6–7, and lost about one-fifth of their total strength. During the engagement at Farmington, on May 9, the regiment remained in the trenches at Corinth to protect its brigade's camps and supplies. The regiment became part of the Mobile, Alabama, garrison in July and spent most of its time in camp at Pollard, east of the city. In April, 1863, the regiment received orders to report to the Army of Tennessee at Tullahoma, Tennessee. There the men became part of the Louisiana brigade commanded by General Daniel W. Adams and later by General Randall L. Gibson. The brigade moved to Jackson, Mississippi, in May and joined General Joseph E. Johnston's army. From July 5 to 25, the brigade participated in the Siege of Jackson, and the regiment repulsed an attack on its trenches on July 12. Returning to the Army of Tennessee in northern Georgia, the brigade fought in the Battle of Chickamauga, September 19–20. Company F captured two enemy cannons, and the regiment lost 153 of the 350 officers and enlisted men engaged. The regiment repulsed several attacks during the Battle of Missionary Ridge, November 25, but had to retreat when the Federals outflanked its position. During the winter of 1863–64, the regiment camped near Dalton, Georgia. The men fought in the Atlanta Campaign at Mill Creek Gap, May 8–11; at Resaca, May 14–15; and at New Hope Church, May 25–28. In the battles around Atlanta, the regiment fought at Atlanta, July 22; Ezra Church, July 28; and Jonesboro, August 31. The regiment went with the army into Tennessee. On November 30, the men arrived too late to participate in the fighting at Franklin. They did see heavy fighting in the Battle of Nashville, December 15–16. From Nashville, the army retreated to Tupelo, Mississippi. After several months there, the brigade received orders to report to Mobile. The men participated in the Siege of Spanish Fort, March 27–April 8, 1865. When Mobile was evacuated, the regiment was consolidated as part of a new unit, the Pelican Regiment. Companies A, E, and I became Company A; Companies C, F, G, and K became Company D; and Companies B, D, and H became Company E. On May 8, the men surrendered at Gainesville, Alabama.

BIBLIOGRAPHY

"Andrew Pickens Butler." Confederate Veteran, VIII (1900), 326–27.
Durham, Ken. "'Dear Rebecca': The Civil War Letters of William Edwards Paxton." Louisiana History, XX (1979), 169–96.
Harris, D. W., and B. M. Hulse. The History of Claiborne Parish, Louisiana. New Orleans, 1886.

20th Regiment
(Lovell Regiment)

COLONELS. Augustus Reichard, resigned July 7, 1863; Leon Von Zinken.

LIEUTENANT COLONELS. Samuel Boyd, resigned June 4, 1862; Leon Von Zinken, promoted colonel July 7, 1863; Samuel L. Bishop.

MAJORS. Leon Von Zinken, promoted lieutenant colonel June 4, 1862; Charles Guillett, killed January 2, 1863; Samuel L. Bishop, promoted lieutenant colonel July 7, 1863.

COMPANIES AND THEIR COMMANDERS

Company A, Steuben Guards (Orleans). Gebhard Kehrwald, deserted December 16, 1863; Richard Hackett.

Company B (1st), Louisiana Musketeers (Orleans), detached in February, 1862. Charles Assenheimer.

Company B (2nd), Noel Rangers (Huckins Guard) (Orleans). Alexander Dresel.

Company C, Reichard Rifles (Orleans). Herrmann Muller, retired November 2, 1864; John Schaedel.

Company D, Turner Guards (Orleans). L. C. Buncken, resigned November 10, 1862; Theodore Schneider, killed September 20, 1863; Theodore Eichholtz, died of wounds December 1, 1863; Samuel Sutter.

Company E (1st), Orleans Blues Company A (Orleans), detached in February, 1862. Richard Herrick.

Company E (2nd) (Orleans), added July 23, 1862. Albert A. Lipscomb.

Company F, Florence Guards (Orleans). H. Brummerstadt, killed January 2, 1863; Edmund Lachenmeyer.

Company G, Orleans Blues Company B (Orleans). Patrick Clark, resigned May 17, 1862; Thomas M. Ryan, died of wounds January 20, 1863; Adolphus P. Webre, killed July 28, 1864; John D. Caulfield.

Company H, Stanley Guards (Orleans). H. H. Rainey, resigned April 20, 1862; James Cousley, dropped May 26, 1862; Fred W. Airey.

Company I, Forstall Guards (Mann Rifles) (Orleans). William Boyd, resigned May 26, 1862; Robert L. Keene.

Company K, Jameson Light Guards (Orleans). Thomas O'Neil, resigned April 23, 1862; Samuel L. Bishop, promoted major July 7, 1863; Daniel Maegher, deserted July 17, 1863; Charles J. Harper.

This regiment was organized at Camp Lewis in New Orleans on January 3, 1862, by the addition of six independent companies to the 6th Louisiana Battalion. The regiment had a strength of 879 men. On January 4, the men moved to Camp Benjamin. Several companies served on detached duty at Fort Jackson, Pass Manchac, and Berwick. On March 11, the regiment left for Corinth, Mississippi. The men fought in the Battle of Shiloh, April 6–7. In the battle, Colonel Reichard had his horse shot from under him and Major Von Zinken lost three horses. The regiment participated in a skirmish at Monterey on April 29 and in the Battle of Farmington on May 9. After spending several months at Tupelo, the regiment accompanied the army on its invasion of Kentucky, August–October. The men fought in the Battle of Perryville, October 8. When the army went into winter quarters at Shelbyville, Tennessee, General Braxton

Bragg ordered the consolidation of the regiment with the 13th Louisiana because of the heavy losses the two units had suffered. This consolidation occurred November 30. Each regiment made up five companies of the new unit. On February 3, 1865, at Mobile, Alabama, the consolidation was dissolved and the 20th Louisiana was combined with the 1st Louisiana Regulars and 16th Louisiana to form a new unit. This unit participated in the Siege of Spanish Fort, March 27–April 8. After the evacuation of Mobile, the men of the 20th Louisiana were combined into one company, designated Company H, Pelican Regiment. As such, they surrendered at Gainesville on May 8.

21st Regiment
(McCown Regiment)

COLONEL. J. B. G. Kennedy.
LIEUTENANT COLONEL. West Steever.
MAJOR. John Newman.

COMPANIES AND THEIR COMMANDERS

Company A, Bonford Guards (Orleans). M. Stern, resigned July 3, 1862.

Company B, Campbell Guards (Orleans). Henry N. Soria.

Company C, Huckins Guard (Noel Rangers) (Orleans), became Company B, 20th Louisiana Regiment, July 23, 1862. Alexander Dresel.

Company D, McClelland Guards Company A (Orleans). Bernard Moses.

Company E, Kosicinski Guards (Whamm Rifle Guards) (Orleans). L. Cedrowski, resigned January 4, 1862; D. Vancourt.

Company F, Askew Greys (Orleans). S. Q. Willis.

Company G (Orleans). H. L. Levy.

Company H, McClelland Guards Company C (Orleans). Gustave A. Moses, dropped May 24, 1862; Augustus Moses.

Company I, McClelland Guards Company B (Orleans). J. Simons.

Company K, Dugue Guards(?) (Orleans). J. W. Wing(?).

This regiment was organized at Columbus, Kentucky, on February 9, 1862, by the addition of four companies to the 5th Louisiana Battalion. The new regiment had a strength of 784 men. On February 23, a portion of the regiment marched to Island No. 10 and began erecting batteries for heavy artillery pieces. The rest of the regiment soon reported at Island No. 10 and continued the work already started. The regiment left for Fort Pillow on March 17 and served in the garrison there until the fort was evacuated in May. From Fort Pillow, the men went to Corinth, Mississippi. They fought in a skirmish near there on May 28. The regiment went with the army to Tupelo. On July 28, General Braxton Bragg ordered the regiment disbanded and the men assigned to other Louisiana units in the army. Illness had reduced the effective strength of the regiment while it was at Corinth.

22nd Regiment
(Patton's 21st Regiment)

COLONELS. Martin L. Smith, promoted brigadier general April 11, 1862; Edward Higgins, transferred; Isaac W. Patton.
LIEUTENANT COLONELS. Edward Higgins, promoted colonel April 11, 1862; Edward Ivy, transferred; John T. Plattsmier.
MAJORS. Edward Ivy, promoted lieutenant colonel April 11, 1862; George Purvis.

COMPANIES AND THEIR COMMANDERS

Company A, Perseverance Guards (Orleans). John Rareshide, transferred(?); David H. Todd.
Company B, Black Jagers (Orleans). Charles F. Rabenhorst, transferred to 13th and 20th Consolidated Louisiana Regiment; Charles Green.
Company C, Scotch Rifle Guards (Orleans). George Purves, promoted major April 11, 1862(?); William R. McKenzie.
Company D, Marion Guards (Orleans). R. L. Robertson, Jr., transferred to Trans-Mississippi Department June, 1862; James Ryan, killed May, 1863.
Company E, Washington Light Infantry (Orleans). John T. Plattsmier, promoted lieutenant colonel February, 1863; Ambrose A. Plattsmier.
Company F, Screwmen's Guards Company A (Orleans). Isaac W. Patton, promoted major and brigade quartermaster July, 1862.
Company G, Screwmen's Guards Company B (Orleans). James G. Batchelor.

Company H, Sappers and Miners (Orleans). James Ryan, transferred
to Company D.
Company I, Jager Company (Orleans). Frederick Peter.
*Company K, Miles' Legion Artillery Company A (Orleans), assigned
but served as independent unit.* Claude Gibson.

This regiment was organized at New Orleans on March 28, 1862,
with 961 men. The men were trained to operate heavy artillery
pieces, and they occupied several fortifications along the Louisiana
coast during the Federal campaign against New Orleans. Company
A was at Fort Pike and Companies B and C at Fort Macomb. Company D manned the ten guns at Battery Bienvenue. Company E held
Tower Dupre, and Company F occupied the Proctorsville Battery.
Companies H and I made up part of the garrison at Fort Jackson. The
men of the two latter companies became prisoners when the fort
surrendered, on April 27. On April 25, Company F participated
in the engagement with the Federal fleet at the McGehee Lines
opposite Chalmette. The regiment reorganized at Camp Moore on
May 24 and formed four companies. From Camp Moore, the regiment went to Vicksburg, Mississippi, and served in the river batteries there during the first Federal attack on the city, which ended
on July 27. The four companies were consolidated into two and remained this way until November. At that time, the regiment moved
to Snyder's Bluff above Vicksburg on the Yazoo River, and the four
companies were restored to their separate organizations. Some of
the men captured at Fort Jackson and at New Orleans joined the
regiment at Snyder's Bluff. Enough men reported to necessitate the
formation of a fifth company. The regiment fired on Federal gunboats and forced them to retreat on December 27. About January,
1863, the regiment's designation was changed to the 21st Louisiana
Regiment. A detachment from the regiment participated in the
defense of Fort Pemberton on the upper Yazoo River, March 11–17.
The regiment repulsed a naval and land attack on Snyder's Bluff,
April 30–May 1. When General Ulysses S. Grant's Union army
neared Vicksburg, the regiment evacuated the works at Snyder's
Bluff and reported for duty at the city. During the Siege of Vicksburg,
May 19–July 4, the regiment, reinforced by two companies of the
22nd (old 23rd) Louisiana Regiment, held an earthwork on the Jackson Road known as the Great Redoubt, or Fort Beauregard. During

the siege, 16 men were killed, 50 were wounded, and 1 deserted. After the surrender, the men went into a parole camp at Enterprise. They remained there until January 26, 1864, at which time they were merged with the remnants of seven other regiments to form the 22nd Louisiana Consolidated Regiment.

BIBLIOGRAPHY
Bergeron, Arthur W., Jr. "'They Bore Themselves with Distinguished Gallantry': The Twenty-Second Louisiana Infantry." *Louisiana History*, XIII (1972), 253–82.

22nd Consolidated Regiment

COLONEL. Isaac W. Patton.
LIEUTENANT COLONEL. J. O. Landry, transferred to the Trans-Mississippi Department May 26, 1864.
MAJOR. Washington Marks.

COMPANIES AND THEIR COMMANDERS

Company A (Company A, 23rd Louisiana). Emanuel Blum.
Company B (Company B, 23rd Louisiana). Edward Durrive, Jr.
Company C (Company C, 23rd Louisiana). Samuel Barnes.
Company D (Company D, 23rd Louisiana). James C. Theard.
Company E (Company E, 23rd Louisiana). A. Selle.
Company F (26th, 27th, and 31st Louisiana). Walter S. Jones, detached February 9, 1864; William H. Wells.
Company G (17th and 29th Louisiana). Samuel Brewer.
Company H (3rd Louisiana). C. A. Brashear.
Company I (Companies A and B, 22nd Louisiana). Ambrose A. Plattsmier.
Company K (Companies C, D, and E, 22nd Louisiana). James Gibney.

This regiment was organized at Enterprise, Mississippi, on January 26, 1864, from the remnants of the 3rd, 17th, 22nd (later 21st), 23rd (later 22nd), 26th, 29th, and 31st Louisiana regiments in the parole camp there. The new unit had 780 men on its rolls. On February 3, the regiment received orders to report to Mobile, Alabama. There the men garrisoned several redoubts and batteries around the city. During the next few months, the men drilled as heavy artillerists and performed guard duty. The regiment moved to Pollard on May 22 to guard the railroad to Montgomery from Federal raids out of Pensacola. On July 22, the men moved to Pine Barren's Creek to meet such a raid, but the enemy retreated to Pensacola before any fighting could occur. The passage of the forts guarding the mouth of Mobile Bay by Admiral David G. Farragut's Union fleet resulted in orders on August 4 for the regiment to return to Mobile. Again the men occupied various batteries in the city's defenses. Later in the fall, the regiment moved to the Eastern Shore defenses. Two companies garrisoned Battery Huger on the Appalachee River, and three companies held nearby Battery Tracy on the Blakely River. Four companies made up part of the Spanish Fort defenses. The latter companies participated in the defense of Spanish Fort, March 27–April 8, 1865. The men at Battery Huger and Battery Tracy fired their guns in support of the earthworks at Spanish Fort. When the latter were evacuated, the men of the regiment united at Huger and Tracy until they too were evacuated, on April 12. The regiment moved to Meridian, Mississippi, and was surrendered there on May 8.

BIBLIOGRAPHY

Bergeron, Arthur W., Jr. "The Twenty-Second Louisiana Consolidated Infantry in the Defense of Mobile, 1864–1865." *Alabama Historical Quarterly*, XXXVIII (1976), 204–13.

23rd Regiment
(Later 22nd Regiment)

COLONELS. Paul E. Theard, resigned May 1, 1862; Charles H. Herrick, died May 22, 1863.

LIEUTENANT COLONELS. William S. Lovell, transferred; A. Louis Tissot, resigned October 1, 1862; Samuel Jones.

MAJOR. Washington Marks.

COMPANIES AND THEIR COMMANDERS

Company A, 1st Company Orleans Artillery (Orleans). Francisco Gomez, killed May 21, 1863.

Company B, 2nd Company Orleans Artillery (Orleans). James P. Morlot, resigned March 18, 1863.

Company C, 3rd Company Orleans Artillery (Orleans). George Stromeyer, dropped March 1, 1863.

Company D, 4th Company Orleans Artillery (Orleans). James C. Theard.

Company E, McCall Guards (Orleans). Charles H. Herrick, promoted colonel May 25, 1862.

Company F (Orleans). Edward Durrive, Jr.

Company G, Twiggs Rifles (Orleans). David H. Marks, resigned May 2, 1862.

Company H, Twiggs Rifles Company B (Orleans). Washington Marks, promoted major May 2, 1863; Marion H. Marks.

Company I, Allen Guards (Orleans). Samuel Jones, promoted lieutenant colonel.

Company K, Tirailleurs d'Orleans (Orleans). A. Louis Tissot, promoted lieutenant colonel May 25, 1862; Samuel Barnes.

This regiment was organized in New Orleans, possibly at Camp Lewis, in January, 1862, by the addition of six companies to the Orleans Artillery Battalion, a state militia unit. In March, the regiment was mustered into Confederate service with approximately 841 men. The various companies occupied at that time or soon received assignment to different fortifications along the Gulf Coast. Companies A, B, C, and D defended Fort Livingston; Companies E and G, Fort Guion on Bayou Lafourche; Companies F and K, Fort Pike; Company H, Fort Quitman on Grand Caillou Bayou; and Company I, Fort Jackson. The latter company was captured at Fort Jackson on April 26. When General Mansfield Lovell ordered the evacuation of New Orleans, most of the companies disbanded, and the men went home, fearing orders compelling them to leave the state. Companies E, F, and K, with small numbers of men from other companies, reported to Lovell at Camp Moore. On May 25, these men reorganized themselves into four companies. They received orders to report to Vicksburg, Mississippi, and arrived there on June 11. The men took part in the defense of the city by manning some of the heavy artillery in the river batteries until the enemy abandoned its operations on July 27. During the fall and winter, the regiment continued to serve in the Vicksburg river batteries and received reinforcements in the form of men of the unit who were exchanged after having been captured at New Orleans. Sometime in early 1863, the regiment's designation was changed to the 22nd Louisiana Regiment. In March, 1863, the men went to Fort Pemberton near Yazoo City, where they exchanged shots with Federal gunboats on several occasions. When General Ulysses S. Grant's Union army approached Vicksburg in May, the regiment returned to the city to participate in its defense. Companies A and B served with the 1st Louisiana Heavy Artillery in the river batteries, and Companies C and D fought in the trenches with the 21st (old 22nd) Louisiana Regiment. These four companies were surrendered with the garrison on July 4 and paroled. Captain Durrive's company had remained at Yazoo City because it had been acting independently from the other companies. In early July, this company moved to Jackson, and the men participated in the fighting there until the city was evacuated, on July 16. The company remained in central Mississippi until winter, when it went to Mobile, Alabama. Most of the men captured at Vicksburg went into a parole camp at Enterprise. On January 26, 1864, they were united with the remnants of the 21st Louisiana Regiment and with men from several other Louisiana regiments to form the 22nd Louisiana Consolidated Regiment.

BIBLIOGRAPHY

Ellis, Lewis E. "Reminiscences of New Orleans, Jackson and Vicksburg." *Confederate Annals*, I (August, 1883), 47–55.

24th Regiment
(Crescent Regiment)

COLONELS. Marshall J. Smith, resigned July 28, 1862; George P. McPheeters, killed October 27, 1862; Abel W. Bosworth.

LIEUTENANT COLONELS. George P. McPheeters, promoted colonel July 28, 1862; George Soule.

MAJORS. Abel W. Bosworth, promoted colonel October 27, 1862; Myford McDougall.

COMPANIES AND THEIR COMMANDERS

Company A, Crescent City Guards Company B (Orleans). George Soule, promoted lieutenant colonel July 28, 1862; Henry B. Stevens.

Company B, Crescent Rifles Company D (Orleans). Andrew F. Haynes, died of wounds May 20, 1862; William C. C. Claiborne, Jr.

Company C, Louisiana Guards Company D (Orleans). George H. Graham, killed April 6, 1862; Josiah T. Watts; Thomas W. Dressar, captured October 27, 1862, and did not return; Charles Hardenburg.

Company D, Beauregard Rangers (Orleans). Jules Vienne, resigned May 19, 1862; Richard S. Venables.

Company E, Twiggs Guards (Orleans). M. A. Tarleton, resigned July 29, 1862; T. Lytt Lyons, transferred; Eugene H. Holmes, captured April 20, 1863, and never returned to the regiment.

Company F, Crescent City Guards Company C (Orleans). William S. Austin; Raney Greene, Jr.

Company G, Marion Rangers (Ruggles Guards) (Orleans). George H. Helme, resigned June 19, 1862; George H. Braughan.

Company H (1st), Washington Guards (Orleans). Abel W. Bosworth, promoted major.

Company H (3rd), Crescent Blues Company A (Orleans). John Knight, wounded April 6, 1862, dropped April 23, 1862; Seth R. Field.

Company I (1st) (2nd Company H), Orleans Cadets Company B (Orleans), disbanded April, 1862. Sylvester F. Parmalee, resigned May 3, 1862.

Company I (2nd), Davidson Guards (Orleans). James D. Hill.

Company K, Sumter Rifles (Orleans). Charles C. Campbell, killed April 6, 1862; Myford McDougall, promoted major October 27, 1862; David Collie, Jr.

Company L, Alexandria Rifles (Rapides), men transferred to 16th Louisiana Regiment July, 1862. John P. Davidson, resigned June 15, 1862; Andrew D. Lewis, resigned July 4, 1862.

This state militia regiment transferred to Confederate service in New Orleans on March 6, 1862, for ninety days with 945 men. The regiment went immediately to Corinth, Mississippi, to reinforce General Pierre G. T. Beauregard's army. On April 6, the regiment played an important role in the capture of two Federal divisions at the Hornet's Nest during the Battle of Shiloh. The next day, the men supported the 5th Company, Washington Artillery, and prevented the enemy from capturing three of the battery's guns. In the battle,

23 of the regiment's men were killed, 84 were wounded, and 20 were missing. Retreating with the army to Corinth, the regiment was disbanded on June 3 by General Braxton Bragg at the expiration of its enlistment. Most of the men went into the 18th Louisiana Regiment. On September 17, the War Department reorganized the regiment and ordered it to report to General Richard Taylor in south Louisiana. The reorganization occurred at New Iberia on October 16, when Colonel McPheeters reclaimed the men serving with the 18th Louisiana. On October 27, the regiment fought in the Battle of Labadieville and retreated with the army to the lower Bayou Teche. After spending several weeks at Bisland, the men moved to Avery Island on December 19. The regiment went to Butte a la Rose on January 11, 1863. On February 16, Companies F, G, and H, while on picket on the Grand River, fired on and drove off the enemy steamer *Grey Cloud*. The regiment returned to Bisland on April 7 and fought in the battle there on April 12 and 13. Retreating with Taylor's army through Opelousas and Alexandria to Natchitoches, the regiment returned to south Louisiana in June. The men garrisoned Brashear City in June and July while the army conducted operations on Bayou Lafourche. During the next three months, the regiment marched with General Alfred Mouton's brigade back and forth across south Louisiana. On November 3, the 11th and 12th Louisiana Infantry battalions were added to the regiment at Simmesport to form the Consolidated Crescent Regiment.

BIBLIOGRAPHY
"John Dimitry." *Confederate Veteran*, XI (1903), 72–73.
"Memorial to Louisianians at Shiloh." *Confederate Veteran*, XXII (1914), 342–43.

25th Regiment

COLONELS. Stuart W. Fisk, killed December 31, 1862; J. C. Lewis, killed August 31, 1864; Frank C. Zacharie.

LIEUTENANT COLONELS. J. C. Lewis, promoted colonel December 31, 1862; Frank C. Zacharie, promoted colonel August 31, 1864; Calvin H. Moore.

MAJORS. Frank C. Zacharie, promoted lieutenant colonel December 31, 1862; Calvin H. Moore, promoted lieutenant colonel August 31, 1864.

COMPANIES AND THEIR COMMANDERS

Company A, Caddo Guards (Caddo). William Robson, dropped June 27, 1864; Charles W. Lewis.

Company B (Franklin). Calvin H. Moore, promoted major December 31, 1862; Clement H. Watson.

Company C (Concordia). Samuel C. Scott, died October 15, 1862; John M. Clayton.

Company D, Morehouse Avengers (Morehouse). Benjamin K. Fluker, died May 12, 1862.

Company E (Union). James M. Lupo, retired August 14, 1864.

Company F (Concordia). W. T. Miller, resigned January 8, 1864; George L. Walton.

Company G (Claiborne). Seaborne Aycock, killed August 31, 1864; W. J. Lesley.

Company H, Caddo Pioneers (Caddo). William F. Mellen, retired August 22, 1864.

Company I (Catahoula). Hugh Keenan, died October 9, 1863.

Company K (Carroll). Thomas C. Scarborough, resigned November 1, 1862; W. R. C. Lyons.

This regiment was organized March 26, 1862, at New Orleans with 1,018 men. Ordered to Corinth, Mississippi, the regiment traveled by steamer to Memphis and from there by train to its destination. The men arrived at Corinth on April 11 and later marched to Monterey, Tennessee. During the operations around Corinth the next month, the regiment participated in several skirmishes. On May 9, the men saw their first battle at Farmington, at which 2 men were killed and 29 were wounded. The regiment's brigade commander wrote that the men "behaved like veterans" during the engagement. When Corinth was evacuated, the regiment marched to Tupelo and remained in camp there until August. The men then went with the army on its invasion of Kentucky and fought in the Battle of Perryville, October 8. On November 30, the regiment was consolidated into five companies and united with the 16th Louisiana Regiment to form the 16th and 25th Louisiana Consolidated Regiment. This unit was broken up on February 3, 1865, and the men of the 25th Louisiana were merged with those of the 4th Louisiana Battalion. They fought in the Siege of Spanish Fort near Mobile, Alabama, March 27–April 8. After the evacuation of Mobile, the 25th was consolidated again. Companies A, B, E, G, I, and K became Company B; and Companies C, D, F, and H became Company C, Pelican Regiment. This unit surrendered at Gainesville on May 8.

BIBLIOGRAPHY

Duff, William Hiram. *Terrors and Horrors of Prison Life.* [Lake Charles, La., 1907(?)].

———. *The Truth: A Piano in Confederate Trenches.* [Monroe, La., 1913(?)].

Harris, D. W., and B. W. Hulse. *The History of Claiborne Parish, Louisiana.* New Orleans, 1886.

"Inquiry for and about Veterans." *Confederate Veteran,* XVI (1908), 347–48.

26th Regiment

COLONELS. Alexander DeClouet, resigned November 10, 1862; Duncan S. Cage, resigned December 30, 1862; Winchester Hall.

LIEUTENANT COLONELS. Duncan S. Cage, promoted colonel November 10, 1862; Winchester Hall, promoted colonel December 30, 1862; William C. Crow, resigned(?) March 4, 1865.

MAJORS. Winchester Hall, promoted lieutenant colonel November 10, 1862; William C. Crow, promoted lieutenant colonel December 30, 1862; W. Whitmel Martin, killed June 22, 1863; Cleophas Lagarde, promoted lieutenant colonel March 4, 1865; Manda W. Bateman.

COMPANIES AND THEIR COMMANDERS

Company A, Lafayette Prairie Boys (Lafayette). Eraste Mouton.

Company B, Lovell Rifles (St. Mary). Manda W. Bateman, promoted major March 4, 1865; Jared Y. Sanders II.

Company C, Assumption Creoles (Assumption). W. Whitmel Martin, promoted major December 30, 1862; Lovincy Himel.

Company D, Bragg Cadets (Lafourche). Cleophas Lagarde, promoted major June 22, 1863; Lewis Guion.

Company E, Grivot Fancy Guards (Lafayette). William C. Crow, promoted major November 10, 1862.

Company F, Grivot Guards Company C (Terrebonne). John J. Shaffer.

Company G, Prudhomme Guards (Natchitoches). Octave Metoyer.

Company H, Grivot Guards Company B (Terrebonne). William A. Bisland.

Company I, Allen Rifles (Lafourche). Caleb J. Tucker, killed December 28, 1862; Lovincey A. Webre.

Company K, Pickett Guards (Terrebonne). C. O. Delahoussaye, resigned October, 1862; Felix G. Winder, killed May 19, 1863; Richard C. West.

This regiment was organized at Camp Lovell, Berwick City, on April 3, 1862, with eight companies and 805 men. Several weeks later, the regiment went to New Orleans, where two additional companies joined it. At the evacuation of the Crescent City, the regiment went by railroad to Camp Moore. The men moved to Jackson, Mississippi, on May 6 and spent the next two weeks there and at Edwards' Depot. On May 19, they went to Vicksburg and performed picket duty during the opening stages of the first Federal attack on the city. The regiment returned to Edwards' Depot on June 18 and remained there through the summer. In September, the regiment once again went into camp at Vicksburg. The men participated in the defense of Chickasaw Bluffs, December 25–29. They captured more than 300 enemy soldiers in an attack on the enemy's flank on December 29. In the last week of March, 1863, the regiment traveled to Deer Creek in northeast Mississippi and was entrenched there in anticipation of an enemy attack. During the Siege of Vicksburg, May 19–July 4, the regiment served in the trenches on the left flank of the Confederate lines. The men went home on parole after the surrender of the garrison. Some men began gathering in a parole camp at Pineville in June, 1864. After being declared exchanged in August, more men reported to the camp during the closing months of the year. Many men did not report for duty after being exchanged but remained at their homes. As part of General Allen Thomas' brigade, the regiment did picket and guard duty at Fort Buhlow and Fort Randolph near Pineville. The men continued this duty until late April, 1865. At that time, the brigade moved to a camp on Bayou Cotile. The men spent a few days there and marched to Camp Salubrity near Natchitoches. On May 19, the brigade was dismissed to go home in anticipation of the surrender of the Trans-Mississippi Department. During the war, 38 men of the regiment were killed or mortally wounded and 69 died of disease.

BIBLIOGRAPHY

"Capt. John J. Shaffer." *Confederate Veteran*, XXVII (1919), 146.

Hall, Winchester. *The Story of the 26th Louisiana Infantry.* N.p., 1890(?).

Sanders, Mary Elizabeth, ed. "Diary in Gray: Civil War Letters and Diary of Jared Young Sanders II." *Louisiana Genealogical Register*, XVI (1969), 300–308; XVII (1970), 15–22, 114–20, 214–21, 358–65; XVIII (1971), 78–81, 141–47, 290–98, 378–86; XIX (1972), 92–96, 126.

27th Regiment

COLONELS. Leon D. Marks, mortally wounded June 28, 1863; Alexander S. Norwood.

LIEUTENANT COLONEL. L. L. McLaurin, mortally wounded June 21, 1863.

MAJORS. George Tucker, resigned October 29, 1862; Alexander S. Norwood, promoted colonel June 28, 1863; Jesse M. Cooper.

COMPANIES AND THEIR COMMANDERS

Company A, Skipwith Guards (East Feliciana), became Company A, Gober's Regiment Mounted Infantry. Alexander S. Norwood, promoted major October 29, 1862; L. P. Talbert, died March 14, 1863; Joseph A. Norwood.

Company B, Boeuf River Rebels (Franklin). W. S. McIntosh, resigned August 22, 1864.

Company C, Rapides Terribles (Rapides). Joseph T. Hatch, resigned November 15, 1864.

Company D, Iberville Guards (Iberville). Edward W. Robertson.

Company E, Sparta Guards (Bienville). Robert W. Campbell.

Company F, Winn Rebels (Winn). Jesse M. Cooper, promoted major June 28, 1863; William B. Stovall.

Company G, Dixie Rebels (DeSoto). O. L. Durham, resigned May 15, 1862; Claiborne J. Foster.

Company H, Spencer Guards (St. Helena[?]), became Company D,

Gober's Regiment Mounted Infantry. John T. Spencer; Thaddeus
C. S. Robertson.
Company I, Caddo Confederates (Caddo). T. C. Lewis.
Company K, McLaurin Invincibles (Natchitoches). J. H. Garrett.

This regiment was organized at Camp Moore in April, 1862, with
973 men. The regiment left for Vicksburg, Mississippi, on May 1 and
arrived on May 4. During the first Federal campaign against Vicksburg, May 18–July 27, the men did picket duty north and south
of the city. The regiment did guard and picket duty in Vicksburg
from the fall of 1862 through the early spring of 1863. On May 18,
1863, the men skirmished with the enemy as General Ulysses S.
Grant's army surrounded Vicksburg. The regiment held part of the
line of entrenchments during the siege of the city, May 19–July 4.
The men repulsed an attack on May 19 and were said to have captured the first enemy flag and prisoners taken during the siege. In
the course of the siege, 58 men of the regiment were killed and 96
were wounded. Following the surrender and their parole, the men
went into camp for a time at Enterprise. Most of the men then went
home on furlough. Perhaps a majority of the men remained at home
even after the government declared them exchanged in the fall of
1863. In the summer of 1864, six companies, reduced in strength, reorganized at Alexandria. Companies A and H reorganized at Clinton, Louisiana, and became part of Gober's Regiment Mounted Infantry. One source states that Company D never reorganized, but
some records show at least part of it at Clinton in June, 1864. The
regiment occupied a camp at Pineville until the end of the war. Occasionally, detachments would help garrison Fort Buhlow and Fort
Randolph near the town. Many of the men began dispersing to their
homes in late April, 1865. The remnants of the regiment marched to
Mansfield and disbanded there about May 19.

BIBLIOGRAPHY
"Civil War Records of the Walker Family." In *The Walker Family of
Mississippi, Louisiana and Texas,* compiled by Dorothy Lyons
Sutphin. N.p., 1970, pp. 99–105.
[Harewell, J. D.]. "Why Did He Eat Mule Meat." *Confederate Vet-
eran,* XXIX (1921), 357.
In Memoriam Claiborne Jasper Foster, 1834–1898. Chicago, n.d.
McGinty, Garnie W., ed. "The Human Side of War: Letters Between

a Bienville Parish Civil War Soldier and His Wife." *North Louisiana Historical Association Journal*, XIII (1982), 59–81.

[Perry, Lynch]. "Vicksburg, Some New History in the Experience of Gen. Francis A. Shoup." *Confederate Veteran*, II (1894), 172–74.

Sanders, Mary Elizabeth, ed. "Letters of a Confederate Soldier, 1862–1863." *Louisiana Historical Quarterly*, XXIX (1946), 1129–40.

Winters, John D., ed. "Letter from a North Louisiana Soldier: The First Vicksburg Campaign, 1862." *North Louisiana Historical Association Journal*, VI (1975), 98–104.

28th Regiment

COLONELS. Henry Gray, promoted brigadier general April 15, 1864; Thomas W. Pool.

LIEUTENANT COLONELS. William Walker, killed April 8, 1864; Isaac W. Melton.

MAJOR. Thomas W. Pool, promoted colonel April 15, 1864.

COMPANIES AND THEIR COMMANDERS

Company A, Bienville Stars (Bienville). Isaac W. Melton, promoted lieutenant colonel April 15, 1864; Daniel H. Sheppard.

Company B, Marks Guards (Bossier). John W. Rabb, resigned September 26, 1862; Thomas W. Abney.

Company C (Jackson). William F. Clark, resigned May 31, 1864; Edwin C. Kidd, resigned January, 1865.

Company D, Claiborne Invincibles (Claiborne). Marcus O. Cheatham.

Company E (Winn). John T. Lewis.

Company F, Jackson Volunteers (Jackson). Robert H. Bradford.

Company G (Winn). David Hardy.

Company H (Bienville). James Brice.

Company I (Jackson). Rufus S. Richards, resigned May 23, 1864; Virgil M. Eiland.

Company K (Winn). Darling P. Morris, resigned October 24, 1863; Austin C. Banks, resigned December 7, 1863; Benjamin F. Fort.

This regiment was organized at Monroe in April or May, 1862, with 902 men. The regiment moved to Vienna and drilled there for several months before going into camp near Milliken's Bend. In November, the regiment received orders to report to General Richard Taylor in south Louisiana. The men were in camp at Avery Island for a short time and then moved to Fort Bisland near Centerville. On March 28, 1863, a detachment helped capture the Federal gunboat *Diana* in a skirmish on the Atchafalaya River. Company K went aboard the gunboat when it was refurbished for active service. The regiment fought in the Battle of Fort Bisland, April 12–13, and was instrumental in the Confederate victory in the Battle of Irish Bend, April 14. With Taylor's army, the regiment retreated to Natchitoches but returned to south Louisiana in June. During the summer and fall, Colonel Gray commanded General Alfred Mouton's brigade in its various marches back and forth across the southern part of the state. The brigade marched to Monroe in December and remained there until January, 1864. At that time, it marched to Pineville and went into camp. When the Federals began marching up the Red River in mid-March, the brigade crossed over to Alexandria and began retreating toward Natchitoches. The regiment distinguished itself in the Confederate attack at the Battle of Mansfield, April 8. During the Battle of Pleasant Hill, April 9, the brigade remained in reserve until late in the day and saw little fighting. The regiment participated in the Battle of Yellow Bayou, May 18, and again suffered numerous casualties. In August, the brigade marched to Monroe and from there went into southern Arkansas until late in the year. It then returned to Alexandria via Minden. The regiment camped on Bayou Cotile until May, 1865, when it marched to Mansfield. There the men disbanded on May 19, just prior to the surrender of the Trans-Mississippi Department.

BIBLIOGRAPHY

Harris, D. W., and B. W. Hulse. *The History of Claiborne Parish, Louisiana.* New Orleans, 1886.

Jones, Terry L. "The 28th Louisiana Volunteers in the Civil War." *North Louisiana Historical Association Journal,* IX (1978), 85–95.

Sliger, J. E. "How General Taylor Fought the Battle of Mansfield, La." *Confederate Veteran,* XXXI (1923), 456–58.

29th Regiment

COLONELS. Allen Thomas, promoted brigadier general February 4, 1864; J. O. Landry.

LIEUTENANT COLONELS. J. O. Landry, promoted colonel February 4, 1864; Charles M. Peques.

MAJOR. Charles M. Peques, promoted lieutenant colonel February 4, 1864.

COMPANIES AND THEIR COMMANDERS

Company A, Creole Rebels (St. Landry). E. P. Doremus.

Company B, Elam Guards (DeSoto). A. B. Harley.

Company C, Watts Guards(?). E. B. Sloan.

Company D, Carroll Rebels (Carroll). William F. Norman.

Company E, Ascension Guards (Ascension). D. Landry, absent without leave from January 4, 1863; J. M. Baldwin.

Company F. Gustave Bredon, Jr., promoted assistant quartermaster December 22, 1862; J. L. Wemple.

Company G. Francis Newman.

Company H (Assumption). Emile E. Lauve.

Company I, Calcasieu Tigers (Calcasieu). James W. Bryan.

Company K, Sons of St. Landry (St. Landry). Napoleon Robin, resigned November 30, 1862; M. L. Lyons.

This regiment was organized at Camp Moore on May 3, 1862, by the addition of five companies to a battalion formed by Thomas for state service. The regiment left for Vicksburg, Mississippi, on May 20, and arrived the next day. During the first Federal attack on Vicksburg, May 18–July 27, the regiment did picket and guard duty near Warrenton, south of the city. The men remained in the Vicksburg area through the summer and fall, drilling and doing picket duty. On December 27, the regiment moved to Chickasaw Bluffs north of Vicksburg to assist in the defense of that area. The regiment repulsed enemy attacks on December 28 and 29; 9 men were killed, 25 were wounded, and 9 were missing. Again the regiment went through a period of inactivity, until the beginning of the Siege of Vicksburg, May 19, 1863. The regiment originally occupied trenches on the Confederate left flank near Fort Hill. On May 22, the regiment moved to the support of General John H. Forney's division during one of the major Union assaults. After this attack, the men returned to their old position. During the siege, 16 men of the regiment were killed and 57 were wounded. Paroled after the surrender on July 4, the remaining men marched to a camp at Enterprise. The men went home on furlough after several months in this camp. In the summer of 1864, the regiment was ordered into camp near Alexandria and returned to active duty. Many of the men chose not to return to duty and remained at their homes. The regiment remained in the Alexandria-Pineville area until May, 1865. At that time, it marched to Mansfield, where the men disbanded on May 19.

30th Regiment
(Sumter Regiment)

COLONEL. Gustavus A. Breaux, dropped February, 1863.
LIEUTENANT COLONEL. Thomas Shields.
MAJOR. Charles J. Bell.

COMPANIES AND THEIR COMMANDERS

Company A, Algiers Guards (Orleans). Norbert Trepagnier.
Company B (Orleans), organized by addition of remnants of Henry Clay Guards, St. James Guards, and Sumter Greys Companies A and B to Lewis Guards. Henry P. Jones.
Company C (1st), Henry Clay Guards (Orleans), most of company captured at New Orleans April 25, 1862. Charles E. Morrison, promoted assistant quartermaster May 16, 1862.
Company C (2nd), American Rifles (Orleans). Roger T. Boyle.
Company D, Valcour Aime Guards (Orleans), added at Camp Moore. Arthur Picolet.
Company E, Pickett Cadets (Orleans), added at Camp Moore. Charles W. Cushman.
Company F, Orleans Guards (Orleans), remnants of Orleans Guards Battalion, added at Camp Moore. Louis Fortin.
Company G, Stephens Guards (St. John the Baptist). Lezin P. Becnel.
Company H, Richard Musketeers (Lafourche), added at Camp Moore, disbanded March 4, 1863. C. De La Bretonne.
Company I, Dardennes Guards (Iberville), disbanded March 4, 1863. Aubrey Bevin.

Company K, Tirailleurs of St. James (St. James), furloughed May 15, 1862, and never returned. J. Adam Gaudet.

This regiment was organized at Camp Moore on May 15, 1862, with 804 men. The unit had originally been mustered into state service in New Orleans on December 17, 1861, as the Sumter Regiment and was transferred to Confederate service for ninety days on March 1, 1862. Upon the evacuation of New Orleans, April 25, three and a half companies remained in the city and were captured. The other six and a half companies went to Camp Moore. There General Mansfield Lovell added four new companies to bring the unit back to regimental strength. Company K went home on furlough and never returned, since the enemy controlled that portion of the state. The regiment remained at Camp Moore until August 5, when it participated in the Battle of Baton Rouge. In that battle, 58 men of the regiment were killed, wounded, or missing. The remaining men marched to Port Hudson after the battle and became part of the garrison there. They did outpost and picket duty and helped construct the entrenchments in the area. In February, 1863, the War Department ordered the reduction of the regiment to a battalion of seven companies. On March 4, Companies H and I were disbanded and the men were distributed among the other companies. The new 30th Louisiana Battalion retained the regiment's number, and records frequently call it the 30th Louisiana Regiment.

31st Regiment

COLONEL. Charles H. Morrison.
LIEUTENANT COLONELS. Sidney H. Griffin, killed June 27, 1863; James W. Draughan.
MAJORS. Thomas C. Humble, died January 7, 1863; James W. Draughan, promoted lieutenant colonel June 27, 1863; Robert D. Bridger.

COMPANIES AND THEIR COMMANDERS

Company A, Confederate Defenders (Carroll). James W. Draughan, promoted major January 7, 1863; Edward J. Delony.
Company B, Caldwell Avengers (Caldwell). Robert D. Bridger, promoted major June 27, 1863; James Duke.

Company C. David Bryant, killed December 29, 1862; Warren M. Scott.

Company D, Catahoula Fencibles (Catahoula). John Ker.

Company E, Gladden Avengers (Claiborne). Shelby Baucum.

Company F, Catahoula Avengers (Catahoula). S. F. Routh, died November 30, 1862; John Y. Snyder.

Company G. Charles W. Hodge, resigned October 10, 1864; Savoy O. Larche.

Company H, Confederate Warriors. William W. Farmer.

Company I, Sparrow Cadets (Union). John A. White, resigned November, 1864; Charles H. Griffin.

Company K. Flavius J. Hundley.

This regiment was organized June 11, 1862, at Monroe from Morrison's Battalion, which had been formed May 14. The men remained at Monroe drilling until June, when they moved to a camp in Madison Parish about eight miles from Vicksburg, Mississippi. Then they moved to Tallulah and New Carthage. In August, the regiment went to Milliken's Bend to unload a shipment of arms intended for General Albert Pike's Indian brigade. On August 18, an enemy gunboat steamed up and captured the transport *Fair Play* with all of the weapons still on it. The regiment retreated to Tallaluh, pursued by a small force landed from the gunboat. During the next few months, the men camped at Tallulah, Delhi, and Trenton. In November, the regiment received orders to go to Jackson, Mississippi. There the Catahoula Battalion was added to the regiment to give it ten companies. The men fought in the Battle of Chickasaw Bayou, December 26–29, and helped repulse several enemy attacks. During the winter and early spring of 1863, the regiment remained at Vicksburg, drilling and doing picket duty. The men participated in the closing stages of the Battle of Port Gibson, May 1, and covered the retreat of the Confederate forces. They picketed the crossings of the Big Black River until the Confederate army retreated past the river into the Vicksburg defenses. The regiment fought in the trenches during the Siege of Vicksburg, May 19–July 4, and went home on parole after the surrender. Many of the men decided they had seen enough fighting and remained at their homes until the war ended. In January, 1864, some of the men went into a parole camp at Vienna but returned home on furlough after a few weeks. After the men were declared officially exchanged, they went into camp at Minden in June. They spent two weeks there, moved to Shreveport, and soon went to Pineville. The regiment formed part of General Allen Thomas' brigade and acted as a support for Fort Buhlow and Fort Randolph near Pineville until February, 1865. At that time, it moved to Bayou Cotile, remaining there until May. The men marched to Mansfield and were disbanded just prior to the surrender of the Trans-Mississippi Department.

BIBLIOGRAPHY

Cawthon, John A., ed. "Letters of a North Louisiana Private to His Wife, 1862–1865." *Mississippi Valley Historical Review*, XXX (1943–44), 533–50.

Harris, D. W., and B. M. Hulse. *The History of Claiborne Parish, Louisiana*. New Orleans, 1886.

Vandiver, Frank E., ed. "A Collection of Louisiana Confederate Letters." *Louisiana Historical Quarterly*, XXVI (1943), 937–74.

32nd Regiment
(Miles' Legion)

COLONEL. William R. Miles
LIEUTENANT COLONEL. Frederick B. Brand.
MAJOR. James T. Coleman.

COMPANIES AND THEIR COMMANDERS

Company A, Butler Avengers (Orleans). J. G. Mackey, resigned April 6, 1864; Lewis E. Woods.

Company B, St. Tammany Guards (St. Tammany). P. F. Mancosas, resigned December 4, 1862; William B. Cook.

Company C (St. Tammany). J. B. Turner, killed May 21, 1863; George J. Wilson.

Company D, Taylor Guards (St. Landry). Tacitus G. Calvit, resigned December 19, 1862; William Dejean.

Company E (St. Tammany). Charles W. Gallagher.

Company F, Denis Rifles (Orleans). Robert C. Weatherly.

Company G, Alfred Davis Guards (Mississippi). Edward Lynn, resigned August 28, 1862; James M. Searles, resigned February 16, 1863; James O'Neill.

Company H, Voorhies Guards (Orleans). William W. Carloss.

The formal organization of the legion occurred at Camp Moore on May 16 or 17, 1862, but the infantry companies had all been in service for several months. The unit always used the name Miles' Legion; it never went by the designation 32nd Regiment. On June 1, the legion left for Grand Gulf, Mississippi. A portion of it fought in a skirmish near there on June 24. The legion received orders in late August to report for duty at Port Hudson. There the men did picket and guard duty and assisted in the construction of earthwork defenses. A small group of volunteers from the legion sailed on the cottonclad *Dr. Beatty* and on February 24 participated in the capture of the Federal ironclad *Indianola* near New Carthage on the Mississippi River. From April 29 to May 3, the legion took part in the unsuccessful efforts to stop Colonel Benjamin Grierson's Federal cavalry raiders from reaching Baton Rouge. The legion played an important role in the Battle of Plains Store, May 21. In this battle, the first significant engagement for the unit, 89 of its men were killed, wounded, or missing. During the Siege of Port Hudson, May 23–July 9, the legion held most of the trenches on the Confederate right wing and repulsed all attacks thrown against it. Around 150 men of the unit deserted and went into Union lines as the siege dragged on. At the end of the siege, the enlisted men went home on parole and the officers went into Federal prisons. In early 1864, the men on the east side of the Mississippi River were reorganized, mounted, and assigned to Gober's Regiment Mounted Infantry. Large numbers of the men west of the Mississippi River, particularly those who had been conscripted, remained at their homes rather than returning to service when declared exchanged in the fall of 1863. A small number of men gathered in camp at Alexandria in the summer of 1864 and, with some new recruits, were reorganized as the 15th Louisiana Battalion Sharpshooters.

BIBLIOGRAPHY
Bergeron, Arthur W., Jr., and Lawrence L. Hewitt. *Miles' Legion: A History and Roster*. Baton Rouge, 1983.

33rd Regiment

COLONEL. Franklin H. Clack.
LIEUTENANT COLONEL. Valsin A. Fournet.
MAJOR. Gabriel A. Fournet.

COMPANIES AND THEIR COMMANDERS (organization incomplete)

Company A (Company B, 12th Louisiana Battalion). Arthur W. Hyatt.

Company I (Company H, 10th Louisiana Battalion). Simeon Belden.

This regiment was organized near Donaldsonville about October 10, 1862, by the consolidating of the 10th and 12th Louisiana battalions. Most of the regiment remained near Donaldsonville performing picket duty along the Mississippi River below the town. A portion of the regiment occupied the post at Bayou Des Allemands. On October 25, the men near Donaldsonville fell back down Bayou Lafourche when a large enemy force landed south of the town. They participated in the Battle of Labadieville, October 27. Though the records are sketchy, it appears most of these men retreated from their position without putting up a fight. The regiment was reunited several days later at Brashear City and retreated with the army to Bisland on Bayou Teche. On November 22, General Richard Taylor broke up the regiment and restored the battalion organizations, largely because of the discontent created by the consolidation.

Consolidated Crescent Regiment

COLONELS. James H. Beard, killed April 8, 1864; Abel W. Bosworth.

LIEUTENANT COLONELS. Franklin H. Clack, mortally wounded April 8, 1864; Arthur W. Hyatt.

MAJORS. Mercer Canfield, killed April 8, 1864; Hugh N. Montgomery, transferred October 17, 1864; James J. Yarborough.

COMPANIES AND THEIR COMMANDERS

Company A. Seth R. Field, killed April 8, 1864; J. M. Bonner.

Company B. William B. Spencer, captured April 1, 1864; Abram H. Thigpen.

Company C. William C. C. Claiborne, Jr.

Company D. Charles D. Moore, killed April 8, 1864; W. J. Self.

Company E. Hugh N. Montgomery, promoted major April 8, 1864; Edward F. Moore.

Company F. William M. Fuller, killed April 8, 1864; H. E. H. Buck.

Company G. Charles Hardenburg.
Company H, St. Martin Rangers (St. Martin). Edward T. King.
Company I. William J. Calvit.
Company K. John Houston, resigned(?); Joseph B. Johnson.
Company L. Henry B. Stevens, transferred to Company O; J. M. Fair.
Company N. David Collie, Jr.
Company O. George W. Tyson, resigned(?); Henry B. Stevens.
Company P. L. D. DeBlanc.

This regiment was formed at Simmesport on November 2, 1863, by the addition of the 11th and 12th Louisiana battalions to the Crescent (24th) Regiment. With General Alfred Mouton's brigade, the regiment marched from Simmesport to Monroe to support troops crossing weapons over the Mississippi River from the east. The brigade left Monroe on January 30, 1864, and arrived at Pineville on February 10. When General Nathaniel P. Banks's Union army began its Red River Campaign in mid-March, the brigade crossed to the south side of the river and retreated through Natchitoches toward Shreveport. The regiment played a major role in the Battle of Mansfield, April 8. In the attack on the enemy, more than 175 of the regiment's men were killed or wounded; and the regiment became the only Louisiana regiment to lose all 3 field officers in one battle. The next day, April 9, at the Battle of Pleasant Hill, the regiment saw only limited fighting since its division constituted the army's reserve force. Pursuing Banks's army back down the Red River, the regiment participated in the Battle of Yellow Bayou, May 18. Portions, if not all, of the regiment supported the 2nd Louisiana Battery in a skirmish with enemy gunboats on the Atchafalaya River north of Simmesport on June 8. When the army marched through north Louisiana into southern Arkansas in the fall, the regiment remained at Alexandria and then marched to Shreveport. After several months in the garrison at Shreveport, the regiment returned to Alexandria. The brigade joined the regiment there in January, 1865, and occupied camps in the vicinity until spring. In May, the brigade marched to Mansfield; it disbanded there on May 19, prior to the surrender of the Trans-Mississippi Department.

1st Battalion

LIEUTENANT COLONELS. Charles D. Dreux, killed July 5, 1861; N. H. Rightor.

MAJORS. N. H. Rightor, promoted July 5, 1861; James H. Beard.

COMPANIES AND THEIR COMMANDERS

Company A, Louisiana Guards (Orleans). Samuel M. Todd, resigned(?); Charles E. Fenner.

Company B, Crescent Rifles Company A (Orleans). Stuart W. Fisk, resigned(?); Thaddeus A. Smith.

Company C, Louisiana Guards Company C (Orleans), transferred from 1st Louisiana Regiment July 16, 1861. Francis Rawle.

Company D, Shreveport Greys (Caddo), assigned to 1st Louisiana Regiment June 27, 1862. James H. Beard, promoted major July 15, 1861; B. L. Moore, resigned(?); William E. Moore.

Company E, Grivot Guards (Terrebonne). F. S. Goode, resigned January 11, 1862; J. B. Dunn.

Company F, Orleans Cadets (Orleans). William R. Collins.

The five original companies of this battalion went to Pensacola, Florida, in mid-April, 1861, as a part of the 1st Louisiana Regulars Infantry Regiment, which had not yet completed its organization. By late May, the remainder of the 1st Regulars' companies had finished recruiting and had reported for duty at Pensacola. The five original companies then received orders to go to Virginia and left on May 30. On June 11, at Richmond, the companies were organized as the 1st Louisiana Infantry Battalion. They soon moved to join the garrison at Yorktown. Colonel Dreux took 20 men from each company on July 5 to ambush some enemy soldiers near Newport News. In the brief skirmish that occurred, Dreux and 1 other man were killed. Dreux thus became the first Louisiana officer, and probably the first Confederate officer, killed in the war. The battalion continued to do picket duty on the Peninsula until April, 1862, when General George B. McClellan's Union army began operations against the Confederate defenses. On April 5, the men fought in a skirmish near the junction of the Warwick and Yorktown roads. Their term of enlistment expired during these operations, but the men agreed to remain in service until the operations ended. On May 1, just prior to the retreat of the army to Richmond, the battalion disbanded. Many of the men enlisted in a battery formed by Captain Fenner. The term of service of Company D had not expired, and it was assigned to the 1st Louisiana Regiment. In all, some 545 men served in the battalion. There were no battle deaths besides the 2 on July 5, 1861, but 16 men died of disease.

BIBLIOGRAPHY

[Allen, Columbus H.]. "About the Death of Col. C. D. Dreux." *Confederate Veteran*, XV (1907), 307.

Dreux-Rightor Louisiana Battalion, 1861–1911. [New Orleans(?), 1911].

"First Volunteers from Louisiana." *Confederate Veteran*, III (1895), 146.

Lamare, Just M. "Col. C. D. Dreux." *Confederate Veteran*, XXX (1922), 20–21.

Lowe, R. G., "The Dreux Battalion." *Confederate Veteran*, V (1897), 54–56.

Meynier, A. *Life and Military Services of Col. Charles D. Dreux*. New Orleans, 1883.

[Renaud, J. K.]. "The Orleans Cadets." *Confederate Veteran*, XXIX (1921), 207–208.

———. "The Romance of a Rich Young Man." *Confederate Veteran*, XXXI (1923), 256–58.

Warren, Charles. "Dreaux's Battalion." *Confederate Veteran*, XXIII (1915), 32.

1st Special Battalion

MAJOR. Chatham R. Wheat, killed June 27, 1862.

COMPANIES AND THEIR COMMANDERS

Company A, Walker Guards (Orleans). Robert A. Harris.

Company B, Tiger Rifles (Orleans). Alex White.

Company C, Delta Rangers (Orleans). Henry C. Gardner, resigned July 1, 1862; Thaddeus A. Ripley.

Company D (1st), Catahoula Guerrillas (Catahoula), transferred to 7th Louisiana Battalion October 1, 1861. Jonathan W. Buhoup.

Company D (2nd), Old Dominion Guards (Orleans), organized as Company E, became independent company mounted infantry September 1, 1862. Obed P. Miller.

Company E, Wheat's Life Guards (Orleans), added September 1, 1861. Robert G. Atkins.

The most famous Louisiana unit of the war, this battalion took the nickname "Louisiana Tigers" from its Company B. Its reputation led in time to the nickname being applied to all the Louisiana units in Virginia. Though generally represented as being completely out-fitted in Zouave uniforms, the battalion had only one such company—the Tiger Rifles. The battalion began organizing at Camp Walker in New Orleans. It moved to Camp Moore and completed its organization on June 6, 1861, with five companies and 416 men. Ordered to Virginia, the battalion became the first Louisiana unit to be engaged in the war, when it fought a skirmish at Seneca Falls on the Potomac River on June 28. The men played an important role in the Battle of First Manassas, July 21, by helping to hold back the Union flank attack until more troops could come up and form a defensive line. In the battle, 8 of the battalion's men were killed, 38 were wounded, and 2 were missing. The battalion was assigned to General Richard Taylor's Louisiana brigade along with the 6th, 7th, 8th, and 9th Louisiana regiments later in the month. That winter, the men drilled and did picket duty. They sometimes fought with other Confederate units and among themselves. One of the internal fracases led to the December 9 execution by firing squad of two men of Company B, the first men executed in the Army of Northern Virginia. Taylor's brigade joined General Stonewall Jackson's army in the Shenandoah Valley in May, 1862. The battalion played the major role in the capture of Front Royal, May 23. On May 25, the battalion was detached on the left flank of the army and saw no fighting in the Battle of Winchester. The brigade distinguished itself again in the Battle of Port Republic, June 9. Rejoining the Army of Northern Virginia near Richmond, the brigade participated in the Battle of Gaines' Mill, June 27. In that fight, Major Wheat and 5 other men were killed and 16 men were wounded. The battalion was so reduced in strength by the end of the Seven Days' Campaign, and the men were so hard to control following Wheat's death, that it was recommended that the battalion be disbanded. This occurred on August 15. During the war, 39 men of the battalion were killed, 15 died of disease, 2 were executed, and 1 died in an accident.

BIBLIOGRAPHY

Drane, J. W. "Louisiana Tigers at Fair Oaks, Va." *Confederate Veteran*, XIV (1906), 521.

Dufour, Charles L. *Gentle Tiger: The Gallant Life of Roberdeau Wheat*. Baton Rouge, 1957.

Laurence, Debra N. "Letters from a North Louisiana Tiger." *North Louisiana Historical Association Journal*, X (1979), 130–47.

Minnich, J. W. "Picturesque Soldiery." *Confederate Veteran*, XXXI (1923), 295–97.

Moore, Alison. *He Died Furious*. Baton Rouge, 1983.

———. *Old Bob Wheat—High Private*. Baton Rouge, 1957.

"Sketch of Major Chatham Roberdeau Wheat." *Southern Bivouac*, II (1883–84), 385–92.

Steffen, Randy, and Ronald E. Youngquist. "1st Special Battalion, Louisiana Infantry (Wheat's Tigers), 1861–1862." *Military Collector and Historian*, XI (1959), 10.

Steuart, Richard D. "Wheat's Tigers and Others." *Confederate Veteran*, XXXI (1923), 326.

Wheat, Leo. "Memoir of Gen. C. R. Wheat, Commander of the 'Louisiana Tiger Battalion.'" *Southern Historical Society Papers*, XVII (1889), 47–60.

1st State Battalion

MAJOR. William H. Terrell.

COMPANIES AND THEIR COMMANDERS

Company A, Winn Reserves (Winn). W. T. Hardee; F. M. Sharp.

Company B, Young Greys (DeSoto). John W. Stuart.

Company C, Jackson Volunteers (Jackson). J. R. Kavanaugh, resigned July 29, 1863; M. B. Kidd.

This battalion originated as independent companies in the Louisiana State Army. They went into Camp DeSoto near Pineville in April, 1863, and shortly thereafter received orders to report to Fort DeRussy. When that fort was evacuated, in early May, the companies fell back to Shreveport. There, on May 7, this battalion was formed with two companies. Company C was added on June 29. The battalion remained at Shreveport until September, when Companies

A and C returned to Camp DeSoto. Company B stayed at Shreveport for an unknown length of time. Apparently, the men did guard duty around Alexandria and drilled while at Camp DeSoto. On February 15, 1864, the battalion was transferred to the Louisiana State Guard. In March, the battalion was disbanded, and the companies were mounted and assigned to the 2nd Louisiana State Guards Cavalry Battalion.

1st Zouave Battalion

LIEUTENANT COLONELS. George A. G. Coppens, killed September 17, 1862; Marie A. Coppens, retired on account of wounds November 17, 1864.
MAJORS. Waldhemar Hyllested, captured August 29, 1862; Fulgence De Bordenave.

COMPANIES AND THEIR COMMANDERS

Company A (Orleans). Marie A. Coppens, resigned May 1, 1861; Leopold Lange.
Company B (Orleans). Fulgence De Bordenave, promoted major September 17, 1862; Joseph Demourelle.
Company C (Orleans). Howard H. Zacharie, resigned(?); Hortaire M. Andry.
Company D (Orleans). Nemoura Lauve; Charles P. J. Mansoni; Louis M. Ducros.
Company E (1st) (Orleans), detached as Orleans Heavy Artillery. Paul F. DeGournay.
Company E (2nd), 1st Company Foot Rifles (Orleans), added from 7th Louisiana Battalion August, 1862. Charles M. Rene, resigned August 12, 1862; John Peralta.
Company F (Orleans). Marie A. Coppens, promoted lieutenant colonel September 17, 1862; Jules Dupuy, suspended by court martial September or October, 1864.
Company G, Crescent Blues Company B (Orleans), added from 7th Louisiana Battalion May 31, 1862, transferred to 15th Louisiana Regiment August, 1862. McGavock Goodwyn.
Company H, Catahoula Guerrillas (Catahoula), added from 7th Louisiana Battalion May 31, 1862, transferred to 15th Louisiana Regiment August, 1862. Samuel W. Spencer.

This battalion was organized at Pensacola, Florida, on April 2, 1861, with six companies of 616 men. In June, the battalion proceeded to Virginia and received orders to join the garrison at Yorktown. Company E, originally recruited as an artillery unit, was assigned to help build the earthwork defenses. In August, this company was permanently removed from the battalion and made a heavy artillery company. The battalion moved to Williamsburg about the same time because of illnesses occurring at Yorktown. At Williamsburg, the battalion helped man Fort Magruder. The men accompanied the Peninsula Army when it retreated to Richmond in May, 1862. Companies B and C, 7th Louisiana Battalion, reported to Coppens in late May and served with the battalion through the Seven Days' Campaign. During this time, the combined unit was called the Regiment of Louisiana Zouaves and Chasseurs. On May 31, the battalion went into the Battle of Fair Oaks with 225 officers and men and lost nearly half that number. The battalion fought next in the Battle of Beaver Dam Creek, June 27, where 5 of its men were killed and 42 were wounded. At the end of July, the battalion was assigned to the 2nd Louisiana Brigade, along with the 1st, 2nd, 9th, 10th, and 15th Louisiana regiments. The brigade participated in the Battle of Second Manassas, August 28–30, and the Battle of Sharpsburg, September 17. On November 10, the battalion was reorganized. It was in reserve during the Battle of Fredericksburg, December 13. In January, 1863, the battalion was assigned to the Richmond defenses. After about a month there, the men were sent to the Blackwater River in southeast Virginia. There they did guard and picket duty and helped bring in conscripts and deserters. This duty continued until April, 1863, when the battalion joined General James Longstreet's corps in its operations near Suffolk. Once Longstreet returned to the Army of Northern Virginia, the men resumed their former duties. They remained in southeastern Virginia and northern North Carolina for the remainder of the battalion's existence. At various times, the battalion was stationed at Hicksford, Virginia, and Murfree's Depot, Franklin Depot, and Weldon, North Carolina. On January 29, 1864, the men fought in a skirmish near Windsor, North Carolina. They skirmished with the enemy near Suffolk in March. Part of the battalion participated in a fight near Fort Powhatan, Virginia. The last recorded activity of the battalion was a raid at Hicksford on December 9, in which 1 man was killed and 6 were wounded. During its war service, 52 of the battalion's men were killed, 26 died of disease, and 2 died by accident.

BIBLIOGRAPHY

[DeGournay, P. F.]. "D'Gournay's Battalion of Artillery." *Confederate Veteran*, XIII (1905), 30–33.

Minnich, J. W. "Picturesque Soldiery." *Confederate Veteran*, XXXI (1923), 295–97.

———. "With the Louisiana Zouaves." *Confederate Veteran*, XXXVI (1928), 425.

Wallace, Lee A., Jr. "Coppens' Louisiana Zouaves." *Civil War History*, VIII (1962), 269–82.

2nd Special Battalion

MAJOR. Felix Dumonteil.

COMPANIES AND THEIR COMMANDERS

Louisiana Rebels (Orleans). John M. Leggett.

Orleans Blues (Orleans). William B. Barnett.

St. James Guards (St. James). Adolph Strauss, resigned June 21, 1861; Emile Lacoul.

Orleans Rangers (Orleans). Edward Crevon.

Shepherd Guards (Orleans). Alfred Philips.

This battalion was organized on June 14, 1861, probably at Camp Moore. On July 22, the St. James Guards were detached, and six new companies were added to the remaining four to form the 10th Louisiana Regiment.

2nd Zouave Battalion

MAJOR. St. Leon Dupeire, resigned January 14, 1863.

COMPANIES AND THEIR COMMANDERS

Company A (Orleans). Oscar Dupeire, Jr., resigned December 29, 1862; J. R. Ducros.

Company B (Orleans). J. B. Fleitas.

Governor Thomas O. Moore apparently authorized the formation of this battalion in June, 1861, but it was not until March, 1862, that Company A was mustered into Confederate service in New Orleans. Company B was mustered in on April 22. The two companies numbered 165 men. At the evacuation of New Orleans, the companies went to Camp Moore. The battalion was probably formally organized there in early May. General Mansfield Lovell ordered the battalion to Vicksburg, Mississippi. The men probably did picket duty near the city during the first Federal campaign against it, from May 19 to July 27. On July 5, the Secretary of War ordered the battalion to report to the 1st Louisiana Zouave Battalion in Virginia, probably intending to form a Zouave regiment. Major Dupeire protested the order, and the battalion was allowed to remain at Vicksburg. On October 3 and 4, the battalion fought in the Battle of Corinth; 2 of its men were killed and 14 were wounded. The battalion returned to Vicksburg following the battle. Later, the companies were attached to Waul's Texas Legion. The men served with the legion during the Siege of Vicksburg, May 19–July 4, 1863. At the surrender of Vicksburg, the men went home on parole. In late 1863, Major Dupeire attempted to collect some of the men and recruit new men to form a battalion of mounted troops in south Louisiana. He succeeded in forming two companies and went into camp at Bayou Portage. On November 23, Federal troops surprised and overran the camp, capturing the battalion flag, 1 officer, and 25 enlisted men. General Richard Taylor broke up the battalion in January, 1864, because it had very few men left in it.

3rd Battalion

LIEUTENANT COLONELS. Charles M. Bradford, resigned June 5, 1862; Edmund Pendleton.

MAJORS. Edmund Pendleton, promoted lieutenant colonel June 5, 1862; Robert A. Wilkinson.

COMPANIES AND THEIR COMMANDERS

Company A, Askew Guards Company B (Orleans). Andrew Brady.
Company B (1st), Quitman Rangers (Orleans), transferred to 14th Louisiana Regiment November 27, 1861. Henry Gillum.

Company B (2nd), Empire Rangers (Orleans). Robert A. Wilkinson, promoted major June 5, 1862; Henry J. Egan.

Company C, Grosse Tete Creoles (Iberville). William Patrick, killed June 26, 1862; William Bowman.

Company D, St. Ceran Rifles (Orleans). Levi T. Jennings, disabled June 26, 1862.

Company E, Grivot Rifles (Orleans). J. S. West, appointed assistant quartermaster October 1, 1861.

Company F, St. James Rifles (Orleans). Adolphe Strauss, dropped 1861; Francis Divine, resigned November 23, 1861; William H. Murphy.

Company G, Davenport Rebels (Morehouse). William C. Michie.

Company H, Bogart Guards (Orleans). George J. Mahe, resigned October 17, 1861; Joseph F. Wetherup.

This battalion was originally organized as the 2nd Regiment, Polish Brigade, at Camp Pulaski near Amite on June 16, 1861, with 678 men. When the eight companies arrived at Richmond, Virginia, in August, the War Department ordered them formed into a battalion; and this organization occurred on September 7. The battalion was ordered to Norfolk and spent the winter in camp there. On March 20, 1862, the battalion received orders to report to Goldsborough, North Carolina. There it became part of General James R. Anderson's brigade. In April, the brigade moved by railroad to Fredericksburg, Virginia, and remained there until May, when it joined the Army of Northern Virginia near Richmond. The battalion fought in the Battle of Beaver Dam Creek, June 26. At the Battle of Frayser's Farm, June 30, the battalion was present but not engaged. In August, two companies were added to the battalion to form the 15th Louisiana Regiment.

BIBLIOGRAPHY

Hicks, E. M. "Stories of Service in Virginia." *Confederate Veteran,* XX (1912), 561–62.

Mann, J. T. *Hanged as a Spy at Barrancas, Florida, During Civil War.* Pensacola, 1906.

[McChesney, Wallace H.]. "Capt. Charles W. McLellan." *Confederate Veteran,* VI (1898), 506–507.

4th Battalion

LIEUTENANT COLONEL. John McEnery, detached August 18, 1864, because of wounds.

MAJORS. George C. Waddill, resigned December, 1861; John McEnery, promoted lieutenant colonel May 20, 1862; Duncan Buie, detached after August, 1864; Samuel L. Bishop, temporarily.

COMPANIES AND THEIR COMMANDERS

Company A, Madison Infantry (Madison). W. J. Powell.

Company B, Ouachita Blues (Ouachita). John McEnery, promoted major March, 1862; Frank N. Marks, killed September 19, 1863; A. B. Hardy, dropped June 28, 1864.

Company C, Franklin Life Guard (Franklin). Duncan Buie, promoted major May 30, 1862; J. Laurence Ward.

Company D, Carroll Rebels (Carroll). Edward L. Coleman, killed September 19, 1863; L. E. Stowers.

Company E, Natchez Rebels (Mississippi). Alfred V. Davis, resigned November 14, 1861; T. Alex Bisland.

Company F, Ouachita Rebels (Ouachita). James H. Walker, resigned April 23, 1863; Thomas N. Conner.

This battalion was organized on July 10, 1861, in Richmond, Virginia, with five companies and 561 men. The battalion acted as President Jefferson Davis' bodyguard and as guards at Libby Prison until the fall. After being reorganized on September 19, the battalion moved to what is now West Virginia. There the men served in the Kanawha Valley and skirmished with the enemy at Cotton Hill, November 1–10. In December, the battalion returned to Richmond but remained there only a short time. The battalion received orders to travel by train and report for duty in South Carolina. It was assigned to occupy Skidway Island on the Georgia coast south of Savannah. On March 17, 1862, the battalion moved to the Isle of Hope; and on April 21, it moved to Camp Mercer near Savannah. About this time, Company F joined the battalion. On June 4, the battalion moved to Charleston, South Carolina, and was assigned to duty on James Island. The men fought in a skirmish on the island on June 10. They arrived on the field at the Battle of Secessionville, June 16, in time to repulse the second enemy attack. In the battle, 6 men of the battalion were killed and 22 were wounded. On July 7, the battalion returned to Savannah and did picket and guard duty there until December 14. The men moved to Wilmington, North Carolina, where they stayed until February, 1863. Returning to Savannah, the battalion was once again on the move in May. Early in that month, the men went to Jackson, Mississippi. They fought in the Battle of Jackson, May 14, and then served in General Joseph E. Johnston's army to protect the city during the Siege of Vicksburg. The battalion participated in the Siege of Jackson, July 9–16, and in August reported to the Army of Tennessee in northern Georgia. At the Battle of Chickamauga, September 19–20, the men saw heavy fighting on the first day. Every commissioned officer present, except 1 lieutenant, was killed or wounded; and more than 50 percent of the enlisted men became casualties. On November 12, the battalion was assigned to General Randall L. Gibson's Louisiana brigade and fought in the Battle of Missionary Ridge, November 25. The brigade spent the winter and early spring at Dalton, Georgia. During the Atlanta Campaign, the battalion participated in the battles of Resaca, May 13–16, and New Hope Church, May 25–28. At the Battle of Ezra Church, July 28, the battalion captured an enemy artillery flag. The men fought on August 31 in the Battle of Jonesboro. During the invasion of Tennessee, November–December, the battalion guarded a pontoon bridge over the Duck River and saw no fighting. In February, 1865, at Mobile, Alabama, the battalion was consolidated with the 25th Louisiana Regiment. The men participated in the Siege of Spanish Fort, March 27–April 8. Following the evacuation of Mobile, Companies A, B, and D of the battalion became Company F, and Companies C, E, and F became Company G of the Pelican Regiment. They surrendered as such at Gainesville on May 8, 1865.

BIBLIOGRAPHY

Lea, H. J. "The Fourth Louisiana Battalion at the Battle of Secessionville, S.C." *Confederate Veteran*, XXXI (1923), 14–16.

———. "In the Battle of New Hope Church." *Confederate Veteran*, XXXI (1923), 61–62.

———. "With the Fourth Louisiana Battalion." *Confederate Veteran*, XXVII (1919), 339–40.

"Service with the 4th Louisiana Battalion." *Confederate Veteran*, XIX (1911), 542–43.

5th Battalion

LIEUTENANT COLONEL. J. B. G. Kennedy.
MAJOR. John Newman.

COMPANIES AND THEIR COMMANDERS

Company A, Bonford Guards (Orleans). M. Stern.
Company B, Campbell Guards (Orleans). Henry N. Soria.
Company C, Huckins Guard (Noel Rangers) (Orleans). Alex. Dresel.
Company D, McClelland Guards (Orleans). Bernard Moses.
Company E, Kosicinski Guards (Whamm Rifle Guards) (Orleans).
   L. Cedrowski, resigned January 4, 1862; D. Vancourt.
Company F, Askew Greys (Orleans). S. Q. Willis.

These six companies had made up part of the Jackson Regiment, Louisiana Militia, which was organized June 29, 1861, in New Orleans. They reported at Columbus, Kentucky, in August, 1861. General Leonidas Polk ordered them organized as the 5th Louisiana Battalion. During the Battle of Belmont, November 7, the men supported the heavy artillery batteries at Columbus. On February 9, 1862, four new companies were added to the battalion to create the 21st Louisiana Regiment.

6th Battalion
(Lovell Battalion)

MAJOR. Augustus Reichard

COMPANIES AND THEIR COMMANDERS

Turner Guards (Orleans). L. C. Buncken.
Steuben Guards (Orleans). F. Burger.
Reichard Rifles (Orleans). F. Reitmeyer.
Louisiana Volunteers (Musketeers) (Orleans). Charles Assenheimer.

This battalion was organized at Camp Lewis, New Orleans, in September, 1861, with 315 men. On January 3, 1862, the battalion was merged into the 20th Louisiana Regiment.

7th Battalion
(St. Paul's Foot Rifles, Chasseurs-a-Pied, Washington Battalion)

MAJORS. Henry St. Paul, resigned; McGavock Goodwyn, acting.

COMPANIES AND THEIR COMMANDERS

Company A, 1st Company Foot Rifles (Orleans). Edgar Macom.
Company B, Catahoula Guerrillas (Catahoula). Jonathan W. Buhoup, died January, 1862; Samuel W. Spencer.
Company C, Crescent Blues Company B (Orleans). McGavock Goodwyn.

This battalion was formed at Manassas, Virginia, on October 1, 1861, by the combination of the 1st Company Foot Rifles and Crescent Blues Company B. The men were assigned to the Washington Artillery Battalion as sharpshooters. On November 1, the Catahoula Guerrillas joined the battalion from the 1st Louisiana Special Battalion, giving the unit a total strength of 246 men. The battalion moved to Yorktown in March, 1862, when the army evacuated Manassas. During the Battle of Williamsburg, May 5, the men occupied a redoubt near Fort Magruder and suffered only 2 casualties—1 man killed and 1 wounded. On May 31, the battalion was attached to the 1st Louisiana Zouave Battalion, and the new unit was called the Regiment of Louisiana Zouaves and Chasseurs. The men fought in the battles of Fair Oaks, May 31–June 1, and Beaver Dam Creek, June 27, during the Seven Days' Campaign. On June 24, Companies B and C had received orders to report to the 3rd Louisiana Battalion; but because of the marches and fighting during the campaign, they could not do so until August 1. On that day, those two companies joined the 3rd Louisiana Battalion, which then became the 15th Louisiana Regiment. Company A remained with the 1st Louisiana Zouaves Battalion, becoming its second Company E.

BIBLIOGRAPHY
Laurence, Debra Nance. "Letters from a North Louisiana Tiger." *North Louisiana Historical Association Journal,* X (1979), 130–47.

8th Battalion

LIEUTENANT COLONEL. William E. Pinkney.
MAJOR. Fred N. Ogden.

COMPANIES AND THEIR COMMANDERS

Company A, Linton Light Infantry (Orleans). Paulin Grandpre.
Company B, Tunica Volunteers (West Feliciana). Ruffin C. Barrow.
Company C, Hickory Guards (Cotton Plant Guards[?]) (Orleans).
John Cavanaugh.
Company D, Crescent Artillery (Orleans). Henry F. Wade, Jr.
Company E (Orleans). Toby Hart.
Company F (St. Landry). B. F. White, resigned July 1, 1862; Thomas N.
McCrory.

This battalion was organized in New Orleans in February, 1862, with
402 men. The battalion helped occupy the McGehee Lines opposite
Chalmette when Admiral David G. Farragut's Union fleet approached
New Orleans on April 25. The men fired all of their cartridges at the
enemy vessels and then retreated into the nearby swamps. Many of
them made their way via Bayou Lafourche to Donaldsonville and
then by boat to Port Hudson. From there, they went to Camp Moore.
On May 5, General Mansfield Lovell reorganized the remnants of
the battalion into three companies as the 8th Louisiana Heavy Artillery Battalion.

9th Battalion

LIEUTENANT COLONEL. Samuel Boyd, retired because of wounds
received August 5, 1862.
MAJORS. Thomas Bynum, resigned May 2, 1863; Bolling R. Chinn,
acting.

COMPANIES AND THEIR COMMANDERS

Company A, Campaigners (East Baton Rouge). Thomas Bynum,
promoted major September 13, 1862; William L. Burnett, died
August 7, 1863; T. Winthrop Brown.
Company B, Baton Rouge Invincibles (East Baton Rouge). Thomas J.
Buffington, appointed surgeon September 15, 1862; B. F. Burnett.

Company C, Lemmon Guards (East Baton Rouge). Bolling R. Chinn.
Company D, Caruthers Sharpshooters (Livingston). William D. L.
McRae, resigned November 5, 1862; Alfred Bradley.
Cavalry Company, Plains Store Rangers (East Baton Rouge). John W.
Jones, resigned October 30, 1862; Gilbert C. Mills.

Companies A, B, and C and Jones's cavalry company were mustered
into service as part of Stewart's Legion. They moved to Jackson, Mississippi, where General Mansfield Lovell ordered them to Camp
Moore. There the companies were organized as the 9th Louisiana
Battalion on May 15, 1862. In early July, Company D was added
to the battalion but remained on duty at Ponchatoula. The other
companies of the battalion fought in the Battle of Baton Rouge, August 5; 5 of their men were killed, 27 were wounded, and 17 were
missing. Men of the 6th Michigan Infantry captured the battalion's
flag during the fighting. After the battle, the men camped on the
Comite River. They occupied Baton Rouge when the enemy evacuated the town late in the month. Company D joined the battalion
around this time. When the Federals reoccupied the town in December, the battalion moved to Port Hudson. There the men did
guard and picket duty and assisted in the construction of earthworks. One source indicates the battalion was stationed at Clinton
for a brief period early in 1863. In early May, 1863, the battalion left
Port Hudson on its way to Jackson, Mississippi, but returned when
the Federals began moving against Port Hudson. The men fought in
the siege, May 23–July 9, and occupied part of the trenches on the
Confederate right flank. Many of the men deserted during the siege.
After the surrender, the men went home on parole. The cavalry company had remained outside the lines during the siege, and it became
part of a temporary cavalry battalion commanded by Captain John B.
Cage. In early 1864, the remnants of the battalion were consolidated
into one company, mounted, and attached to Gober's Louisiana
Regiment Mounted Infantry.

BIBLIOGRAPHY
Carpenter, Horace. "Plain Living at Johnson's Island." *Century Magazine,* XLI (1891), 705–18.

10th Battalion
(Yellow Jacket Battalion)

LIEUTENANT COLONELS. Valsin A. Fournet, resigned June 10, 1863; Gabriel A. Fournet.

MAJORS. Gabriel A. Fournet, promoted lieutenant colonel June 10, 1863; Arthur F. Simon.

COMPANIES AND THEIR COMMANDERS

Company A (St. Martin). Alexander Thibodeau, resigned(?); Valery Thibodeau.

Company B (St. Martin). Desire Beraud.

Company C (St. Martin). Louis DeBlanc, resigned(?); Nicholas Cormier.

Company D, Hussars of the Teche (St. Martin). Bernard D. Dauterive, resigned August 27, 1863.

Company E (St. Martin). Achille Berard.

Company F (St. Martin). Joseph Hebert.

Company G, St. Martin Rangers (St. Martin). A. S. Hayes.

Company H, Grivot Rangers (St. Martin). Simeon Belden, resigned(?); William Robert.

This battalion was organized at St. Martinville on April 7, 1862, with six companies. The battalion entered Camp Pratt near New Iberia on May 23 for drilling and instruction. From June 12 to July 8, the battalion conducted operations along the railroad between Brashear City and New Orleans, including a skirmish near Raceland on June 22. The battalion returned to Camp Pratt, where two more companies joined it. In mid-September, the battalion moved to a camp near Donaldsonville. Three companies participated in an engagement at Koch's Plantation on September 24. About October 10, the battalion was merged with the 12th Louisiana Battalion to form the 33rd Louisiana Regiment. This regiment was broken up on November 22 at Camp Bisland on Bayou Teche, and the battalion resumed its separate identity. The men remained in camp there through the winter and early spring. On April 12 and 13, 1863, the battalion participated in the Battle of Fort Bisland. During the army's retreat toward Opelousas, most of the men deserted to their homes. Lieutenant Colonel Fournet temporarily mounted the remnants of the battalion, and in late May the men skirmished with the enemy near Franklin. When the army returned to south Louisiana in June, the battalion went into Camp Pratt briefly and then conducted a campaign against Jayhawkers near Hineston. The men rejoined the army in late July or early August at Vermilionville and were dismounted. During September and October, the battalion marched around south Louisiana as part of General Alfred Mouton's infantry brigade. On November 14, at Simmesport, the battalion was reorganized into four companies and merged with the 18th Louisiana Regiment to form the 18th Louisiana Consolidated Regiment. Many of the men who had deserted the battalion reentered service in early 1864 by joining the 7th Louisiana Cavalry Regiment.

11th Battalion

LIEUTENANT COLONELS. Jacob D. Shelley, resigned August 3, 1863; James H. Beard.

MAJOR. James H. Beard, promoted lieutenant colonel August 3, 1863.

COMPANIES AND THEIR COMMANDERS

Company A (DeSoto). Augustus H. Jordan, resigned October 24, 1863; Marshal D. Flenniken.

Company B (Natchitoches). George W. Holloway, resigned(?) 1863; John Houston.

Company C (Natchitoches). Joseph A. Carrell, resigned March 19, 1863; William M. Fuller.

Company D (DeSoto). James J. Yarbrough.

Company E, Sabine Guards (Sabine). Sherod S. Holland.

Company F (Catahoula). William B. Spencer.

Company G (Natchitoches and Texas[?]). Charles D. Moore.

This battalion was organized at Monroe on May 14, 1862, with six companies and 580 men. The men remained in the Monroe area through the fall doing picket duty and drilling. In December, the battalion moved to Rosedale to protect the Bayou Grosse Tete region from enemy incursions from Baton Rouge. Early in 1863, the battalion fell back to the area of Simmesport and Fort DeRussy. The men retreated to Natchitoches in May, when Federal forces advanced against Alexandria. Company F participated in the defense of Fort Beauregard at Harrisonburg on May 10 and 11. The battalion accompanied General Richard Taylor's army into south Louisiana in June and participated in all of the marches of General Alfred Mouton's infantry brigade during the summer and fall. On November 3, the battalion was united with the Crescent (24th) Regiment and 12th Louisiana Battalion at Simmesport to form the Consolidated Crescent Regiment.

12th Battalion
(Confederate Guards Response Battalion)

LIEUTENANT COLONEL. Franklin H. Clack.
MAJORS. Franklin H. Clack, promoted lieutenant colonel September, 1862; Mercer Canfield.

COMPANIES AND THEIR COMMANDERS

Company A, Mounted Rangers (Rapides). Mercer Canfield, promoted major September, 1862; William J. Calvit.
Company B (formerly A), Confederate Guards Response Company B (Orleans). George P. Macmurdo, discharged overage July 25, 1862; Arthur W. Hyatt.
Company C (formerly B), Confederate Guards Response Company D (Orleans). Hugh N. Montgomery.
Company D, St. Martin Rangers (St. Martin). Edward T. King.
Company E (Rapides). John Kelso.
Company F (Lafourche). Louis Ranson.

This battalion, sometimes called the 16th Louisiana Battalion, was organized in New Orleans on March 6, 1862, with two companies and 201 men. The battalion went to Corinth, Mississippi. On April 6 and 7, the men fought in the Battle of Shiloh, suffering 46 casualties out of the 150 men who went into the fight. About May 1, the battalion was united with a Florida infantry battalion. The battalion participated in the Battle of Farmington, May 9, but had few casualties. In August, the battalion was ordered to western Louisiana, and its connection with the Florida unit ceased. The battalion reorganized at New Iberia. On September 20, Canfield's company joined the battalion. The men moved to a camp on Bayou Lafourche south of Donaldsonville in early October. About October 10, the battalion was merged with the 10th Louisiana Infantry Battalion to form the 33rd Louisiana Regiment. This regiment was broken up November 22, and the battalion was restored as a separate unit. The men occupied camps near New Iberia during the winter and early spring. They were at New Iberia during the Battle of Bisland, April 12–13, 1863. The battalion joined General Richard Taylor at Franklin on April 14 and fought in the Battle of Irish Bend. The men retreated with the army to Natchitoches. When Taylor led the army back into south Louisiana in June, the battalion remained at Alexandria as a provost guard. There King's and Kelso's companies joined the battalion. King's company acted independently as a heavy artillery battery and was rarely, if ever, with the rest of the battalion. On August 22, the battalion rejoined the army at Vermilionville. There Ranson's newly recruited company joined the battalion. On September 29, the battalion played a major role in the Battle of Stirling's Plantation on Bayou Fordoche. The battalion was merged with the Crescent (24th) Louisiana Regiment and 11th Louisiana Battalion on November 3 at Simmesport to form the Consolidated Crescent Regiment.

13th Battalion
(Orleans Guard Battalion)

MAJOR. Leon Queyrouze.

COMPANIES AND THEIR COMMANDERS

Company A (Orleans). Charles Roman.
Company B (Orleans). Eugene Staes.
Company C (Orleans). Auguste Roche.
Company D, DeClouet Guards (St. Mary). Charles A. Tertrou.

This battalion was mustered into Confederate service for ninety days in New Orleans on March 6, 1862, with 411 men. The battalion went to Corinth, Mississippi, to reinforce the army of General Pierre G. T. Beauregard. On April 6, the battalion participated in the attack at the Battle of Shiloh and lost heavily. At one point, other Confederate soldiers fired on the battalion, mistaking the men for Federals because of their blue uniforms. During the second day of fighting at Shiloh, April 7, the battalion attached itself to the 18th Louisiana Regiment. Total casualties for the battle amounted to 17 men killed,

55 wounded, and 18 missing. The battalion fell back to Corinth with the army and later retreated to Tupelo. On June 6, the battalion was disbanded. Captain Louis Fortin formed a company from the men of the battalion, and this company later joined the 30th Louisiana Regiment.

BIBLIOGRAPHY

[Markle, Edith Hall]. "My Uncle's War Story." *Confederate Veteran*, V (1897), 102–103.

14th Battalion Sharpshooters

MAJOR. John E. Austin.

COMPANIES AND THEIR COMMANDERS

Company A. Thomas W. Peyton, mortally wounded December 31, 1862; William Q. Lowd.
Company B. James Lingan.

This battalion was formed on August 21, 1862, with 200 picked men from the recently disbanded 11th Louisiana Regiment. The men were to serve as sharpshooters and skirmishers for General Daniel W. Adams' (later Randall L. Gibson's) Louisiana brigade in the Army of Tennessee. On October 8, the men participated in the Battle of Perryville, Kentucky, and received praise for their gallant conduct. The battalion fought in the Battle of Murfreesboro, covering the retreat of the brigade after an unsuccessful attack on December 31 and acting as the brigade reserve on January 2, 1863. Losses in the battle amounted to 4 men killed, 9 wounded, and 2 missing. In May, 1863, the brigade went to Jackson, Mississippi, to reinforce General Joseph E. Johnston's army. The men took part in the Siege of Jackson, July 5–25, and afterwards rejoined the Army of Tennessee in northern Georgia. At the Battle of Chickamauga, September 19–20, the men acted first as skirmishers and later as a reserve to protect the brigade's flank and rear. Company A captured two enemy cannons and 86 prisoners. The battalion fought in the Battle of Missionary Ridge, November 25, and retreated with the army to Dalton, Georgia. There the men spent the winter and spring. In the opening stages of the Atlanta Campaign, May, 1864, the battalion saw frequent skirmishing with the enemy. The men fought at Mill Creek

Gap, May 7, and at Resaca, May 15. Only 45 men went into an engagement near Pumpkin Vine Creek on May 25, and 15 of them fell dead or wounded. The battalion participated in the battles of Ezra Church, July 28, and Jonesboro, August 31, during the fighting around Atlanta. When the army invaded Tennessee, in November, the battalion had only 24 men present for duty. They fought in the Battle of Nashville, December 15–16. The army retreated to Tupelo, Mississippi; and in February, 1865, at Mobile, Alabama, the remnants of the battalion were consolidated with the 4th and 13th Louisiana regiments and 30th Louisiana Battalion. This consolidated command fought in the Siege of Spanish Fort, March 27–April 8. After the evacuation of Mobile, the men became Company H, Chalmette Regiment, and surrendered as such at Gainesville on May 8.

BIBLIOGRAPHY

[Chalaron, J. A.]. "Vivid Experiences at Chickamauga." *Confederate Veteran*, III (1895), 278–79.

15th Battalion Sharpshooters

MAJOR. Robert C. Weatherly.

COMPANIES AND THEIR COMMANDERS

Company A. James B. Martin.
Company B. William W. Carloss.
Company C. James Hill.
Company D. Commander unknown.
Company E. Commander unknown.

This battalion was organized about July, 1864, probably at Pineville, from men of Miles' Louisiana Legion on parole west of the Mississippi River and from new recruits. The battalion was assigned to General Allen Thomas' brigade at Pineville and did guard duty there during most of its service. Some of the men appear to have served as pickets along the upper Atchafalaya River early in 1865. Thomas' brigade moved across Red River to Bayou Cotile in April, 1865, and soon marched to Natchitoches. On May 19, the brigade was disbanded at Mansfield in anticipation of the surrender of the Trans-Mississippi Department.

30th Battalion

LIEUTENANT COLONEL. Thomas Shields, killed July 28, 1864.
MAJORS. Charles J. Bell, killed July 28, 1864; Arthur Picolet.

COMPANIES AND THEIR COMMANDERS

Company A, Algiers Guards (Orleans). Norbert Trepagnier, dropped September 8, 1863; Octave F. Vallette.
Company B (Orleans). Henry P. Jones, died November 26, 1864.
Company C, American Rifles (Orleans). Roger T. Boyle.
Company D, Valcour Aime Guards (Orleans). Arthur Picolet, promoted major July 28, 1864; Ed. N. Ganucheau.
Company E, Pickett Cadets (Orleans). Charles W. Cushman, killed December 16, 1864.
Company F, Orleans Guards (Orleans). Louis Fortin, killed August 14, 1864; A. J. Vienne, killed August 25, 1864; F. O. Trepagnier.
Company G, Stephens Guards (St. John the Baptist). Michael A. Becnel, dropped August 27, 1863; Lezin P. Becnel, died of wounds August 2, 1864.

This battalion was formed at Port Hudson on March 4, 1863, when two companies of the 30th Louisiana Infantry Regiment were disbanded and their men distributed among the remaining seven companies. Frequently, the records refer to the battalion as a regiment. The battalion occupied part of the entrenchments at Port Hudson until May 6, when it marched with General Samuel B. Maxey's brigade to Jackson, Mississippi. A small detachment of the battalion remained at Port Hudson and served there during the siege, May 23–July 9, on the right wing of the Confederate defenses. The battalion participated in the Siege of Jackson, July 6–17, and retreated with General Joseph E. Johnston's army to Morton. In August, the men received orders to report at Mobile, Alabama, and they served in the garrison there until November. At that time, the battalion went to Dalton, Georgia, to reinforce the Army of Tennessee, which had just retreated from Chattanooga. The battalion returned to Mobile after a couple of months and garrisoned Fort Gaines at the mouth of Mobile Bay. On May 21, 1864, the battalion received orders to report to the Army of Tennessee and joined it at New Hope Church. The men became part of General Randall L. Gibson's Louisiana brigade in

July. They fought at Atlanta, July 22, and at Ezra Church, July 28. In the latter battle, the enemy captured the battalion's flag, and nearly three-fourths of the men were killed or wounded. The battalion went with the army on its invasion of Tennessee, and most of the remaining men became prisoners at the Battle of Nashville, December 17. In February, 1865, the remnants of the battalion were consolidated with the 4th and 13th Louisiana regiments and the 14th Louisiana Battalion. The consolidated unit fought in the Siege of Spanish Fort near Mobile, Alabama, March 27–April 8. When it surrendered at Meridian, Mississippi, on May 8, 1865, only 59 officers and enlisted men of the battalion were still present for duty.

Catahoula Battalion

MAJORS. John Ker (acting); Rufus J. Bruce (acting temporarily), from 1st Louisiana Heavy Artillery Regiment.

COMPANIES AND THEIR COMMANDERS

Company A, Catahoula Fencibles (Catahoula). John Ker.
Company B, Catahoula Avengers (Catahoula). S. F. Routh.

This battalion was probably organized May 4, 1862, at Natchez or Vicksburg, Mississippi. The men may have remained at either point for a time during the first Federal campaign against Vicksburg, May 18–July 27. On July 16, General Earl Van Dorn ordered the battalion to Jackson, where Captain Ker assumed command of the post. The men appear to have performed guard and provost duty there during the remainder of their existence as a separate unit. They suffered from typhoid and intermittent fevers during the fall. In November, the battalion was merged with the 31st Louisiana Regiment.

Keary's Battalion

MAJOR. Patrick F. Keary.

COMPANIES AND THEIR COMMANDERS

Company (?). William A. Martin.
Company (?). Robert Lynne.

Company (?). John D. Workman.
Company D. George W. Stafford.

On February 6, 1863, the War Department authorized Keary to raise and organize a battalion of sharpshooters in western Louisiana for use with General Harry T. Hays's Louisiana brigade in the Army of Northern Virginia. Keary and four lieutenants, all from the latter army, reached Alexandria in March and began recruiting. The Federal invasion of the Red River area in May, 1863, temporarily interrupted their efforts. After the enemy retreated, the recruiting began again; and by June, Keary had organized three or four companies with 325 men. Late in June, the battalion moved to Hineston to hunt draft dodgers and Jayhawkers. On August 9, the battalion received orders to report to Shreveport. There the men apparently performed guard duty. In mid-November, the battalion was ordered to Alexandria to serve under General Richard Taylor. Taylor sent the battalion to picket the Black and Ouachita rivers. On December 18, the battalion was disbanded because of conflicts between its organization and the conscript law. The men were assigned to other Louisiana units in Taylor's army. Keary and the four lieutenants returned to their commands in Virginia.

Louisiana Defenders Battalion

MAJOR. Juan Miangolara.

COMPANIES AND THEIR COMMANDERS

Company A (Orleans). T. Viade.
Company B (Orleans). Arthur Picolet.
Company C (Orleans). Jose Domingo.

This battalion was organized in November, 1861, in New Orleans and transferred to Confederate service on March 18, 1862. The battalion went to Camp Lewis. On April 12, it moved to Camp Benjamin. The men received orders to go by steamer from Lake End to Covington when New Orleans was evacuated. On April 29, they marched to Madisonville, and the next day they took steamers to Pass Manchac. They left Pass Manchac for Camp Moore on May 2.

Members of Company B, and possibly men from the other companies, were assigned to the 30th Louisiana Regiment on May 20. The fate of the battalion from this time is unknown. In May, 1863, Miangolara was at Ponchatoula recruiting for his battalion. He left there May 19 for Madisonville because of the approach of Federal troops. The battalion was reported as being in Richmond, Virginia, on September 7, 1863.

Miles' Legion

The infantry companies of this legion were organized early in 1862, and it appears that efforts to form them into a legion occurred in New Orleans prior to the fall of the city on April 25. All of the companies gathered at Camp Moore and were formally mustered into Confederate service on May 16 or 17. They served separately from the artillery and cavalry companies; and their history is discussed under the heading 32nd Louisiana Infantry Regiment, the official but unused designation of the unit. Two artillery companies were assigned to the legion at various times but maintained separate identities during the war. The sections on the 2nd Louisiana Battery and Gibson's Louisiana Battery give the history of the artillery companies. Apparently, the legion did not include cavalry companies until late 1862. At that time, three companies were assigned to the legion; but they never actually operated with the infantry or artillery companies. These three companies served in a temporary organization known as Cage's Louisiana Cavalry Battalion, and their story appears under that heading.

Stewart's Legion

Very little substantial information on the origins of this unit exists. It appears that in February, 1862, General Leonidas Polk authorized Captain R. A. Stewart, commander of the Pointe Coupee Artillery at Columbus, Kentucky, to return to Louisiana and raise some infantry and cavalry to add to his artillery companies. Stewart claimed later that he recruited eight infantry companies and a cavalry squadron and reported for duty at Fort Pillow, Tennessee. Because of the evacuation of Columbus and the resulting confusion, Stewart said, he had to turn over to "other commanders" the infantry companies and one cavalry company. On May 23, General John B. Villepique, commander at Fort Pillow, ordered Stewart back to Louisiana to gather the recruits mustered for his legion. Stewart mustered in three infantry companies and one cavalry company and sent them to Abbeville, Mississippi, where Villepique camped after abandoning Fort Pillow. At Jackson, Mississipi, General Mansfield Lovell stopped the companies, and soon General Earl Van Dorn ordered them to Camp Moore. There they were organized as the 9th Louisiana Infantry Battalion. Their history appears under that heading. On July 2, Stewart resigned as commander of his legion, because he feared he would never succeed in keeping any additional companies he might raise.

Appendix I/Independent Companies

Ben McCulloch Rangers Company Infantry (Orleans). Captain William F. McLean, relieved temporarily; F. M. Imboden. Organized May 19, 1861, in New Orleans. Ordered to Virginia and assigned to duty in the Kanawha Valley. Assigned as 2nd Company A, 59th Virginia Infantry Regiment, on August 1 and officially recognized as such in May, 1862.

Benjamin's Company Cavalry (Rapides, Avoyelles, and Natchitoches). Captain Joseph Benjamin. Organized December 24, 1863, at Alexandria. Served as headquarters guard for the District of West Louisiana. Paroled at Natchitoches in June, 1865.

Bossier Cavalry (Bossier). Captain Thomas W. Fuller, retired(?); Captain William Harrison. Enlisted April 6, 1862, at Monroe. Went to Mississippi. Served as Company B, Wimberly's (later Webb's) Squadron Louisiana Cavalry. Assigned temporarily to the 18th Tennessee Cavalry Battalion as Company G. Later transferred to the 2nd Kentucky Cavalry Regiment. Detached and returned to Louisiana in the spring of 1863. Became Company C, Harrison's Louisiana Cavalry Battalion about December, 1863.

Briarfield Rebels Company Cavalry (Carroll). Captain A. J. McNeill, promoted major April 21, 1862. Mustered in September 1, 1861, at Memphis, Tennessee, as Company D, 1st (6th) Arkansas Cavalry Battalion. Saw some service as a detached company in the Florida Parishes in 1863.

Caddo Light Horse Company Cavalry (Caddo). Captain William B. Denson. Mustered in May 3, 1862, at Shreveport. Served as an escort company in the District of Arkansas. Captured January 11, 1863, at Arkansas Post. Did escort duty again after exchanged. Relieved and ordered to Shreveport November 17, 1863. Became Company A, Harrison's Louisiana Cavalry Battalion, in December, 1863. Some officers and men detached as the nucleus for Company D, Harrison's Battalion.

Calcasieu Rangers Company Cavalry (Rapides). Captain William E.

Ivey. Formed in the fall of 1863 as a home guard unit. Mustered into Confederate service February 20, 1864, at Hineston. Operated against Jayhawkers and deserters in western Louisiana and gathered conscripts for the army. Became Company I, 6th Louisiana Cavalry Regiment, in late 1864 or January, 1865.

Carroll Dragoons Company Cavalry (Carroll). Captain Arthur J. Lott. Organized March 1, 1862. Moved to northern Mississippi. Assigned to the 2nd Mississippi Partisan Rangers Regiment as Company B in October, 1862. The remnants of the company were transferred to the Minden Rangers Company Cavalry in May, 1865.

Caruthers' Sharpshooters Company Infantry (Livingston). Captain William D. L. McRae. Organized April 10, 1862, at Ponchatoula and mustered into Confederate service May 10, 1862, at Camp Moore. Occupied fortifications at Pass Manchac and repulsed attacks by Federal gunboats May 11, 19, and 23. Another Federal gunboat attack on June 17 forced the men to abandon the fortifications and retreat to Ponchatoula. Remained at that town until December, when the men moved to Baton Rouge. Became Company D, 9th Louisiana Infantry Battalion.

Darden Rangers Company Cavalry (Lafourche). Captain Albert G. Cage. Organized April 8, 1862, at Thibodaux. Moved to Memphis, Tennessee. Became 2nd Company F, Wood's Regiment Confederate Cavalry.

Dubecq's Company Cavalry (Avoyelles). Captain J. Dubecq. Organized in 1863 at Marksville. Served as a headquarters guard in the District of West Louisiana.

Grivot Rangers Company Cavalry (St. Landry). Captain S. D. Ashe, resigned September 8, 1862; Captain B. W. Bond. Also known as Bond's Mounted Partisan Rangers. Organized August 21, 1862, at Opelousas from a militia company. Operated along the Mississippi River between Plaquemine and St. Charles Courthouse. In skirmishes at Boutte Station and Bayou Des Allemands, September 4, 1862. Mustered out September 18, 1862, at Thibodaux. Some men joined Company A, 2nd Louisiana Cavalry Regiment.

Jefferson Mounted Guards Company Cavalry (Orleans). Captain Guy Dreux. Organized in March or April, 1862, at New Orleans. Served as a headquarters guard in the Army of Tennessee. Paroled at Meridian, Mississippi, May 10, 1865.

Louisiana Mounted Rangers Company Cavalry (East Baton Rouge).

Captain J. Warren Cole. Organized July 23, 1861, at Port Hudson. Went to Kentucky and then Tennessee. Became part of a temporary unit called Cole's Battalion Cavalry and later of the 2nd Battalion Mississippi and Alabama Cavalry. Disbanded March 29, 1862.

Louisiana Scouts and Sharpshooters Company Infantry (Orleans). Captain William G. Mullen, died August 27, 1863; Louis S. Greenlee. Organized March 12, 1862, at Camp Stevens near New Orleans. Served along the banks of the Mississippi River during Federal operations against Fort Jackson and Fort St. Philip in March and April, 1862. Later mounted and served along the north shore of Lake Pontchartrain. Became Company H, 14th Confederate Cavalry Regiment, September 14, 1863.

Lovell Scouts Company Cavalry (St. Mary). Captain David Ker, resigned September 15, 1862; Captain Alexander A. Pecot. Organized in November, 1861, at Franklin. Stationed around that town until the end of the next year. Operated with General Henry H. Sibley's Texas Cavalry Brigade after December, 1862. Became Company I, 3rd Louisiana (Harrison's) Cavalry Regiment, in the fall of 1863.

Marion Infantry. Captain (?). Did provost duty at Mobile, Alabama.

McWaters' Rangers Company Cavalry (Rapides). Captain James A. McWaters. Organized June 2, 1862, at Alexandria. Operated along the Mississippi River between Plaquemine and St. Charles Courthouse, arresting suspicious persons and stopping trade with the Federals. In skirmishes at Boutte Station and Bayou Des Allemands on September 4, 1862. Became Company G, 2nd Louisiana Cavalry Regiment.

Miller's Mounted Rifles Company Cavalry. Captain Obed P. Miller. Organized September 1, 1862, at Lynchburg, Virginia, from men formerly in 2nd Company D, 1st Louisiana Special Battalion Infantry. Men assigned to Robinson's Horse Artillery in June, 1863.

Minden Rangers Company Cavalry (Bossier). Captain F. D. Wimberly, resigned June 19, 1862; Captain Junius Y. Webb. Organized April 4, 1862; reorganized May 18, 1862. Served as Company A, Wimberly's (later Webb's) Squadron Louisiana Cavalry. Later served temporarily as Company E, 18th Tennessee Cavalry Battalion. Then acted as an escort company in the Department of Mississippi and East Louisiana.

Orleans Light Horse Company Cavalry (Orleans). Captain J. McD.

Taylor, resigned 1861; Thomas L. Leeds, died April 23, 1862; W. Alexander Gordon, resigned October, 1862; Leeds Greenleaf. Organized in 1861 in New Orleans and mustered into Confederate service on March 22, 1862. Served as a corps headquarters guard in the Army of Tennessee. Paroled at Greensboro, North Carolina, on April 26, 1865.

Pargoud Volunteers Company Infantry (Orleans[?]). Captain Alfred A. Lipscomb. Became Company H, 1st Missouri Infantry Regiment.

Pelican Guards Company B (Orleans). Captain John O'Hara. Organized October 26, 1861, in New Orleans. Served aboard floating battery *New Orleans* at Columbus, Kentucky, and Island No. 10, Tennessee. Captured April 8, 1862, at the latter place.

Phillips Rangers Company Cavalry (Ouachita). Captain C. W. Phillips, resigned May 2, 1862. Organized September 14, 1861, at Monroe. Went to Memphis, Tennessee, and became 1st Company F, Wood's Regiment Confederate Cavalry. Transferred to infantry service in April or May, 1862.

Prairie Rangers Company Cavalry (St. Landry). Captain Nathaniel Van Woert, resigned January 9, 1862; Captain William Spencer, resigned(?) June 5, 1862; Captain Samuel M. Todd. Organized July 20, 1861, as a militia company. Joined the St. Landry Militia Cavalry Regiment on April 5, 1862. Transferred to Confederate service on August 20, 1862. Performed scout and courier duty and became headquarters guard for General Richard Taylor. Collected conscripts for the army and operated against Jayhawkers and deserters in southwestern Louisiana. Became Company K, 3rd Louisiana (Harrison's) Cavalry Regiment in the fall of 1863.

Red River Rangers Company Cavalry (Caddo). Captain L. M. Nutt. Organized in 1861 in Shreveport. Served in the District of Arkansas. Many men captured at Arkansas Post, Arkansas, January 11, 1863. After release from prison, these men served with the Army of Tennessee. The men not captured became Company G, 3rd (Harrison's) Louisiana Cavalry Regiment in the fall of 1863.

St. Martin Rangers Company Infantry (St. Martin). Captain E. W. Fuller, died July 15, 1863; Captain Edward T. King. Organized May 14, 1862, near St. Martinville. Operated as cannoneers and crewmen on the gunboats *Music, Cotton,* and *Mary T* until the summer of 1863. Converted into an artillery company at Grand Ecore and became known as King's Louisiana Battery.

Teche Guerrillas Company Cavalry (St. Mary). Captain Bailie P. L. Vinson. Organized May 26, 1864, at Franklin. Did scout and outpost duty on lower Bayou Teche. Paroled June 10, 1865, at Franklin.

Tensas Cavalry Company (Tensas). Captain Isaac F. Harrison, promoted major August 15, 1862; Captain Albert Bondurant. Mustered in August 29, 1861, at Memphis, Tennessee. Became 1st Company A, Wood's Regiment Confederate Cavalry, on October 15, 1861. Detached September 26, 1862, and returned to Louisiana. Became Company A, 15th Louisiana Cavalry Battalion, in December, 1862.

Appendix II/Louisiana Volunteer State Troops

In the early months of 1862 (February–April), Governor Thomas O. Moore arranged with Major General Mansfield Lovell to transfer three brigades of militiamen to Confederate service. Lovell accepted the eleven regiments and two battalions of "Volunteer State Troops" for the defense of New Orleans. It appears, however, that Lovell had few, if any, of the men formally mustered into regular Confederate service. Most of the men went into camps around the city for drill and discipline. Napier Bartlett's *Military Record of Louisiana* places the strength of the three brigades at 9,113 men, but they probably had no more than half that number ready for active duty. Lovell ordered the Chalmette Regiment to the Quarantine Station, six miles upriver from Fort St. Philip, to guard the rear of that bastion. Bartlett gives the following account of the fate of these units: "When the gunboats [of Union Flag Officer David G. Farragut] passed the forts [Jackson and St. Philip] and Lovell carried off all transportation, [the regiments] were disbanded by Gen. [E. L.] Tracy." Farragut's vessels captured and paroled all of the men of the Chalmette Regiment at the Quarantine Station on April 24. Many of the officers and enlisted men of the other units escaped the city before it surrendered and accompanied Lovell's regulars to Camp Moore. Only one unit, the Sumter Regiment, maintained its organization; and it later became the nucleus for the 30th Louisiana Infantry Regiment. Bartlett's account goes on to say, "When [General Benjamin F.] Butler arrived, the officers and men [in New Orleans] were arrested as prisoners of war, paroled, and those who did not take the oath, were exchanged on the 8th of October following, being delivered at Vicksburg." While the majority of these "Volunteer State Troops" took the oath, a number did find their way into Louisiana units on active duty in the Vicksburg area.

The paucity of official records of these units makes it impossible to present separate historical sketches on each one. The rosters of officers that follow are as complete as existing records allow.

Beauregard Regiment

COLONEL. Frank A. Bartlett.
LIEUTENANT COLONEL. George S. Lacey.
MAJOR. George McKnight.

Companies and Their Commanders

Police Guards Company A. Frank J. Read.
Police Guards Company B. James B. Tank.
E. Thompson Guards. Theo. W. Buddecke.
Carondelet Light Infantry. J. A. DeHart.
Belmont Guards. R. H. Browne, resigned March 4, 1862.
McRae Rangers. V. Hebert.
Clay Guards. J. Stuart Derickson, resigned April 15, 1862.
Davidson Guards. J. Davidson Hill.
Glenn Guards. W. H. C. King.
Rhinehart Guards. Daniel Scully.

Cazadores Espanoles

COLONEL. Juan Miangolara.
LIEUTENANT COLONELS. Jose M. Auguera; Neville Soule.
MAJORS. Juan Miangolara; Gaudenzi Marzoni.

Companies and Their Commanders

1st Company. Commander unknown.
2nd Company, Slavonian Rifles. J. B. Pigniole(?).
3rd Company. Lazaro Roca.
4th Company. Ramon Llaurador.
5th Company, Company of Tiradores. Commander unknown.
Company A. Joe Llado.
Company B, Cazadores Espanoles 2nd Company. Manuel Infants;
    Gabriel Sequi y Gahona; U. Marinoni.
Company C, Long Rifles. Joseph Marcou.
Company D, Chasseurs d'Orleans 1814 and 1815. Louis Surgi.
Company E, Slavonian Rifles. S. G. Fabio.
Company F, Garibaldi Guards. Joseph Santini; Gaudenzi Marzoni;
    U. Marinoni.
Company G, Cazadores of St. Bernard. Columbus Reid; Pablo Pons.

Chalmette Regiment

COLONEL. Ignatius Szymanski.
LIEUTENANT COLONEL. George W. Logan.
MAJOR. Eugene Soniat.

COMPANIES AND THEIR COMMANDERS

Company A, Scandinavian Guards. Edward Fry.
Company B, Manassas Rifles. Greenleaf Andrews.
Company C, Plauche Rebels. J. V. Chaery.
Company D, Howard Guards. J. J. E. Massicot.
Company E, Gulf Guards. Louis A. Wiltz.
Company F, Heation Guards. William Chapman.
Company G, Gentilly Rangers. L. G. Oscar Valeton.
Company H, Frappe d'Abord. Theophile Wiltz.
Company I, DeFeriet Guards. Frederick Losberg.
Company K, Clouet Guards. Charles A. Jaquet.

Chasseurs-a-Pied

COLONEL. J. Simon Meilleur.
LIEUTENANT COLONEL. C A. Janvier.
MAJOR. H. J. Rivet.

COMPANIES AND THEIR COMMANDERS

1st Company. Isidore Esclapon, resigned March 4, 1862.
2nd Company. Leopold Aleix.
3rd Company. Louis Gagnet.
4th Company. J. Lafond.
5th Company. Charles A. Rivet.
6th Company, disbanded. A. Hauzut.
7th Company. F. A. Mader.
Pointe Coupee Creoles. Prosper Echelard.
False River Guards. Henri Knaps.
Chasseurs of St. Charles. N. St. Martin.
Ranson Guards. Louis Ranson.

Confederate Guards

COLONEL. John F. Girault.
LIEUTENANT COLONEL. Charles R. Railey.
MAJOR. John J. Noble.

COMPANIES AND THEIR COMMANDERS

Company A. James McCloskey.
Company B. George W. West.
Company C. Joseph Ellison.
Company D. Edward Judice.
Company E. J. D. Dameron.
Company F. John Purcell.
Company G. George W. Race.
Company H. E. Pillsbury.
Company I. James J. Tarleton.
Company K. Simon Green.

Continental Regiment

COLONEL. George Clark.
LIEUTENANT COLONEL. A. W. Merriam.
MAJOR. George H. Hynson.

COMPANIES AND THEIR COMMANDERS

Continental Guards Company A. W. F. Hodgkins.
Kirk Guards. John H. Davidson.
Jackson Rail Road Rifles. T. S. Williams.
Waterman Guards. Warren Davis.
Citizens Guards Company B. S. Woodall.
Calhoun Guards. William Towell.
Magnolia Guards Company B. Frank Roder.
Sumpter Turner Guards. C. K. Gallagher.
G. W. Magee Guards. Addison Thompson.

Jeff Davis Regiment

COLONEL. Alex. Smith.
LIEUTENANT COLONEL. William P. Freret.
MAJOR. John B. Cotton

COMPANIES AND THEIR COMMANDERS

Pochelee Rangers. A. C. Beattie, resigned April 7, 1862.
Carrollton Guards. Ernest Commagere.
Beauregard Tigers. John C. Costley.
Jefferson Rangers. Hugh B. Knox.
Jeff Confederate Guards Company A. J. W. Davis.
Jeff Confederate Guards Company B. Thomas Friend.
Caldwell Guards. J. E. Pitcher.
Bennett and Lurges Guards. Francis Lurges.
Baker Guards. F. Lang.
Gaiser Guards. J. D. Gaiser.

Johnson's Special Battalion

LIEUTENANT COLONEL. W. W. Johnson.
MAJOR. W. H. Winn.

COMPANIES AND THEIR COMMANDERS

Avoyelles Fencibles (Avoyelles). H. W. Verstille.
Chasseurs-a-Pied (Avoyelles). Leon Phillipson.
Creole Rebels (Avoyelles). J. J. Ducote.
Marksville Guards (Avoyelles). Louis Barbin.
Mansura Guards (Avoyelles). E. Joffrion.

King's Special Battalion

LIEUTENANT COLONEL. John E. King.

COMPANIES AND THEIR COMMANDERS

Company A, Calcasieu Volunteers (Calcasieu). Albert Warren.
Company B, Calcasieu Tigers (Calcasieu), assigned to 29th Louisiana Infantry Regiment. James W. Bryan.
Company C, Calcasieu Invincibles (Calcasieu). Warren W. Johnson.
Company D, Calcasieu Guards (Calcasieu). John T. Lindsey.
Company E, Taylor Guards (St. Landry), assigned to Miles' Louisiana Legion (32nd Regiment). Tacitus G. Calvit.

Leeds Guards

COLONEL. Charles J. Leeds.
LIEUTENANT COLONEL. E. Gunnell.
MAJOR. A. G. Brice.

COMPANIES AND THEIR COMMANDERS

Company A, Leeds Guards Company A. John M. Brooks.
Company B, Rescue Guards Company B. James B. Prague.
Company C, Rescue Guards Company A. A. Thompson.
Company D, Leeds Guards Company D. Arch. Mitchell.
Company E, Leeds Guards Company B. Thomas Malone.
Company F, Lovell Guards. Philip McGuire.
Company G, Mechanics Guards. M. J. Downes.
Company H, Fulton Guards. R. A. Hoffman.
Company I, Lovell Light Infantry. J. S. Milliken.

Louisiana Irish Regiment

COLONEL. Patrick B. O'Brien.
LIEUTENANT COLONEL. W. J. Castell.
MAJOR. D. O. D. Sullivan, declined appointment(?).

COMPANIES AND THEIR COMMANDERS

O'Brien Light Infantry. John O'Brien.
Irish Volunteers. L. Doyle.
Johnston Rifles. J. W. Enright.
Emmett Guards Company B. M. J. Brennan.
Cotton Plant Guards. R. Condon.
Laughlin Light Guards. T. O. Laughlin.
Montgomery Guards. Martin Glynn.
Pikemen 61. John Gorman.
Beauregard Guards. E. D. White.
Stephens Guards. M. J. Kernaghan.

Orleans Fire Regiment

COLONEL. S P. Duncan.
LIEUTENANT COLONEL. M. M. Reynolds.
MAJOR. James D. Hill.

COMPANIES AND THEIR COMMANDERS

Milneburg Fire Guards. Charles Evershed.
Orleans Good Will Fire Guards. Benjamin Faith.
Third District Fire Guards. Frank Borge.
Confidence Fire Guards. Joseph Didlot.
City Fire Guards. John Kennedy.
Vigilant Fire Guards. X. Maurer.
Phoenix Fire Guards. Valentine St. Ceran.
Perseverance Fire Guards. W. H. Latham.

Orleans Guard Regiment

COLONEL. Numa Augustin, resigned.
LIEUTENANT COLONEL. Charles Messieu.
MAJORS. Octave Voorhies, resigned February 18, 1862; Leon
    Queyrouze.

COMPANIES AND THEIR COMMANDERS

Company A. Charles Roman.
Company B. P. Oscar Labatut; Eugene Staes.
Company C. Leon Queyrouze, promoted major February 18, 1862;
    Auguste Roche.
Company D. Gustave Cruzat; Victor Burthe.
Company E. E. P. Poupart.
Company F. John Thibaut, resigned October 29, 1861; Pierre Maspero.
Company G. Arthur Poincy.
Company H. Joaquin Viosca, Jr.
Company I. Charles Bienvenu, resigned August 21, 1861; E. A.
    Desmommes; Guy Duplantier.
Company K. S. Plassau.

Sumter Regiment

COLONEL. Gustavus A. Breaux.
LIEUTENANT COLONEL. Thomas Shields.
MAJOR. Charles Bell.

COMPANIES AND THEIR COMMANDERS

Company A, Louisiana State Guards Company A. —— Tarleton.
Company B, Louisiana State Guards Company B. —— Green.
Company C, Louisiana State Guards Company C. —— Pilsbury.
Company D, Sumter Greys Company A. —— Maupay.
Company E, Sumter Greys Company B. H. J. Beebe.
Company F, American Rifles. Roger T. Boyle.
Company G, Crescent Blues Company A. John Knight.
Company H, Lewis Guards. H. Jones.
Company I, Crescent Cadets. F. Cook.
Company K, Beauregard Rifles. —— Masher(?).
Orleans Cadets Company E. —— Planchard(?).
St. John the Baptist Guards. L. LeBourgeois.
St. John the Baptist Rifles. A. J. Deslondes.
Sabine Independents. Isaac Wright.

A Note on Sources

In addition to the sources mentioned in the unit bibliographies, there exist a number of printed and manuscript sources that contain information on more than one Louisiana Confederate unit. These sources have provided much of the data used in the compilation of the historical sketches presented in this book. Rather than repeat their names in each bibliography, I have chosen to discuss them in a brief essay in the hope of emphasizing their strengths and weaknesses.

The most important source of information on Louisiana Confederate units is the immense set, *War of the Rebellion: Official Records of the Union and Confederate Armies* (128 parts in 70 vols.; Washington, D.C., 1880–1901), compiled by the U.S. War Department. These volumes contain battle reports, casualty returns, tables of organization, strength reports, orders, correspondence, and maps. The *General Index* volume and the individual indexes in each volume provide easy access to references concerning a unit. Of a similar nature but of less value is the U.S. Navy Department's *War of the Rebellion: Official Records of the Union and Confederate Navies* (30 vols.; Washington, D.C., 1894–1922). While most of the documents in this publication deal with naval vessels, the volumes do contain references to land units.

In addition to the documents printed in the *Official Records*, the War Department gathered thousands of other Confederate records at the end of the war. These unpublished records now repose in the National Archives as Record Group 109, War Department Collection of Confederate Records. Besides the types of documents printed by the War Department, this collection contains records pertaining to individual units, such as clothing issue returns, extra duty reports, and ration reports. The published guide to this collection—National Archives, *Preliminary Inventory of the War Department Collection of Confederate Records* (Washington, D.C., 1957)—facilitates access to whatever series of records a researcher wishes to use in looking for unit information.

Of great importance to any unit history is the Compiled Service Records of Confederate Soldiers Who Served in Organizations from the State of Louisiana (Microcopy No. 320, 414 reels), a part of Record Group 109 that is available on microfilm. This series contains carded abstracts from regimental and company muster rolls, parole lists, hospital records, prisoner of war records, and other records pertaining to individual soldiers. The microfilm reels also contain carded abstracts from the "Record of Events" portion of muster rolls used in the compilation of the records. These "Record of Events" cards note the date and place of the muster and frequently give brief descriptions of the movements of the unit during the mustering period. Many of the records of the individual soldiers, particularly officers, contain original documents of value to a unit history, such as orders, letters, discharge certificates, requisitions for provisions and supplies, and pay vouchers.

Napier Bartlett's *Military Record of Louisiana* (1875; rpr. Baton Rouge, 1964) contains valuable information on a number of units. Bartlett included in his book a few summary unit histories and extracts from diaries, journals, rosters, reports, and casualty lists. The book has three main sections: units in Virginia, units in the West (for example, Tennessee, Georgia, and Mississippi), and units in the Trans-Mississippi Department. Anecdotes relating to individual soldiers are sprinkled through these sections. Bartlett's memoirs, "A Soldier's Story," and other information on the famed Washington Artillery make up half of the reprint edition. One appendix contains lists of officers for many units when they entered Confederate service. A word of caution: Though this book was compiled relatively soon after the end of the war, it contains some inaccuracies in articles dealing with both units and individual soldiers.

"Louisiana," by John Dimitry, in vol. X of *Confederate Military History*, edited by Clement A. Evans (12 vols.; Atlanta, 1889), summarizes the service of many units. Dimitry apparently drew much of his information from available official sources, and he concentrated on the units that served in the Army of Northern Virginia and the Army of Tennessee. Each original set came with an expanded volume of the state of one's choice, except in a few cases. The expanded version of the "Louisiana" section contains statistical information on almost every unit and short biographies of soldiers who held rank below brigadier general. The reprints of this set do not contain these two very useful appendices. Individual volumes of *Confederate Military History* do not have their own indexes, so a researcher must go to the general index in vol. XII.

Two state publications give lists of Louisiana's Confederate units with brief statistical notations: *Biennial Report of the Secretary of State of the State of Louisiana to His Excellency Samuel D. McEnery, Governor of Louisiana, 1886–1887* (Baton Rouge, 1888) and *Annual Report of the Adjutant General of the State of Louisiana for the Year Ending December 31, 1892* (Baton Rouge, 1893). These two books contain such information as dates of organization, commanding officers, strength figures, casualty totals, and lists of officers killed. In several cases, the lists give background on units formed from other units or the disposition of units that were disbanded. Some errors appear in the books, probably because of faulty information available to the compilers.

Louisiana infantry units formed several distinct brigades in the armies east of the Mississippi River. Two books and an article cover the campaigns of the troops in the Army of Northern Virginia, the most famous of all the state's soldiers. Terry L. Jones's *Lee's Tigers: The Louisiana Infantry in the Army of Northern Virginia* (Baton Rouge, 1987) presents the best picture of the marches, battles, and camp life of the two Louisiana brigades in General Robert E. Lee's army. Jones has woven an excellent story from an impressive collection of primary sources, and his study should serve as a starting point for anyone interested in those units. Larry Hewitt's "Death, Disaster and Destruction: The Louisiana Brigades in the Army of Northern Virginia," Amite (La.) *News Digest*, April 24, May 1, 8, 15, 1985, centers on the high casualty rates of the brigades. Alison Moore's *The Louisiana Tigers* (Baton Rouge, 1961) presents a somewhat favorably biased picture of the Louisiana brigades. It is based on a limited number of printed sources.

Though many of Louisiana's Confederate newspapers have disappeared since the war, the issues that have survived contain numerous items of significance. Unfortunately, extant issues of several papers do not date later than April, 1862, and so have only limited value. Some New Orleans papers published during the Union occupation of the city continued to carry stories and casualty lists pertaining to Confederate units. Newspapers published in states other than Louisiana, particularly Mississippi and Texas, also printed items relating to Louisiana troops. For many years after the war, newspapers in Louisiana published memoirs and reminiscences of Confederate veterans. When approached with some skepticism, these accounts can provide details on units not found elsewhere.

Naturally, manuscript collections in libraries, historical societies, and archival repositories are important sources of information. This is true not only for institutions within the state but also for a large number of institutions around the country. Some of these institutions have published catalogues or inventories to assist in the location of relevant collections, but many of them have not. For example, an excellent guide exists to the manuscripts in the Southern Historical Collection at the University of North Carolina at Chapel Hill, but only an extremely outdated guide to the outstanding collections in the Louisiana State University Department of Archives and Manuscripts is available. The letters, diaries, memoirs, and other writings of Louisiana's Confederate soldiers provide a look behind the official sources to reveal what the war was really like to the men who fought in the units from this state. The details such documents furnish make up the "meat" of the history of any regiment, battalion, or company.

Two collections of official documents deserve special mention. The first group of records are part of the Louisiana Historical Association Collection in the Manuscript Department, Special Collections Division, Howard-Tilton Memorial Library, Tulane University. The original Louisiana Historical Association began collecting Confederate documents in 1889. Now in the Tulane archives, these records contain a wealth of material on Louisiana units. The collection consists of letters, reports, orders, strength returns, muster rolls, diaries, and other documents. Most of the records fall into categories of parent organizations, such as the Army of Tennessee or the District of West Louisiana. A published guide—*Inventory of the Louisiana Historical Association Collection on Deposit in the Howard-Tilton Memorial Library, Tulane University, New Orleans*, compiled by Connie G. Griffith (New Orleans, 1983)—allows the researcher to determine specific boxes and folders of interest.

Lesser known and certainly rarely used are the records preserved by the Louisiana Adjutant General's Library at Jackson Barracks, Chalmette. This collection's strength lies in the documents concerning units, especially cavalry regiments, in Louisiana in 1864 and

1865. Numerous letters, orders, and reports detail the activities of the men on duty in southern Louisiana during the final year of the conflict. Other records make it possible to pick up information on individual soldiers that appears nowhere else. Microfilmed copies of these records are located at the Louisiana State Archives in Baton Rouge. A typescript guide to the microfilmed records can be found at both Jackson Barracks and the State Archives. No research on a cavalry unit located in Louisiana late in the war can be complete without reference to this collection of documents.

The Confederate pension files located at the Louisiana State Archives sometimes provide useful information on units. On their applications, the veterans answered the following questions: When and where did you enlist? Who were your regimental and company officers? Where were you at the surrender? Depending upon the accuracy of a veteran's memory or the documents at his disposal, the answers to these simple questions can present facts and names found nowhere else. Some veterans' records did not establish their eligibility for pensions, so the veterans or their widows sent various documents to the Board of Pension Commissioners to support their claims. These documents included such things as letters recounting incidents from or summaries of the men's war service, affidavits by former comrades, letters written during the war, discharge papers, paroles, and muster rolls or rosters. Though presently indexed only alphabetically by the name of the veteran or widow, these pension files can be worth the time required to go through them.

Several journal articles have described the activities of the artillery batteries that served in the District of West Louisiana. One article is actually a transcription of an official report submitted by Colonel Joseph L. Brent, Chief of Artillery, at the close of the Red River Campaign of 1864: "Operations of the Artillery of the Army of Western Louisiana, After the Battle of Pleasant Hill," *Southern Historical Society Papers*, IX (1881), 257–64. Basing his research on a wide variety of scattered original manuscript sources, Alwyn Barr has produced two articles: "Confederate Artillery in Western Louisiana, 1862–1863," *Civil War History*, IX (1963), 74–85; and "Confederate Artillery in Western Louisiana, 1864," *Louisiana History*, V (1964), 53–73. Barr's articles serve not only to present an overview of military operations but also to point the way to sources for more detailed research.

Finally, the memoirs of some Confederate generals contain factual data or anecdotes about Louisiana units that served under them. Two prime examples are Richard Taylor's *Destruction and Reconstruction: Personal Experiences of the Late War*, ed. Richard B. Harwell (New York, 1955); and Jubal A. Early's *A Memoir of the Last Year of the War for Independence* (Lynchburg, Va., 1867). Taylor led a Louisiana brigade in the Army of Northern Virginia in 1861 and 1862 and commanded the District of West Louisiana from 1862 to 1864. His book contains numerous references to individual units as well as descriptive accounts of battles and campaigns in which these units fought. Early led a division and later a corps in the Army of Northern Virginia from 1862 to 1865. He had Louisianians serving under his command in several campaigns, and he provides valuable information on their performance under fire.

These paragraphs should make it apparent that thorough research on Louisiana Confederate units can prove tedious, time-consuming, and sometimes frustrating. Nevertheless, conscientious researchers will often find their task not only rewarding but fun. Discovering that nugget of golden information in some obscure source gives meaning to the phrase *the thrill of the hunt*.

Index